# THE NEWTON BOYS
## Portrait of an
## Outlaw Gang

For Joline
with best wishes
Claude Stanush

*Original painting of the Newton Boys by Bob Crofut*

# THE NEWTON BOYS
## Portrait of an
## Outlaw Gang

*by Willis and Joe Newton*

as told to

## Claude Stanush
## &
## David Middleton

STATE HOUSE PRESS
Austin, Texas
1994

*Library of Congress Cataloging-in-Publication Data*

Newton, Willis, 1889-
The Newton boys : portrait of an outlaw gang / by
Willis & Joe Newton as told to Claude Stanush
& David Middleton.
p. cm.
Includes index.
ISBN 1-880510-15-4 (hardcover : acid-free paper)
ISBN 1-880510-16-2 (paper cover : acid-free paper)
ISBN 1-880510-17-0 (limited ed. : acid-free paper)
1. Newton, Willis, 1889-  . 2. Newton, Joe, 1901-  .
3. Outlaws—United States—Biography.
4. Gangs—United States—Biography.
5. Robbery—United States—Case studies.
I. Newton, Joe, 1901-  . II. Stanush, Claude, 1918-  .
III. Middleton, David L. IV. Title

HV6446.N49 1994
364.1'552'0973—dc20
93-43267

*Printed in the United States of America*

*cover painting by Bob Crofut*

STATE HOUSE PRESS
P.O. Box 15247
Austin, Texas 78761

# TABLE OF CONTENTS

Prologue                                                          vii
1.   Family History (1830-1890)                                    1
2.   On the Move (1890-1903)                                       11
3.   Wanderlust (1903)                                             37
4.   Hardscrabble Farming (1903-1907)                              47
5.   Tangling with the Law (1907-1908)                             65
6.   Miscarriage of Justice (1909-1910)                            79
7.   Living and Dying in the Texas Pen                             89
8.   The First Train Robbery (1914)                                95
9.   On Trial for Murder and Mayhem  (1916-1917)                  105
10.  In the Texas Pen and Out—Again                               117
11.  Breaking Into the Bank Business (1918)                       131
12.  Dissension in the Gang (1919)                                153
13.  Joe Newton (1914-1919)                                       169
14.  Organizing the Newton Gang (1920-1921)                       181
15.  Working in Canada (1922)                                     203
16.  Upping the Ante: Robbery in Daylight (1923)                  215
17.  Black Gold (1923)                                            231
18.  Toronto Currency Clearing House (July 1923)                  241
19.  Trains, Banks and Funerals (1923-1924)                       253
20.  America's Biggest Train Robbery (June 12, 1924)              267
21.  Life After Leavenworth (1929-1976)                           297
22.  Last Thoughts                                                311
     Epilogue                                                     321

# PROLOGUE

When we first met Willis and Joe Newton in Uvalde, Texas, in the summer of 1973, all we knew about them firsthand was that they had some interesting stories to tell. A rancher friend who lived in Uvalde and had known the Newtons for many years urged us to record these stories "before it's too late, because these fellows are beginning to get old." Willis was eighty-four at the time, Joe seventy-two.

Over the years, we knew, numerous newspaper and magazine articles had been written about the "Newton Boys," describing how four brothers—Willis, Joe, Jess and Willie (Doc) Newton—had formed a gang back in the 1920s and robbed banks and trains from Texas to Canada. Willis, despite being younger than Jess, had organized the gang and was unquestionably its mastermind. Joe was the youngest. Their main claim to fame, according to the many accounts, occurred on June 12, 1924, at Rondout, Illinois, where the Newtons pulled off the biggest train robbery in American history.

By 1973 Jess had died and Doc was living in a nursing home in Uvalde, mentally unstable because of a blow on the head. Willis and Joe, although aging, as our rancher friend had said, were apparently still in good health. In truth, as we discovered later, both were *very* much alive, physically and mentally.

In the public library there was an out-of-print book by J. Marvin Hunter and Noah Rose, *The Album of Gunfighters*, which described the Newton Boys as

PROLOGUE

"daring and desperate outlaws who had engaged in many
gun battles with officers of the law." The rancher, however, told us that the book's assessment of them was
wrong. Yes, the Newtons had robbed eighty banks and
six trains, and had acknowledged carrying off "more loot
than Jesse and Frank James, the Dalton Boys, Butch
Cassidy and all the other famous outlaw gangs put
together." But the real story of the Newton Boys had yet
to be told, our friend said: "You'll know what I mean when
you talk to them."

Willis and Joe were willing. We saw it as a unique
opportunity, not only to satisfy our own curiosity but also
to explore recently popular facets of social history: most
particularly, anti-social behavior from the perspective of
the living rather than from statistics or myth. If Willis
and Joe would speak frankly, we believed they could tell
us of matters not ordinarily accessible to historians but
without which no history of a people would be complete.

There were, in fact, many intriguing questions that
we wanted to ask the Newtons. Since they had grown up
in the latter part of the nineteenth century and the
beginning of the twentieth, at a time when the life expec-
tancy of a bank and train robber must have been very
short indeed, how had they managed to survive to such
ripe old ages? Also, if they were in fact the unusual people
the rancher had described, what had turned them to
careers of crime? What could they tell us about the
psychology of a bank and train robber?

The Newtons had chosen Uvalde, seventy miles west
of San Antonio, for their "retirement," and it seemed an
appropriate home town for them. Founded on the edge
of the Texas frontier in the last century, it too in its youth
had a deserved reputation for lawlessness. By 1973 it
had grown more tranquil and was known not for gun-
happy outlaws and marauding Indians, but for its wide,
pleasant streets shaded by giant pecan trees, for its
distinctive Brush Country honey, and for being the home
town of Vice President John Nance "Cactus Jack" Garner
and Texas Governor Dolph Briscoe—as well as that of the

Newton Boys.

When we finally met Willis and Joe at their homes in Uvalde, they certainly didn't strike us as the kind of men who had once been "desperate outlaws." Nor was there any suggestion they could have been cold-blooded killers like Bonnie and Clyde. Open, friendly, witty and engagingly frank about their past lives, they were also very intelligent. Speaking in a dialect of the rural Southwest, they were highly articulate, even poetic.

Despite all they had in common, there were marked differences between the brothers, both physically in the way they dressed, behaved, and talked, and in their respective views of the world. Willis always dressed like a city man, in a suit with a white shirt, a tie and a sporty, narrow-brimmed hat that Joe referred to as a "dude hat." Joe's attire could have been that of a rancher or well-heeled cowboy; he favored a checkered shirt, gabardine pants, nicely-oiled boots, and a western hat. Willis talked in a high-pitched, raspy voice that ratcheted substantially higher on the scale when emotional, which he frequently became when expressing indignation at brutal police or corrupt politicians and bankers. Joe talked in a slow, easy drawl, the kind natural to the proverbial Westerner. Even when he related harrowing experiences, Joe tended to remain cool, often balancing Willis' anger with lightly humorous asides as if he saw and enjoyed the irony of it all: Willis Newton, convicted bank and train robber, waxing indignant over "crooked" police and politicians.

Although he was frank about his past deeds, Willis never apologized for them, never gave the impression of being repentant, and never pleaded sympathy for his case. His objective throughout our many hours of interviews always seemed to be to set the record straight. He eagerly claimed credit for having been the leader of the gang, the one who had talked his three brothers into joining him in a career of plundering banks and trains. Joe, who had been a cowboy and bronc rider before joining Willis, said with contrition, "*It was the biggest mistake of my life to lay down my saddle and spurs and pick up that pistol.*" But even Joe conceded they had all lived well off the money—dressing in tailor-made clothes, sporting diamond rings and stickpins, driving the best cars, wintering in the best hotels in Denver, St. Louis, Kansas City and Chicago—and that he had enjoyed himself and hadn't withdrawn from the gang even though more than once he had opportunities to do so when his bank account was bulging. "*When you're twenty-one years old, wearing a hundred dollar suit and got several hundred dollars in your pocket, it feels good.*"\*

Yet if Willis and Joe had been no more than ex-bank robbers, we would not have taken the interest in them that we did after our first meeting. Outlaws or not, they turned out to be fascinating people. The stories they had to tell were captivating, and only partly because what they had done was so radically different from what ordinary folks did and do as a matter of course. In a number of subtle ways, what they had done, why they did it, and how they did it all related to, and were revealing of, larger patterns of life in the Southwest.

Having grown up on West Texas farms under oppressive work conditions and with scant opportunities for improving their situations, they knew and could function in the natural world like few people we had ever met. With quick, imaginative minds—even if their creativity was put to use for unconventional purposes—they had a sense of Texas history born from an awareness that they and their families before them had created some of that history.

While acknowledging that he and his brothers had repeatedly broken the law, Willis insisted on distinguish-

---

\* Note the italic typeface used for commentary by Joe. In subsequent chapters, these italics will be used to aid the reader in distinguishing when it is Joe rather than Willis who is talking, even though the tone of the commentary usually indicates whether it is the more aggressive Willis or the softer-spoken Joe.

ing between what they did and the criminal behavior of people such as Bonnie and Clyde. With a snort of disgust he said:

> Bonnie and Clyde was just silly kids bound to get theirselves killed. They killed that old sheriff over at Commerce and that was their undoing. We wasn't at all like them. We wasn't thugs. All we wanted was the money, just like doctors, lawyers and other businessmen. Robbing banks and trains was our way of getting it. That was our business.

Willis added they had never wanted to kill or hurt anybody, and the only reason they carried guns was to protect themselves.

> I always told the boys, "If you have to shoot don't shoot to kill." In fact, we loaded our guns with birdshot a lot of times just so we wouldn't kill anybody.

Whether or not readers will agree with the Newtons' claim to have been professionals just like doctors and lawyers, they did carry out their operations very professionally and efficiently. Most of the time, after carefully mapping a getaway route, they robbed (technically "burglarized") banks late at night, when people were asleep, and in the wintertime when residents of the town tended to be indoors. They usually picked small communities whose banks lacked burglar alarms and whose old-fashioned, square safes were relatively easy to break into. Before prying open a door or window to enter the banks, they would cut telephone and telegraph wires to prevent anyone's spreading an alarm. Once inside, they blew off the doors of the safes with nitroglycerine. Then, with loot packed into gunny sacks, they fled on foot to their car planted in a safe location outside town and accomplished their getaway according to the preconceived plan.

If the Newtons weren't quite the trigger-happy out-laws imagined by the editors of *The Album of Gunfighters*, they were nevertheless daring. They held up some of the banks, and all of the trains, at gunpoint—risky business even if done after scrupulously careful planning. How many robbers would have entered, unmasked, the New Braunfels, Texas, State Bank at noon, made everybody in the place, including an ex-Texas Ranger, lie down on their bellies while they stuffed $104,000 into a pillow slip, and then walked out? How many robbers would have stuck up messengers for the bank clearing house in Toronto, Canada, in broad daylight, again without masks, and after the biggest gun battle of their careers, coolly parked their getaway car—the cash still in it—in a garage a few blocks from the scene of the crime, and gone to a movie? How many would have blown two banks in one night in Hondo, Texas, while the night marshal was drinking coffee in the railroad depot across the street? And especially, we kept asking ourselves, how many would have stopped the Chicago, Milwaukee & St. Paul mail train with seventeen armed clerks aboard and driven away with more than sixty bags of registered mail?

For the record, let it be said that some bystanders and law officers inevitably got hurt, despite Willis' dis-claimer they never wanted that to happen. Our research confirms what the Newtons told us about never having *killed* anybody. Newspaper accounts, magazine stories, and oral history gathered from other informants verify the truth of Willis' remark, even though in two instances nonfamily members of their gang were shot to death while bank robberies were in progress, and several men guarding the currency couriers in the Toronto holdup were wounded. During the Rondout train robbery, Doc Newton was hit by several bullets, one of them almost cutting his tongue in half. Clearly this was a business with a frightening downside and no reasonable expecta-tion of retirement. Indeed, in 1928 the Texas Bankers

Association posted a notice in every bank throughout the State.

REWARD
FIVE THOUSAND DOLLARS FOR DEAD
BANK ROBBERS
NOT ONE CENT FOR LIVE ONES

When we met Willis and Joe in Uvalde, all of these events had happened fifty years earlier, and both brothers looked and behaved more like garrulous old men than gun-toting outlaws. As they described robberies and experiences to us, they joked back and forth, and obviously were enjoying their reminiscences, even some that must have been painful at the time. Yet they almost certainly had been very different people in the 1920s. Anybody meeting them then, with guns in their hands and intent on robbing a bank or train and getting safely away, would not have seen the genial individuals we did at this later date. Willis said he always talked rough to people they encountered during the robberies "to scare them, because that way they weren't apt to cause trouble and nobody would get hurt." By the time of our discussions, they had mellowed and grown reflective; they even looked back on their own escapades with a degree of detachment, as if those adventures had all happened in another lifetime.

On various trips to Uvalde we talked with people who had known both men for some years. They regarded the two as "folk characters," just as they might have regarded Jesse and Frank James or any other historical figure who suddenly appeared on the scene. People were almost unanimously fond of Joe, who they thought would not have embarked on a career of crime if his brother, twelve years older, had not talked him into it. Joe, the former bronc buster, still ran a few cattle on a piece of land and still rode a big, raw-boned, Roman-nosed horse he called, with some humor, Old Paint. He also owned a gasoline station and a drive-in cafe that he rented to others to operate. His wife, Mildred, was a faithful member of a local church; his son, Little Joe, was a sheet metal worker. Joe had several close buddies with whom he drank coffee every day and with whom he swapped yarns and went hunting with hounds for coyotes and wildcats. Raised a good Baptist, Joe never drank liquor even when he was enjoying the high life as a bank robber.

Willis was more of a loner, somewhat more suspect among the local community. "I know some of 'em think I'm still out to rob banks," he told us, "but I'm not gonna rob any more banks—not because I'm too good, I'm just too damn old." When we went with Willis into the First State Bank in Uvalde, owned by former governor Dolph Briscoe, he greeted the tellers and secretaries by name and joshed good-naturedly with them. "These bank people like me," he said, "because we never once robbed the bank here in Uvalde, though we could have easily." Behind his hand he whispered, "We never robbed it because we had to have a place to keep our money."

But even in towns where the Newtons had robbed banks, such as New Braunfels, San Marcos and Boerne, Willis and Joe had friends and were looked upon more as respectable figures of folklore or legend than as reprehensible outlaws. "To tell you the truth, the only exciting thing that ever happened in New Braunfels was when we robbed the bank there in broad daylight," said Willis. Oscar Haas, who was operating a store in the town when the bank was robbed and who later became the historian for New Braunfels and Comal County, was one of the friends Willis and Joe made decades later. Haas said, with a hearty laugh, "Who would ever have thought that the people who robbed the bank would come by years later and introduce themselves."

While driving around the countryside, Willis and Joe liked to stop at the museums in little towns and look at the old photographs, pioneer furniture and farming equipment, old guns and newspaper clippings—some about local banks that the Newtons had robbed—that were the inevitable items on display. The two of them often stopped to chat and have coffee with the curator of the New Braunfels museum. "*We like museums,*" Joe stated. "*I guess it's because Willis and me are like a museum ourselves now.*"

In the small town of Big Foot where there was a copy of *The Album of Gunfighters* describing the Newtons as desperate outlaws, they played a trick on the curator. "Say," Willis said to him, "whatever happened to those rough Newton Boys that they talk about in this book. We heard that they used to live around here." The curator replied, "Yeah, they lived over in Uvalde, but I heard they died years ago." Willis and Joe winked at each other and walked out of the museum without telling the curator who they were.

Near Brackettville, about forty miles west of Uvalde, there is a movie set of the Alamo and a western town which had been built originally for John Wayne and his version of the battle of the Alamo. When films were being shot there, Joe would load Old Paint into his stock trailer and drive to the set, where sometimes both he and his horse were hired as extras. Among the movies he appeared in was one about the Alamo, *The Last Command,* in which Joe laughingly claimed he played roles opposite himself: in one scene he was a Mexican lancer charging the Texans inside the fort, while in another he was a Texan firing at the charging Mexicans, one of whom was himself.

Although we intended from the outset to produce an oral history book about the Newtons, Joe's interest in films suggested a complementary project to us: why not a film about them while the two brothers were still alive and vital? It was not only that Willis and Joe had dramatic stories to tell; they were so relaxed and natural and utterly candid while narrating that we believed they would be ideal subjects for a documentary in a visual medium. We also were convinced that such a film would be of unique value from both historical and sociological viewpoints, particularly in light of recent scholarly interest in social history. When Willis and Joe gave us their stories of life in West Texas in the nineteenth and early part of the twentieth centuries, they did so with such vividness and in such detail that to duplicate it, one would have to endure firsthand the struggles those people underwent to survive. The stories of Texas' political, military and business leaders, and others at the pinacle of society, have been well documented and frequently told, but not so well known are the life histories of those who existed on the bottom, the poor and inarticulate and unrepresented, especially those who for one reason or another, like the Newtons, chose to pursue antisocial ends.

We approached Willis and Joe about doing a documentary film, and they agreed to participate. With substantial help from the film department of Trinity University, and a generous grant from the Texas Commission on the Arts, a division of the National Endowment for the Arts, we produced a sixteen millimeter film in color and sound which had its premiere at Trinity in 1976 under the title, *The Newton Boys: Portrait of an Outlaw Gang*.

Although the film has never made money, it was an instant hit and has generated and sustained interest ever since. Roddy Stinson, columnist for the San Antonio *Express-News*, wrote a review of the initial screening which began as follows: "Willis and Joe Newton were in town Sunday, but they didn't rob any banks. In fact, all they stole were the hearts of about three hundred people at Trinity University's Laurie Auditorium who watched a thirty minute film about their outlaw days." Stinson went on to say that "almost every time Willis opens his mouth in the film, quotable quotes pour forth," and he concluded his review by saying that "as with most good museums, an observer leaves the display of objects from the past somewhat awed by the relics he has seen—and grateful that someone has had sense enough to preserve them."

Since that premiere the film, now among the library holdings at Trinity University, has had various uses. It has been run at both the National Endowments for the Arts and for the Humanities, and was featured as a fund-raiser for a museum in San Marcos (where the Newtons in 1923 used so much nitro in the door of the vault that it blew out the entire front of the bank and rained coins all the way across the street). It also was screened as part of the effort to restore the old Opera House in the Newtons' home town of Uvalde. It was a favorite and a prize winner at film festivals held at Rice University in Houston and the University of California in Los Angeles, and won the gold medals for documentaries at the Texas Film Festival in Austin and the Virgin Islands International Film Festival in 1976. Numerous meetings of historical societies, local civic organizations and academic gatherings such as the Texas Folklore Society have featured the work, and it is regularly shown in history, sociology, criminology, and even gerontology classes at Trinity. In 1990 the film was included as part of a seminar on autobiography held on the campus of Austin College, Sherman, Texas, and funded by the National Endowment for the Humanities.

One consequence of each exposure was to bring the two old robbers back into the public eye. *People* magazine ran a two page spread on them in September 1976, and to his delight Joe was invited to appear on the Johnny Carson show. Many interviews in newspapers and magazines followed, and several Hollywood producers expressed an interest in doing a feature film based on the Newton story.

Finally we were led back to our original intention: the production of a serious, comprehensive book based on the taped interviews. As the Russian novelist Dostoyevsky said when asked why he wrote about criminals, "If you want to understand crime, you have to understand the mind of the criminal." The story of the Newton Boys is the story of Texas and the Southwest seen from a perspective afforded very few historians or scholars. Their behavior may have been anti-social in many respects, but such behavior is a pervasive part not only of Texas history but of all human history. Willis' and Joe's negative view of banks, insurance companies, and police and government officials is a dominant theme in the evolving record of Texas. Their understanding of the corruption in these institutions, as seen from the point of view of folks who would have to be considered "outsiders" throughout their lives, is an essential element in understanding these institutions and is as topical as today's newspapers.

This story, however, is no lurid exposé of crime and corruption. We believe it has sufficient scope and significance to qualify as a version of what historian William H. McNeill termed "mythistory": the stories of the struggle to settle and survive in an environmentally harsh frontier land and of the eternal struggle of humankind with both nature and its own human nature. Much of audiences' attraction to Willis and Joe is based, we believe, on the brothers' assessment of that struggle and the factors which led them both to initial success and eventual failure. Their story is not a "success" story in any conventional sense, but it is a faithful rendition of some of the conditions of human life beyond that found in most academic studies.

When we finished the interviews, Joe seemed to have a sense of great satisfaction, as though a need that had nagged him for a long, long time had finally been met:

> *Many stories have been written about us, most of them full of errors. Some people who said they was eyewitnesses saw ten or twelve of us robbing a bank when maybe there was three or four. That will give you an idea of how accurate these stories were. This is the first time we have had a chance to tell the whole story ourselves. We was the ones who was there, so who knows what happened better than us?*

Altogether we made thirty-five tapes of interviews with the brothers. Willis' account, because he was the instigator and leader of the group, took twenty-four tapes, Joe's account eleven. Having the same events described by two different people was a definite advantage in achieving objectivity, because even brothers working closely together view identical occurrences with different eyes. Generally, Willis and Joe agreed on the overall shape of what happened, but they often differed about details. Their personal feelings about events were also often at odds. Willis wanted to rob the Rondout train because, "I'd always wanted to make me a million dollars, and this was our chance." Joe was against it, "*because everybody who ever tried such a big robbery always got caught some way or the other.*"

What follows, then, is the story of the Newton Boys, their origins, their experiences and the consequences, as told by Willis and Joe Newton in their own unaffected way. The many, many hours of interviews were carefully transcribed according to the guidelines of the American Association for State and Local History [Willa K. Baum, *Transcribing and Editing Oral History*, AASLH, Nashville, 1977], and the original audio tapes have been preserved. In preparing the material for publication, we have felt compelled to edit it for readability, removing the questions posed by the interviewers, deleting "crutch" words, false starts, repetitions and uncompleted constructions, and where necessary correcting unclear statements by drawing on dialogue from the documentary film or from other interviews done with the Newtons and transcribed into notebooks. Both Willis and Joe had a strong narrative sense, and we have in essence maintained the chronological form they gave the material in the taped interviews. All chapter breaks represent editorial choices intended to facilitate reading. We have been scrupulously careful to represent accurately the attitude of the speakers and the tone and style of their language.

Willis and Joe gave us their stories unreservedly, even enthusiastically. Up to the time they died, they were shown and asked to verify the accuracy of each successive typescript of the interviews. We feel comfortable in saying they were fully satisfied that what follows is, in both detail and substance, their story.

*Family photograph.*
*Top row (right to left): Joe, wife Mildred, unidentified,*
*unidentified, Tull, possibly Doc, unidentified.*
*Bottom row: (right to left): unidentifed child, Jess,*
*remaining unidentified.*

# 1

## FAMILY HISTORY (1830-1890)

I "Murder, I guess, didn't mean anything in them days, cause everybody had a gun."

'm Willis Newton and I live in Uvalde, Texas. I was born in Callahan County near the town of Cottonwood southwest of Dallas, January 19, 1889. I was the sixth— there was five older than me, and before they quit raising them there was five younger than me. There was Ivy, Bud, Henry, Dolly, Jess—the ones older than me—and then there was Wylie (who we called Doc), Bill, Tull, Ila, and Joe, who was the baby.

In my time I robbed over eighty banks and six trains. On most of these jobs, Jess, Doc and Joe was with me. Some of them I pulled with the help of other people. I don't want to say how much money it all added up to, but it was more than Jesse James, the Dalton Boys, and Bonnie and Clyde got, all put together.

We wasn't thugs like Bonnie and Clyde. We never wanted to kill anybody. Up to the time of the Chicago train robbery we was just quiet businessmen, like doctors and lawyers and storekeepers. All we wanted was the money, to make money. Robbing banks and trains was our business.

Way back in the early days, Texas and Oklahoma was wide open and they had no laws. Texas had been a state way back yonder, but Oklahoma never become a state until 1907. I've heard it said times and times that Texas and Oklahoma in the early days—the 1840s, 50s, 60s, 70s, and 80s—was mostly set up by people that had done something somewhere else and run to Texas and Oklahoma.

I had an uncle that come from Arkansas in 1888 or '89. He'd stuck a knife in a man and he got away and run and come to Texas and that was the end of it. It was a general rule in the old days that fifty percent or more of them had killed somebody or stole something or violated some law and would come to Oklahoma or Texas and they was never bothered.

They had killed somebody or stole something, but they really wasn't an "outlaw." They was law violators. What we always called "outlaws" in the early days was people that went out and robbed trains and banks. But in them days there was horse thieves and cow thieves and all such as that. That was about all there was to steal. There wasn't hardly no money in the banks in them days. They was cattle thieves and horse thieves and what we called "cut throats." That's people that will just shoot you for nothing to get something off of you. Shoot you and then rob you.

I've heard my mother and my grandmother talk about it, about men who'd just "catch hands" and shoot it out in them days. They'd have a quarrel and shoot it out. Just hold hands and get their pistols and start. Everybody carried a pistol on their hip. If you killed somebody, you said, "Well, he reached for it and I killed him." That's the way it went.

My great-grandfather—I don't know his give name, but his family name was Eads—he was an old Irishman who come from Tennessee. I think it was in 1838 he come to Goliad, him and some more people, and they settled. Well, he lived in Goliad until 1843, and then him and one family that come from Tennessee with him moved to Oakville—where the old town of Oakville is now—and settled just above the crossing where Oakville met the creek. They made their headquarters about a quarter of a mile up the creek and the other family went about two miles from there. He brought fifty head of gentle cattle with him from Goliad.

It was all open range, anybody's country, and so he built his pens and corrals there, and a house. He had a

2

girl, Ivy, which was my grandmother, and two boys named Mart and the other Sam. My great granddaddy just raised cattle there, and run his brand on all the cows that come in home, and in ten years he had that whole country stocked with cattle. He had more cattle than anybody down there.

They'd sell their cattle to the buyers that come through in the spring of the year and drove 'em North. He stayed there until 1854 when some roughs come in and tried to buy him out. He had all that country and all them cattle there, and he wouldn't sell. They kept after him and then they said they was gonna run him out, which they tried to do, but he wouldn't run. They'd come up at night and shoot the dogs and do everything else. Kill some of his cattle.

One day him and the two boys was off bellin' a cow. Had caught a gentle cow and was puttin' a bell on her. That was in 1855. And these ruffians, six or seven of them, rode up on him, took him and put him up on one of the horses and rode away with him. The two boys was only about ten and twelve, or twelve and fourteen years old, and they never went home and told my grand-mother—she's about fifteen then or sixteen—what had happened until it got dark. That they had come and took the old man. She'd been trying to get him to carry a gun, but he was a religious old man and he wouldn't carry a gun. She kept tellin' him that them people was going to kill him.

When she heard what happened, she wanted to get right on a horse to hunt for him, but it was night and she couldn't go until the next morning. She went where them boys told her that they had carried him off from. It was just a few miles right down that creek to where it run into the Nueces River. And there's a big hole of water, a long hole, and a high bluff there. She tracked the horses right to that bluff. And she said the ground was tore up all over there and there was men's tracks and horses' tracks, and everything else. And she knowed that they had throwed him in the river. She had nobody to go to for help—only that one family—and they was all afraid to get away then from the house to do anything. And she just had to let him go as dead. She never heard tell of him anymore. She knowed that they'd throwed him in the river there.

Well, she rode a horse just like a man so she stayed there. They come in on her, then, these outlaws, and tried to buy her out. When she wouldn't sell, they done everything, harrassed her, run part of the cattle off and then come back and shot her dogs at night. But she stayed there until she was about eighteen years old. They had lots of horses too, with the cattle, but the main thing was the cattle. Every spring she'd round up them cattle to get 'em in them pens for the cow buyers. For two or three years she stayed there, selling cattle in the spring of the year.

When she was about eighteen, there was a horse buyer named Anderson come down in that country and she got acquainted with him. He's from Boston, Massachusetts. He talked her into selling her outfit, her claim, and all the cattle and things to these outlaws, because he knowed what they was trying to do and what they would do. So she sold all of these cattle and her rights— she never got a big lot for 'em—out to these outlaws. And the horse buyer, she sold him all the horses. They'd take the horses to San Antone to a horse market.

So they got acquainted and they got married. He bought horses in Mexico and brought them back to them forts, to the government, and sold them. The forts was out on the Pecos River west of Sonora, like Fort Lawrence. They had "calvaries" there. He'd bring the horses there and they'd pick the good, big horses.

Then he'd take the rest into San Antone to the horse market and he'd sell them there.

*Fort Lancaster. That was where our mother was born, at Fort Lancaster. She was named Janetta Pecos, after the Pecos River.*

4

Yeah. That was our mother. Those horses come out of Mexico, and my mother was born right there at the crossing on the Pecos River in 1857. Some old Mexican woman was the doctor. She took care of grandma and brought my mother into the world. Think there's one of them old houses on that crossing yet. That's where she was born.

This Anderson kept going to Mexico to get the horses, and the last trip he took over there, he had between two and three hundred head of horses, bringing 'em across the river at old Langtry. He had, oh, I guess ten or fifteen Mexicans with him but the Mexicans from Mexico run in there one night and stampeded the horses. They had a battle and run all the horses back into Mexico. One Mexican that was with him knowed how to go around another canyon and go the same way that they went with the horses. So they took around this canyon, and the next day they got in ahead of those Mexicans and they had 'em in that canyon and had a battle. Two or three of the Mexicans working for my grandfather got killed and they killed a lot of the other Mexicans, but they got the horses and brought 'em back. Run 'em back across the river and on to that old fort and sold some there, and what there was left he took to San Antone. But he wouldn't go back to Mexico anymore. He took what horses him and my grandmother had and moved up at Round Rock.

That country was all wide open back then. My mother said grass was as high as your waist. My grandmother's brother, Sam, had come up to Round Rock too, and one day some guys come into the town and said they was looking for Sam Eads. Sam heard about it and started up there. Grandma Ivy wouldn't let her brother go. She said, "Stay away from them." But Sam said, "I ain't going to do nothing. I want to see what they want with me." He went off up there without a gun. They arrested him. One said he was a sheriff from way up north somewheres, and they took him out about thirty miles, and two or three weeks after that somebody found him hanging from a limb. He wasn't no horse thief, but it was twice as bad as anything else to steal a horse. They'd hang you for stealing a horse. Just take you out to a limb. A horse thief was the worst thing. Your horse, he was the main transportation in them days. That was the most valuable thing there was, horses. Stealing cows was next. And murder, I guess, didn't mean anything in them days, cause everybody had a gun.

It wasn't long after that that my grandfather was a-cleanin' his pistol—my mother was about a year, two years old, so it was 1859, I guess—and it went off and killed him.

Then grandma married a man by the name of Jobe. They lived there until 1861 when the Civil War started and Jobe had to go to war. Well, my grandmother looked after them horses and pushed 'em even further toward Belton. What's that old town? It's an old stage coach town just outta Belton as you're coming to San Antone, where the first college in Texas was. Salado!

Her and all the women all over that country, they moved to Salado on account of the Indians. And they stayed there till the war was over. About the time the war was over Jobe come back, but he had just come back a year or two when he died with some kind of disease.

Grandma stayed there until about 1868 or '69 and then moved to Lampasas. She always called it Lampasas Springs, but I never heard that except by her. But in them days they called it Lampasas Springs. They stayed there I guess two or three years, and my mother had a aunt that had come to them with a girl about twelve or thirteen years old, and my mother was about the same age. The girls was out playing one day and five Indians rode up and grabbed this Alice—her name was—and away they went. Alice's father and mother was separated, and he was mad at her because she wouldn't live with him, I think is the way it was. They come to find out that he had these Indians to come and grab the girl and he took her and left. And they never heard tell of her for a long time. The girl's mother—she was weakly—she

6

didn't live but a year or two till she just grieved herself to death.

My mother and grandmother stayed there at Lampasas and sold a lot of horses in that country, and then they went to Junction City in the early seventies and went into the sheep business. Then Grandma run sheep all up and down in that country of seven hundred springs for several years. I don't know how many years.

Finally she sold her sheep out and left Junction City and went up to Brown County and back into the horse business, and cattle too. Right where the old standpipe was in Brownwood was a spring, right in the heart of the town, and that's where the cattle watered.

While she was still in Junction my mother was a-goin' to school and she met a man by the name of Johnson and they got married. He was a buffalo hunter. He'd go every year hunting buffalo and come back. They had one boy, Jimmy Johnson. The last time his father went out, Jimmy was a year or two old, and they never heard tell of the father anymore.

The buffalo hunters would go up the Brazos River and then up Salt Fork and way up thataway. Out into the plains. Johnson was a good marksman and he got big pay, you know, for killing the buffalo. That's all he done, just kill buffalo. They killed 'em for the hides, but he never skinned any. He was the killer. They don't know what become of him that last time he went hunting. He just never did show up again.

It was when my mother and grandmother were living in Brown County and were in the cattle business that my mother met my father. He had come from Fordyce, Arkansas. His name was Jim Newton. He had a cousin that lived there and he'd come to visit his cousin. He met my mother at a picnic at a little town down there—I used to know the name but I forgot it now—and that's where my mother and my father met. In '79 or '80. Mighta been '77. Somewheres along there, and eventually they got married.

He went to work along them ranches, and it wasn't

long until that Chisholm Trail to the railroad in Kansas was a-goin', and so every spring he used to go up the Chisholm Trail with a cattle herd and come back in the fall.

One year my grandmother decided she'd take her horses to Oklahoma. Well, she went to a little town right this side of Chickasha, out in that Oklahoma Caddo country. All wide open country. She took her horses up there in 1897. When she was up there, some people found out she was from Texas, and right where she was a-stayin' she found this girl, Alice, that the Indians had stole way back there. Her daddy had took her to Oklahoma. She had married a Indian and she had a big family, a grown boy and everything else. They got to talking and found out who one another was. That's the way my grandmother found her.

The last trip my Daddy made on the Chisholm Trail was in the eighties sometime, him and a partner. In them days the old man drank pretty good, pretty heavy. So they drove them cattle up there to Dodge City, and of course there was just everything in the world you could spend your money for. Whiskey, gambling, and everything else. So they all had a horse and saddle when they started, and him and this old boy they drank a little too heavy and gambled a little too heavy, sold their horses and saddles, and lost the money they got for them. And the wagon train that come with the cattle always had a certain day  it'd go back to Texas, you see. So when it got time for the wagon train to go, if you wasn't there, why they went. They didn't wait for nobody. So my daddy and this old boy was drunk and busted, and when after two or three days they went back to the wagon train, it was gone. Well, there they was. They had to get back to Texas. They didn't have a horse, didn't have a saddle, didn't have anything. I guess no money. They got 'em a little grubstake, a little pack to put on their back and of course they knowed where all the waterholes was. It was in the summertime and fall of the year, so you could lay down and sleep anywheres. So they walked all the way back to Texas, all the way back down the Chisholm Trail.

They'd been up through there two or three times, so they knew how to get back. But they was afraid to steal a horse, for in them days they'd hang you about stealin' a horse. He was tellin' it one time, and I says, "Well, I'll tell you one thing, Pa. If it had been me, I'd a damn sure stole a horse. And if they'd hung me, it'd a-been after the battle."

So then he come back there, and they moved to Cottonwood in Callahan County, in about 1885 I guess. At that time him and my mother had made a trip to Arkansas and back in a covered ox wagon, and he come back to Fort Worth, to Dallas, with the railroad. He worked on the railroad. And then he come back to Brown County where my grandmother lived. They had stayed one year in Arkansas.

Ivy, my oldest sister, was born in Brown County. She was the first. Bud was born in Arkansas when they was back there. Then they come back to Brown County and Henry was born, and Dolly. And all the rest of us was born at Cottonwood. There was eleven children altogether. Joe was the youngest. He was born in 1901. I was born in 1889, January the nineteenth. In Cottonwood in the house they called the White House, a big old two-story house, snow white, and everybody called it the White House.

*I was born in one of those double log cabins out there, one old log cabin on this side, one on that side, and a hallway or breezeway between where you could sit out in the chairs and get your fresh air.*

Jess was born about two miles over there at what they called the Whitt Place. On down come me, then Doc was born right over there at a little old house, I forget the name of the place. Then my other brother that died, Billy, he was born right there by the edge of town. Then Tully. He was born in a log house about two mile from Cottonwood. Then Ila, my youngest sister, and then Joe, he was born over there at the double log house. All of us within a mile or two, just in a circle around town. We could almost throw a rock from one farm to another, where we lived around Cottonwood.

# 2

## ON THE MOVE (1890-1903)

> "My daddy was a cyclone farmer
> . . . . always looking for a honey
> pond and fritter tree."

**M**ost of his life, my daddy was a farmer. We called him a "cyclone" farmer because he blew all over the country. Never stayed in one place. He moved every year, even if he made a good cotton crop. He'd say, "Well, boys, we're going to turn over a new leaf," and, "That's the best place over there," and then we'd move, move, move, maybe just over the fence. He'd say, "We're going to make a better cotton crop over there, boys. This place ain't no good." Hell, he'd rent a place, we didn't have no land. I don't know of any place that we ever stayed more than one year until 1903, and then he stayed two or three years in one place. That was just his nature.

From Cottonwood, where my daddy and mother come in '85 after they had been to Arkansas and where the last of us was all born, we moved to Scurry County. That's out west of Abilene. Around Sweetwater, out there. And we made the first cotton crop out there in 1892, in Scurry County northwest of Sweetwater, twelve miles east of Snyder, the county seat. And boy, antelopes—when we went there antelopes was just like quail. Everywhere you looked there was antelopes.

Pa just broke the ground and turned it over with a turning plow and two old horses. Then he went back and took what we called a Georgia Stock and heel sweep, and taken an old middle buster and run a row off with one horse and then the other one followed with a planter— with one horse to the planter. He planted about twenty acres of cotton and made a bale to the acre.

11

Down around Sweetwater they was already raising some cotton, but not up there in Scurry County. I remember taking my daddy a bucket of water over in the field as he was plowing in the summer or spring of 1893 when I was four years old, and there was lots of rattlesnakes out there. I was walking down a plowed furrow, and he had just turned this old sod, turned it over in big flat clods, and I was walking down there to take him this water. I was wearing a dress. And there laid a big rattlesnake, right up on that clod of dirt where I was walking up that furrow. Boy! I flew to the house, dropped my water and hollered, "Maw, yattlemake! yattlemake!" I couldn't talk plain [laughs].

That fall I remember us picking cotton a bale to the acre. And I remember it coming a big rain. All out on that prairie there was prairie dogs, just a prairie dog town as far as you could see. They'd put up a mound—it was all flat country—they'd roll up a big mound around so the water couldn't run in their hole when it rained. And you could look out at that end and see five hundred prairie dogs, oh, any time of the day. And you could look on farther and you'd see five hundred antelopes. The whole country was covered with antelopes.

Then when it'd rain, why we'd go out there—it was all water down in them flats—and we'd take a hoe and dig them mounds down and run that water in them holes and drown the prairie dogs out and catch them. Sometimes you'd put it in this hole and it'd just run and run and run and run and run a big stream, and directly you could see them coming out of that hole and that hole. They'd have five or six or seven holes, maybe, all connected up.

Another thing I remember, that fall we'd put the cottonseed in a little old house there to feed the cattle on. And we'd catch them prairie dogs and put them in that house. So that cotton was put in there about the first of October, a load of cottonseed. Well, we had put prairie dogs in there. And about two months later we went to leave there and the old man he went in there to shovel

12

and load all that cottonseed, and he dug a prairie dog out of them cottonseed. He'd been in there two months. See, they can go for months and months without water. In that old, dry country, you know, the only time they get water is when it rains or dews. That old prairie dog had done had him a bed built back in there and a hole dug and he was living on cottonseed, but he was getting pretty thin. Well, we got that poor old feller out.

We stayed there that one year, then the old man had had all of West Texas he wanted. He wanted to move so we picked our cotton, but we didn't gather half of it, and hauled it thirty miles to Sweetwater where we sold it. He wanted to go back to Cottonwood. So back to Cottonwood we headed, and I guess we moved about December of 1893. We camped one time before we got to Sweetwater, and next night we camped in Sweetwater. There was a creek there that they called Sweetwater Creek, and I imagined the water in it was sweet. Along the road there was a fence and wood steps so that you could walk over that fence down to the creek to a water hole where people that camped got water. I remember getting me a bottle, and I went down there and just drank and drank all I could drink and got me a bottle, an old quart bottle, to take some back with me. So I come back over them steps and went to get in the wagon and I dropped my bottle of water and spilled it all. I cried and raised the devil until they went back and got me another bottle of sweet water.

Most of the water in that part of the country is gyp water. Sweetwater wasn't. It was just a running creek. Sweetwater Creek and Sweetwater town, the county seat of Nolan County, is named after that water. It's good water, but they don't use it now. They've got big lakes all over. But when the town was settled there, that was their water, that creek was.

Pa was always restless. Taking trips looking for honey ponds and fritter trees, you know. For God's Country, we used to call it, where you could just find honey and get some fritters and pick 'em and go to eatin'

13

'em. But he wouldn't stay long. He'd stay awhile, about two or three months, and then he'd come back to Cottonwood. He never found God's Country even though he looked for it all his life.

In the little towns in Texas back then, First Monday was a trade day, and the big business in them days was trading horses. Daddy thought he was a horse trader, and he'd keep old poor horses around, and stand 'em up and feed 'em and curry 'em as work horses and he held 'em out in the grass. And we'd say, "Pa, that old horse ain't any good." And he'd say, "Boys, he'll be a damn good old horse, if he ever gets fat." But he never got fat. He'd keep him awhile, and then come First Monday and he'd take him and trade him off. Get what he could for him and get another one. The problem was, he could take a two hundred dollar horse and make five trades and be afoot.

He could eat more butter and drink more milk than any man I ever seen in my life, but he wouldn't have a cow around him. Up until 1901 Grandma would give my Ma some cows and he'd get shed of them. Then Grandma would give her some more. People had so many cows around the place that lots of times they'd let you take one up to your house, if it had a calf, and milk it. The old man, he wouldn't have them around. He was crazy about horses. That was in his nature too.

I never cared anything about horses. Never rode but one horse, I guess, in my life.

*First Monday of every month, Trades Day, everybody'd go into town and take everything they wanted to trade, horses, cows, chickens, wagons, plows. And Pa'd go in and trade. Sometimes the whole family would go, but mostly our daddy and one or two of the boys would go.*

*My grandmother had give my mother some cows way back there, and first thing she knowed he'd traded them off for horses! That may be where I got my love of horses. I guess it must have been bred in me. Jess was a*

14

*Jim Newton, father of the Newton Boys*

*horseman, and Tull too. There was three of us that were horse people, cowboys, and worked with horses and always had horses all our lives.*

In 1894 the old man bought a gin over there at Cottonwood. We lived down in a house right across from the graveyard, and we'd always call it the Graveyard Place. That was where my brother Billy was born, in the fall of 1894 when I was five. I remember that very well.

Well, Pa run that gin there in the fall of '94. And the old cotton, it'd come down and they'd feed it into the bin with suction and it would fall into a big hopper and it wouldn't all come over to where it was supposed to run down to the gin stands. The gin stands was where big blades would separate the cotton from the seeds. When the hopper was full, cotton would run into the stand, but when it would get low, why you'd have to take a rake and sit there and reach over and rake it. He put me at that job and I was five years old. "Raking cotton," we called it. Oh, boy, that was a job.

The next year in '95 we moved over to the Kelly Place. A man named John Kelly had lived on it. We made a cotton crop there that year, but Pa still had the gin. It didn't take no money to buy a gin, really. He was the best gin man in the whole country. He could make a gin himself. Paid so much out of what he made, out of ginning cotton, to get it built. And then we had a thing that we ground corn, you know, for meal. A big old wheel thing you'd grind corn with. On Saturday, we just ground corn. We'd take so much corn for a toll. A man knowed how much he had, and we'd pour his corn up and then we had another little box we'd pour into, and that's what we charged him for grinding his meal.

Pa run the gin there that year in '95, and the next year we moved about four mile. That was a long move. I don't know what we called that place, but we had a name. Whoever had lived there before, that's what we called it.

So in 1896 we made a cotton crop over there, but Pa still run the gin, you see. That's where Tully was born, October the first, 1896. Among the kids, now, that's going on down the line. When the old man got all of his own cotton out over there, then he went to running the gin that fall. There was a house across from the gin, and when we got through gathering the cotton over there, we all moved over into the house by the gin. I think by that time Bud was big enough to help with the gin. Bud and Henry both.

The house right there by the gin was where my grandmother used to live. It might have belonged to her at that time. Well, Pa finished up all the ginning just a little while before Christmas, but his daddy had died in Arkansas. They had a lot of pine timber and a lot of land stuff, and so they had cut it and they divided it and sent him about two hundred dollars. For his share of the timber and stuff they'd sold. He'd been away from there, I guess twenty years. And we had an uncle out there in West Texas too, Uncle Henry, he'd been out in this country about fifteen years. Them two decided they'd go back to Arkansas visiting for Christmas. So they took me and Doc with them because we didn't have to pay to ride the train.

So, we went back to Fordyce, Arkansas, to where they lived down in Calhoun County, out in the country about fifteen miles. I was about seven years old and Doc was five. My daddy's little old shotgun he'd had when he was a boy was still there at his old home, a single barrel, and it would still shoot. That's the first gun that I ever loaded and shot in my life, that had belonged to my daddy when he was a boy. He kept them in meat during the Civil War with that gun, killing deer. Deer was everywhere and they had them old rail fences. He'd load the gun up and he said he'd get to a crack in the fence and deer would come by, about five, six, seven of them. He'd shoot them right behind the shoulders with that shotgun. He knowed what he was told by the old ones on how to shoot them, see, and the deer was just thick around there.

They wouldn't let us have the gun, but I had a cousin there called Albert, about a year older than me, and one Sunday we stole that gun out. You loaded it with powder, you know. It was a muzzle loader and you used a ram rod. So we went down squirrel hunting and I loaded that old gun up. We'd knock them squirrels down around there.

There was a lot of niggers lived down there. We went down there, old Texas boys, and I had that shotgun and I'd point it at them and they'd just go in all directions. Well, we scared about half the niggers that lived down in the bottom there that day. Finally they got word, Uncle

Henry and my daddy did, that we was down there and had that shotgun. So they come and found us that evening and settled everybody down and brought us on back.

We stayed there I guess two or three weeks and visited everybody in the country. It was Christmas and everybody was coming in on horseback and in their buggies and wagons. You could hear them old wagons rattling in every direction. It was a family reunion. Uncle Henry had been gone fifteen years and my daddy had been gone twenty.

Way back there, Uncle Henry had had a fight with some fellow down there and stuck his knife in him. That's when he come to Texas, on the run from Arkansas [laughs]. Well, they got word out there that the sheriff was going to arrest Uncle Henry when he got ready to leave. He wouldn't bother him while he was around there, but said when he got ready to go back to Fordyce and get on the train, he was going to arrest Uncle Henry for that old case. So they got the word around and Uncle Henry went to a town about fifteen miles on down the track from Fordyce to catch the train. So when they took us back in the wagon to Fordyce to catch the train, sure enough the old law was there to arrest Uncle Henry. But Uncle Henry wasn't there. They asked around where he was at, and our folks said he wasn't going to go for a few days. That he was still over there. But he was way down the track at the next station.

Later Uncle Henry got on the train to come on back. We come down to a canyon of the Ouachita River on that little old train, and boy!, the water was just touching the bridge. Them old bridges was weak in them days, and they stopped and blowed the whistle and got out to examine it. The engineer and fireman and conductor did, before they'd cross it. Finally they decided to cross it. Uncle Henry said, "Come on here, boys. We'll get on the back end of the coach and if it breaks this thing down, we'll jump in the water and I'll get you out." So my daddy and him took us back to the back end to the back coach, but the train went on across all right.

Before that there had been rain, rain, rain, rain. The Ouachita was a big river and it was just lapping at the bottom of the bridge up there. But we rode that train to Fort Worth and then changed over onto the Texas Pacific and come on back home.

Well, Pa then rented a place in what we called "the mountains," in the northern part of Callahan County, from old Luke Cathy, and we called it the Cathy Place. It was twenty miles north from Cottonwood, the farthest we'd ever farmed away from there. That was mountain country. Big, blackland farm up there. Grass, good grass and everything. Every little creek was full of water. It rained so much it was just fish, fish, fish. We lived on fish half the time and on rabbits the other half. Plenty of good jackrabbits. When I left Arkansas they had give me an old single-shot .22 target rifle. They was all single shots in them days. You just broke the barrel and put one bullet in it. When we got to them mountains I went to shooting my target and boy!, it wasn't a little time until I was knocking jackrabbits over at thirty or forty steps.

We stayed up there and made a crop that year, a good crop, too. Then it turned out that somebody had bought a lot of stuff, groceries and stuff, from old John Searles down in Putnam, and had mortgaged their crop to him. He needed somebody to pick it. Since my daddy bought his groceries from Searles, we went down there to pick this cotton and picked about ten bales. I think he give us thirty-five cents a hundred for picking it. Then we went back up to the mountains to our place and I guess we had thirty bales there, but it wasn't worth but three cents a pound, about fifteen dollars the bale. We got about ten or fifteen bales there, then just had to turn around and give them over to John Searles because he had a mortgage on our crop too.

I don't think my daddy got enough money that year to pay for the groceries and clothing and everything for us ten or eleven kids. Our yearly bill come to about $250, and that was a big price.

That's when the old man went down there and got drunk and cussed Searles out. Told him he felt like they was using a brace of pistols on him. My daddy bought his dry goods in one store from old man Shackelford, and his groceries from Searles across the track, at the other store. He told Searles, "Everytime I buy from one of you, I think both of you charges." He whooped them up around there.

He was an easy old man, my daddy. Too good for his own good. That's why he had to get drunk to tell John Searles off. If somebody tried to help him and give him something, he'd monkey around and give them more back than they'd give him. Luke Cathy always tried to help him, but he'd never let it happen. He'd turn around and give something to Luke or do something, and there went our edge.

Luke was an old-time wet roper—they was like vigilantes but they called them wet ropers in them days—and my daddy knowed all about him. If somebody did something wrong, or was accused of stealing a cow, or if they thought he was violating the law in some way, and they couldn't catch him, them wet ropers would take him out and whip him with a wet rope and tell him to leave the country. In order to get shed of him, see. There was an organization of them in Cottonwood. They was all over the country.

In Cottonwood, my daddy knowed every one of the wet ropers—two of the Huffs, old man Breeden, John Searles, Luke Cathy. He seen the head man, Willis Huff, kill a man and he wouldn't tell on him. Some guy out there had killed a man, and he was in a store shooting at Willis Huff's brother. He had shot him in the leg already when Willis grabbed up a Winchester and went around the other way—to go where the guy couldn't see him—and he raised up and killed the guy. Just plugged him, killed him dead, then dropped the Winchester and walked away. Nobody seen it but my daddy. With his big, loud mouth he got to talking around there, and Willis come up to him and told him, "Jim, you're the only man that's seen this. We're all good friends. Let's don't tell anybody."

After that, the old man dried up. If anybody said anything about him seeing the shooting, he said, "That's a damn lie." When he went before the grand jury he said, "No, I didn't see anything about it." And when it went to trial, he said, "No, I didn't see Willis shoot nobody." After that, he was ace high with all the wet ropers, but he wouldn't join them. He wouldn't do a thing like that. They was kind of like the Ku Klux Klan. They took the law into their own hands, and my daddy wouldn't go out and jump someone up and whip him. He wasn't a violator; he never violated a law in his life.

The wet ropers didn't go after a guy just because they didn't like him, though. The guy had to be doing something and he didn't belong in the country, see, but the law didn't have the dope on him. In them days there was lots of fellows that prowled, stole cows here, horses there—things like that. The wet ropers was pretty well law-abiding citizens, or supposed to be. But I heard my daddy cussing them out and saying every one of them was thieves themselves.

See, old Shufford and the others was all men that owned ranches and farms and houses all around in that country, but they had just stole it, really. They come there early and took it, got it for nothing, until they had a hold on the whole country. Then the other guys that didn't have anything, they lived in little shacks around there, trying to make a living. Maybe they did get a cow or a yearling once in awhile to eat, but there was no market in them days so you couldn't sell it. That was the big thieves, trying to run the little thieves out of the country.

Once there was a guy in the mountains that they was going to go whip because he was supposed to have got a cow off of old Breeden, who had all them mountains back in there. The mountain folks had got wind of it, that they was coming. They had to come up through a little gap in the mountains, and the mountain gang set a trap there and aimed to throw down on them. My daddy got next to this too and went and told Willis Huff, "You damn fool. Don't you go over there tonight with them. They're waiting for you to kill you."

That night the wet ropers had a big meeting. Willis was kind of the head man. He didn't tell them what he had found out. At the meeting, they was discussing, "Well, Brother Breeden"—they called each other "Brother" this and that—"Well, Brother Breeden, I believe he's done something. . . . Now, Brother Shufford, I don't think we've got the . . . ." And so on.

Finally Willis Huff says, "I'm going home. When you get through arguing, you better go on home too." He didn't tell them the others was laying for them. So they argued and argued around there and finally left. Half of them would have been killed too, if it hadn't been for my daddy. He was friends to both sides and he didn't want to see anybody get killed.

Finally it got out who they all was. Somebody swore who it was that went and whipped up on a guy, and they come with warrants and arrested Dick Huff, Willis Huff, Shufford, Breeden—oh, there was fifteen or twenty of them, and I knowed them all after I growed up. They took them to Baird and put them in jail. My daddy went to see them and they was talking, "Now, Brother Breeden, if we can just . . . .Well, Brother Shufford, all we want is justice. Just justice." Willis Huff listened to this and said, "Justice, hell. We don't want justice! If they give us justice, they'll hang every damn one of us."

They never done anything with them wet ropers, but it wasn't long after they got out of jail that they disbanded. It had got a little more civilized around there, and now everybody knew who every one of them was.

So we made that crop there at the mountain and went and picked John Searles' cotton. Camped out while we was doing that because it was ten miles back to where we lived. We had us a place by a waterhole there where we left a covered wagon that had our bedding in it and cooking utensils. Then we made our pallets to sleep on the ground.

Then from the mountains we moved down south a ways to what we called the Goether Place, because old man Goether owned it. That was a little north of Putnam and about ten miles back toward Cottonwood. The old man was inching his way back toward Cottonwood [laughs].

My sister Ila was born there in 1898, August the fourth. I can remember all the dates of every one of us that was borned after me. We made a crop there and the old man took to carpentering. He was a pretty good jackleg carpenter and there were houses to build. He got a dollar a day then, and boy!, he thought he was making all the money in the world at that price. That's when I crippled my right foot.

I was nine years old and helping on a house. Somebody had sharpened a hatchet and told me to take it back up and give it to my daddy. I was walking along, slinging it back and forth, and it slipped out of my hand and cut my heel string plumb in two. Plumb in two! Well, there was nothing to do about it. If I had been taken in somewhere and had something done about it, maybe I'd have been all right. All we done was put turpentine and sugar on it. It took five or six months before it ever growed back to where I could walk, and meantime it drawed my foot up a little. That foot on my right leg now is a number and a half smaller, six and one-half, and my left foot is an eight. And my leg is a little smaller all the way up there. I hobbled around there that year.

From there we moved down to Cottonwood, and because we had a little money the old man bought a place over on Turkey Creek. I think there was 160 acres of land. I think he paid $100 or $200 down. For $500 or $1,000 you could buy 80 or 160 acres of ground in them days. But the old man would buy them and he never could get them paid for. Just make a down payment is all.

All that country was wide open, no fences or anything. This was the last of 1898, first of 1899. My oldest sister, Ivy, had went back to Arkansas and stayed one summer, and she got married to Bud Bowing. They come back to Cottonwood while we was living up at the Goether Place, and when the old man bought the land on Turkey Creek, we all moved there.

My brother-in-law had bought him a little house and moved it over there on our land. The old man told him, "Now you can have sixty acres over there. You clear it off and you plant your crop, and I'll give you the land. Then you can pay your part of what I've got to pay."

My sister was going to give birth to a baby about March or April, but she took the measles just about the time she was going to have the baby and it killed her, her and the baby both. So her husband quit the place and sold the house and went back to Arkansas. That was in the early spring, in March or April.

In the summer, my brother Henry died. He had inflammatory rheumatism and it affected his heart. He was sick, and one night he got up and went out and set down on the porch and just fell over dead. That was about four months after Ivy died. He was sixteen. We buried them both in Cottonwood.

That was quite a shock to the family. They was the first kids, and there we lost two within three or four months. My mother had never read a Bible until that day, and she read it from then on every day until she died. She was always a Baptist, but they had no church building. They'd have church services on Sunday in tents stretched up, and they'd all bring their barbeque and pies. The older people talked about where they come from and where they was going and what they was doing. When I was a little kid, I used to go to them. That was one time I got plenty to eat. On the Fourth of July they'd have a big meeting. They'd have a big brush arbor, and they'd hold their meetings at night. A prayer meeting in the evening and the main service was at night on account of the heat. We used to get in that old wagon and hang our feet out at the back end, and rattle, rattle, rattle, here we'd go. Had quilts in the wagon, and if us kids got sleepy in church, we'd go lie down in the wagon and go to sleep.

In the summer time was when they had them, out-doors. But they had a little old church meeting at the school every Sunday. They used the schoolhouse and the church for the same thing, all over that country. Later on they built churches, but the earliest ones was the schoolhouse. There wasn't so many people to go to church, and they was pretty well scattered in that country.

My mother used to read all them outlaw books, and then she'd tell us kids about them at night. My first outlaw I can remember was Harry Tracy. In 1902 him and David Merrill escaped out of the penitentiary in Oregon. Went over the walls. They was partners in there and partners when they got out. I got the Chicago *Blade* and the *Saturday Ledger*. Every Saturday there'd be a story about Harry Tracy and I'd read it. So there come out a story that Harry Tracy got afraid of Merrill and they took their pistols and agreed that they'd walk ten steps and then shoot. But the story was that Harry Tracy, he turned at nine and killed Merrill. That's the story.

Well, Harry he run about two, three, four months, up through Oregon and into Washington. I seen several times where they'd run onto him, get him hemmed up—he was a big, stout man—and there was several stories where they'd get him hemmed up and he'd grab somebody and throw him on his back and run and they wouldn't shoot him and he'd get away. But finally he went up there in Washington, it was in the summertime, and he got into a man's barn to sleep. I think he got some food from this man's house and the man snitched on him. He was in this barn and they come up with a lot of men and surrounded him. He jumped out of a window and broke his leg, and he crawled off out into a wheat field, two or three hundred yards, and they wouldn't go out there. And before he'd let them take him, he killed hisself. [The story of their daring prison break, during which they killed three guards, and subsequent flight from pursuing lawmen was carried for days in both the Chicago *Tribune* and the New York *Times*, beginning

June 10, 1902.].

Well, that was my first outlaw that I read about. Of course I'd been told about the Jameses and Daltons and all of that, but they was all dead in my days. Harry Tracy was the first living outlaw in my days. I thought he was a hero. I cried when they killed him. They was out there running him and trying to kill him and he was trying to get away. He never tried to kill nobody when they run him. He wanted to get out of the country and he had to fight. Boy, he battled it out with them. I liked that. They was trying to kill him and he was trying to get out of that country and save his life. But he didn't make it.

Jesse James and the Daltons—I read their stories and things, and I believed all that stuff in them days. But now there's a lot of it I know was bunko. One thing about the Jameses and Daltons that never set right with me: they hated the North and they'd ride into town to rob a bank or something and they'd go to shooting people before they robbed the bank. Then they'd rob the bank and shoot everybody they could as they rode on out.

Well, I never did believe in that kind of murder. I liked to read their stories and hear their stories and everything, but I never believed in that kind of stuff. If they was robbing there and somebody tried to kill them and they had to shoot back to save their own life, why that's different. But they just shot them as they went in and as they went out.

My mother, she said, "Willis, I guess if I had been a man, I'd a-been a bank robber or outlaw too." I'm the only one that took after my mother completely. She read every outlaw story that come along. Read nothing but outlaw stories until after my sister and brother died. After that, whenever my mother had nothing to do, she read that Bible. She would read three, four, five stories, and then she'd tell us kids everything in there when we went to sleep. She could take that book and read two or three verses that I couldn't understand. Then she would sit down and explain everything that was in there. It would take her an hour. Word to word, she would explain what

*Janetta Pecos Anderson Newton,*
*mother of the Newton Boys*

it all meant.

Or if we got hold of one of them Wild West stories ourselves, we'd bring it in and get Ma to read it. Then at night when we went to bed, she'd tell us the story, and she could tell it word for word. She told you all of it, the Bible or any of them other stories.

She had a pretty good education, I suppose, seventh or eighth grade, where she went to school. I don't know if they had high school in her days or not. But she went to school and she could read and write, everything like that.

After Ivy and Henry died she grieved for two or three years. My mother always said she had all her troubles in the daytime. She worried about her troubles and let them bother her in the daytime. Somebody said to her, "Don't you worry about the boys? I don't see how you can sleep." That's when she told the story of what she done, how she worried. "But when night come and I went to bed, I laid my troubles right over there with my Bible and went to sleep. When I get up in the morning, I pick them up again and go with them all day. When night comes, I lay them aside." She said that until the day she died.

It was awful hard on her, but life ain't miserable for no kids. You got all that youth, and as long as you got quite a bit of little things to eat, you can sleep anywhere. Oh, life was lean, but we didn't know it. Everything was hard in them days. There was nothing soft like now. As long as you got something to eat and a few clothes to wear, there was nothing else to bother you about. No shows to go to or nothing like the kids got now, my God! I played baseball when I was around Cottonwood there until I was about eleven or twelve. And boy!, I was the shortstop, and I was the champion. There was no way in the world to fan me out. I hit that ball every time they throwed it through. But that was the last time I ever played baseball.

Before that, when we were five or six or seven, we had all kinds of games, leap frog and all such as that. We'd go down on them creeks where there was Spanish oaks. They don't break, they bend. And we could get on them and play dog and squirrel. We'd leap from tree to tree, grab a limb and go on to the other maybe for three hundred yards and never hit the ground. That was dog and squirrel. One was the squirrel, and the other one was the dog after him in the trees, and you jumped from tree to tree, tree to tree, tree to tree. If you caught him, then somebody else would take out, and he'd get to be the squirrel. If you didn't catch him when the trees cleared out, he'd jump down on the ground and he's the winner.

We lived there right on the bank of Turkey Creek for two or three years, and we'd go out hunting there. There was squirrels, you'd get ten, fifteen of them every time you wanted squirrel. Hunting, that was our main thing. We'd leave home sometimes before breakfast to keep the old man from telling us there was something we had to do. We'd hit them mountains and creeks and be gone all day. Every Sunday we'd hit them woods and wouldn't get back until dark. Usually got a whipping for staying out all day. We'd get off so far, it'd take us an hour to walk back. Maybe if we got hungry, we'd roast us a rabbit or a squirrel. Sometimes we went without eating all day long. And run all over them mountains just like a jackrabbit, barefooted over them rocks.

Only thing that bothered us was the devil cactus, gets about six or eight inches high, and it's got them old thorns on it just like wire. But I've had my foot so tough that when I stepped on a cactus it would just screech and them stickers wouldn't stick in [laughs]. We could get around a fire and stand, and coals would pop out. You'd get your foot on it and you wouldn't know it until it burnt through that old thick place, and when that happened, boy!, it'd take five minutes to cool off! You just run all over the place, screaming and carrying that foot. Hurt, my God!

In summer, we'd hit them water holes. We'd go off to this creek and that creek and swim half the day. We'd hunt and hunt and then maybe we'd come in and swim in one of them holes until dark. There was little water snakes in there, and a few moccasins, but they never bothered you. Nobody in our family was ever bitten by a snake. There wasn't many rattlesnakes in that country, you know. Rattlesnakes is down here around Uvalde. I guess they grow under the ground down here some- wheres.

So we buried both Ivy and Henry. This was in late 1899. By this time, the old man didn't like the place on Turkey Creek, so he sold it. Somebody come along and give him his money back and about fifty or a hundred dollars extra. He moved us back to Cottonwood. He rented a place there and was going to truck farm, raise cabbage and potatoes. Had him about twenty or thirty acres of rich valley land right down on a good creek. Since an old man named Respus had lived there before, we called it the Respus Place. That was in 1900.

That year we didn't have no cotton, and wouldn't you know it, cotton went up to ten cents a pound! It had always been three cents and five cents, but that year it shot up to ten, and we didn't have a crop. We always missed it [laughs].

So of course he worked at the gin again that fall, all fall. We did pretty good with our vegetables. I guess he made a little money. We raised potatoes and cabbage and corn and we'd take a wagon load to Cisco or to Albany north of there. That was the end of the railroad. Then we'd take a load down to Coleman, about thirty or thirty-five miles. By late fall, all the crop was gathered but the sweet potatoes. We plowed them up in September or October, and oh boy!, did we make sweet potatoes! Got ten cents a bushel for them yellow yams.

When it come time for my mother to buy us kids some clothes, we loaded up a wagon with potatoes and yams and other stuff and went up and sold it all out at Cisco. We got ten or twelve dollars out of the load, and Pa give Ma ten dollars to buy us kids all our winter clothes. That's what he give her every year, ten dollars to buy cloth to make clothes for eight, nine, ten kids. She made them on her fingers too, with a needle and thread. Didn't have no sewing machine.

From there, we moved again to another place, I forget now what we used to call it. We had a name for it. That was in 1901, and that's when Joe was born, at that place, January 8, 1901. Of course we planted a crop there, and Pa give it to my mother and us kids to take care of. We had eight or ten acres of cotton. Then he took out on one of them wild goose chases to New Mexico about January or February and took Jess with him. Pa was always looking for a honey pond and fritter tree. Just get in the wagon and drive. He was going up to Cloudcroft and cut timber, crossties and trees for lumber. But when he got up there, it was high altitude and he couldn't get his breath. He stayed up there for two or three months, though, and that's when I went to school, when he left.

Until that time I had never been to school, so I was twelve years old then. I'd wanted to go to school, but the old man always had something for us to do. When he left, I told my mother, "I'm going to start to school now." We lived about two miles from the school.

I had been picking cotton that fall and I didn't have no shoes. Some way I had got hold of a first reader, but I didn't know my ABC's. Jess had started a month or two before that, in December I think it was, and he went about a month. He never learned his ABC's, and then the old man pulled him out and took him to New Mexico. My mother had made all my clothes. I had a little old shirt and a homemade pair of pants. No shoes. And I had a coat that Wendy Robertson—she had three or four boys—gave me because her kids had outgrown it.

It was two miles, and there was a field right at our house where you could stay right next to the woods and keep that winter off you on cold days. So here I went. I never had nothing to take to eat because all we had at home was a little meat and bread, and I was ashamed to take that. So I took nothing. Oh, if it was right cold, I might get me a chunk of meat and wrap a piece of bread around it, put it in paper, and take it in my bosom here.

There were three teachers. Al Urban had the high school; Rawl Ely was teaching in the middle school; and Miss Dora was teaching from the first to the fourth grade. She was a nice woman. Didn't have no kids of her own, and that year she had adopted a girl, Bessie Ivy, whose mother had died. Bessie was about ten or twelve, my age. Miss Dora's husband run a drugstore there.

In a week or two, God! I could read everything in the first reader. Miss Dora Norton, the teacher, she took an interest in me because I was learning so fast. I didn't have no spelling book, but she took a nickel or a dime and bought one second handed from some other kid and give it to me.

Every morning I'd come in, and pretty soon I was running off and leaving them other kids. It wasn't two or three weeks that Miss Dora said, "Willis, get your mother to get you a second reader."

"We ain't got no money to buy me any books." The next morning when I went to school, she came and laid me down a used second reader.

It come natural for me to spell. I run over that spelling book once or twice, and I could shut it up and spell almost every word down. In two or three weeks, I could. If you missed a word, she didn't say anything about it. Then you could pick it up, one of the others of you, and spell it right, and you'd get them "ahead marks." I had four or five of them ahead marks every morning, when kids would miss them words and the next one wouldn't know and I'd pick them up and run ahead.

Finally she taught me arithmetic, and soon I could divide, multiply, subtract—I could come right on down them columns to the bottom. Other kids would whisper, "Willis, show me how to do this. Tell me what this is." She was watching so I was afraid to show them, but once in awhile, I'd slip them a little and help them.

One morning she gave me a third reader and put me in the third class. I don't think there was a kid that I started in with that wasn't still in the first. There might have been some made second reader, but I doubt it. Here I go in my spelling book, arithmetic book, third reader. I was flying along. God! It just come natural to me, learning did. Only about a week before I had to quit, Miss Dora gave me a fourth grade speller, and I'll never forget the two words in it that I missed. I could spell them all right, but when two words sounded the same, she'd give you one and then she'd say, "What's next?"

She had let one kid try the word. It was "straight" and "strait." I'll never forget that. He took the first one and she said, "What's next?" to me. I was in too much of a hurry, and I run back and spelled the other one, and she said, "No, you missed." I got turned down, and I cried. The other word was "bulk," b-u-l-k. I'd say "bolk," because I hadn't been spelling very long and I said it that way. Then I'd start, "b-o-" and I missed that one.

From school, it was four or five hundred yards to the brush. At noon, because I didn't have any lunch, I'd run back there into the brush and stay until they rung the bell at fifteen minutes to one to start up school again. Make them kids think I had went home to dinner, you see.

Then I had to quit school because the seat of my pants ravelled out. Ma had sewed them and sewed them but you could see all up and down there it was ravelling, and I was ashamed to wear them ravelly pants. Walk by anybody, and they could see them. Ma had got her an old sewing machine. A man had come by with an old Singer, a peddle foot machine that he had took in on a new one somewheres. It worked all right. He sold it to my mother for two dollars. She paid him a dollar and after some time—I don't know when it was—she sent him the other dollar. She worked them pants up as good as she could. I had pulled them off on the bed and laid there while she patched them, but with just three weeks left in the year, I quit.

Miss Dora met my mother over in town and asked her, "Where's Willis?"

"His clothes just got too bad and he won't go to school. He didn't mind going barefoot, but his clothes got too bad."

"Well," she said, "he's the smartest pupil I ever had in school in my life. If you give him an education, there's no telling what he'll do. And if you don't give him an education, there's no telling what he will do." But I never got to go anymore. That ended my school, there in Cottonwood.

My daddy had been out in New Mexico about three or four months. I guess until June. He wrote from there to Tom Marr to send him ten dollars. He didn't have enough money to get back on. Marr was a one-armed man, the tax assessor, and he had been friends with my daddy all his life. When Pa got back, we had two little mules that we used on the wagon, and he couldn't get ten dollars to pay Marr back, so he sold him the mules. I don't know how much he got for them.

We had Polly still. That was the colt we raised up when we come to Scurry County. We kept her and she was about twenty-four years old when she died. The old man bought another horse, so then we had horses for the wagon, not mules. He went off to work the gin that fall at Cottonwood. Me and Doc plowed that cotton with Polly and kept the weeds out of it all summer. When the cows would come into it at night, we chased them and shot at them with the .22 target rifle and run them out. In the end we made a bale of cotton, a good bale of cotton, and me and Doc picked it. I was twelve then and Doc was ten.

That was my mother's cotton, because her and us kids raised and picked it. It was worth eight or nine or ten cents a pound, about forty or fifty dollars then. She was going to use that to buy our clothes and stuff.

We took it over and ginned it, and in place of bringing it back home to unload it, we just let them lay it out there in the cotton yard. Then when we got ready to go to Cisco, we'd go by there and they'd load it for her. We were going to have plenty of money that fall.

But the old man went to Cisco for something before she went. She was keeping her bale of cotton until a while before Christmas. The old man had got the seed. We give him the cotton seed. Besides that, they owed him something at the gin, and he went by there and got more seed, but then he loaded up Ma's bale of cotton too and took it to Cisco to sell. She didn't know about it. I knew he was doing it, but I couldn't get home. I had been picking cotton for other folks around there that fall, and

I had to go along with him when he went to Cisco. I had my own money, and I bought my first suit and my first pair of shoes.

There wasn't nothing I could do about it, but as soon as we got back, I snitched on him. Told Ma he took the cotton to Cisco and sold it. Well, boy, you talk about a mad woman. She cried and cried. Said, "As hard as we worked for that bale of cotton to get our clothes this winter, our stuff for Christmas, and other things—fought them cows all summer, picked and ginned it, and then he took it!"

He always borrowed around, so he owed somebody something, you know. Had to take that cotton to pay a debt. Well, that was terrible, but there was nothing she could do about it. That was in 1901.

From Cottonwood, we moved down to a little town they called Tin Can, about twelve or fifteen miles east of there. A guy name of Booth had a big gin down there and he wanted my daddy to come and get started next summer repairing it. He'd start in about July or August and he'd have two months work, fixing the stands by hand and getting the old boiler cleaned out and everything. He would get a dollar a day until he went to ginning, and two dollars a day running the gins. He could make a gin, you know.

When we got down there, we had a little cotton crop, about ten or fifteen acres. Us kids gathered the cotton. Ma never picked cotton in her life, but she was out there with us in the field to see if we picked cotton. We got three or four bales and sold it that fall.

I always went out and worked for someone to make me some extra money. A boy named Jimmy Robb was selling the paper over there in Cottonwood, what they called the *Saturday Blade* and the Chicago *Ledger*. You got them both for a nickel. The *Saturday Blade* had the weekly news in it, and the Chicago *Ledger* had continued stories. You'd get a dozen, and when you sold them, you gave the company three cents for each copy and kept two cents. That interested me.

So I subscribed for a dozen papers and sold them to the farmers around there. Every time I did that, I had to send in thirty-six cents and made me twenty-four cents. Did it all fall. The first thing I bought, I went over to the store and they had what they called cream candy in them days. It come in big buckets, just loose. It was soft and sweet and s-o-o good. I bought me a nickel's worth of that cream candy. They give it to you in a paper sack, and I got half a pound. All I could eat.

I was helping the old man get the gin back in shape. You had to crawl back into the boiler through a manhole and brush the scale off the inside of it. They fired them with cordwood, four foot long. It run an old steam engine. And I'd get me a dollar every year for working inside the boiler. A man couldn't get in there, but I would crawl way back in there and work for hours on the scale with a brush. But God! I made me a big, flat dollar there. Skinny Newton. Little old skinny thing, I could crawl through a knothole.

Gin time run up until Christmas, and then it played out. Maybe after Christmas somebody would bring in remnants and we'd gin them up. So we stayed there until after Christmas on that place. I was working for an old man name of Square Wells. He had a boy called Shelby and he had married a woman that owned a place there, Miss Black. Her son by a previous marriage was Lee. Shelby and Lee was both about nineteen. I hoed cotton for Square Wells and picked for them all that fall.

That winter, after Christmas, we moved back to Cisco and the old man went to working at the cottonseed oil mill. He got a dollar a day shoveling seeds into the conveyor that took it down to the stands and cut it. Soon they found out he was an expert gin stand man, and they put him on the stands that took the rest of the seed off the cotton. He worked twelve hours a night at that and got a buck fifty. That was really a job! Us kids monkeyed around in Cisco and didn't have nothing to do but prowl around.

# 3

## WANDERLUST (1903)

"We went everywhere—Fort Worth, Abilene, out West, Big Springs, all over Texas. Rode under them rods that held the train cars together."

When we moved into Cisco, they called Jess "Big Snakes" and me "Little Snakes." Doc was younger. He was staying at home, but me and Jess had taken out and went anywhere we wanted to. That's where we first rode us a train. There was a freight train that come to Cisco, and out there about seven mile was a station they called Delmar Switch. It was about seven mile towards the county seat of Callahan County. We thought they stopped at every station, so we got on between the box cars, you know, and that's a rough place. We was going to get off at Delmar and come back, but they didn't stop, and here we went, twenty-five miles to Baird, and us between them cars. You talk about scared! [laughs].

Rattle, rattle, bump, bump—oh, I was never so happy to get off a train in all my life. I don't think I'd have rode another one for a year, but we had to get back home. So that night we went down there and one was going so we got in a cattle car. There was a door open in the end of the car and we both sat in that door and hugged the sides. The door we sat in was a little door. You could open it. It was where you'd come down from the top and go in, and there was this little door, oh, about three foot wide. It was for the brakeman, I guess, if he come over the top and wants to go down in the car. We wanted up there because it was warmer up there. The wind didn't hit you.

So we hugged our arms together and rode that cattle car back to Cisco, and boy-oh-boy!, was I glad when we got back. That was in 1903.

After that, we went everywhere—Fort Worth, Abilene, out West, Big Springs, all over Texas. I rode them under the rods, just laying on the rods if there was a bad brakeman. We'd get down there because he couldn't get us off. Couldn't get to us. The train was running, so he had no chance. When the train stopped we'd get off too, before he got there, and hide on him. It starts up, we'd get another one. Them rods held the cars together. The brakeman didn't shoot at you, but one of them threw a rock. He knowed I was down there and leaned down and throwed a big rock at me. Didn't miss me by two foot, and if he'd a hit me, he'd have chopped me up. Oh, them brakemen was mean, dirty rats them days. I always said if I got growed, I'd get even for the hell they gave us kids.

Years later I got my chance, and I made an old boy jump off one. The train was running coming from Wichita Falls, and one night me and O.C. Wells was on it. We both had pistols, and we seen this brakeman coming. O.C., he hid over on that end of the car, and I got in this end. It was an open car, a coal car. So here come the brakeman and jumped me and was raising hell at me. We wanted him to get tough. Then he seen O.C. duck down. "What's that son-of-a-so-and-so?" and he run over there and he had a club. They all had clubs to turn the brake. They used to didn't have them air brakes, so when they'd switch a car they had a club about four feet long that they'd stick through that brake and help to turn it. It was made of heavy oak, like a sledge hammer handle, and they could kill you with that. So here he run over at O.C and was about to bust him with that, and O.C. comes out with his gun! Then I come right up at his back. And you talk about begging!

That train was running about thirty miles an hour—I was just sorry it wasn't going sixty—and I says, "Get down there on them handle bars." He got down and I didn't do a thing but stomp the gentleman's hands until he fell off. Last we seen of him, he was going thataway. We seen him turning summer-sets, going over and over and over. After that we never rode that cross road there for a long time, or if we did, we'd just ride it at night.

I made lots of them beg after I got big enough to have sense. I carried a pistol and tamed them tough brake-men.

Early in the spring, must have been February or March, an old boy come to Cisco on a horse leading two burros. Us kids went out to where he was at and went to talking to him. His name was Frank Light, from down close to Stephenville. He had been out in West Texas, in Abilene, and had got them burros there. He had a fight with an old boy down there and had hit him with a pair of brass knucks and nearly killed him. The law got after him and he left. He was the only boy in his family and there was two girls and he had got homesick.

I got to talking to him and asked, "Can I ride this burro?"

He said yeah, so Jess and me got on the burros and rode about ten miles to Eastland. Along the way he said, "What are you doing here? Why don't you come home with me and you can work for us?"

So when we got to Eastland, I was ready to go. Jess wanted to go back, but I wouldn't. He followed us for about a mile, and then he wouldn't go on and he had to go back home. Outside of Eastland, an old couple lived. They was in their sixties, well-to-do, their kids all married off. When he had come out, Frank had stayed with them and they told him if he ever come back, to stop and stay the night with them. We rode in there that night and I was welcome. They give us a good supper and bed and a breakfast, then we pulled out and went about twenty or twenty-five miles over to where Frank lived. Got in there that night. That was right after Christmas and they had a little cotton to pick, so I helped them and they said I could stay as long as I wanted, that they would give me board and clothes. Next fall they said they would send me to school if I wanted. School was about half over then, so I didn't care about going then.

I hadn't told my mother or anybody that I was leaving, but Jess told them when he got back that I'd went on with this boy Frank. Me and Frank had two horses, and where Frank went, usually I'd go with him. I ran a turning plow, picked cotton, any kind of work they could do, I could do. That went on up to the last of May or first of June, along in there.

They had big meetings at the churches then, you know, where everybody would take their food and have singing all day. Frank's family had been over visiting people about ten miles away. They called me "Muffin." They told those people about what a smart boy old Muffin was, and this old man says, "Why don't you let him come and stay with us? You don't need him and we'll feed him and send him to school."

We was going to go over to let that old man and lady see me, and I wanted to wear my long pants. Frank's family had bought me a suit of clothes, short kneepants, and shoes, and then they had made another pair of pants that was long. They said, "No, you've got to wear the short suit we bought."

I didn't want to. And Frank was going off to a party that night, to a dance, and I wanted to go with him and he wouldn't let me. We was going to that big church meeting the next day about eight or ten miles away, and we was going to start early. Well, this all made me mad, especially Frank not letting me go with him that night.

The log houses in them days had the kitchen separate from the house where they lived. Frank's room, where I was at, was right even with the kitchen. Just raise up the window and there it was. They was cooking that day, cakes and pies and everything, grub to take to that big meeting.

I found me a shoe box in the room there and put my short suit in it, my good shoes, and what little stuff I had with me. They couldn't see me from the kitchen, what I was doing, and I would come and sit in the window and talk and monkey around. Along about five or six o'clock in the evening, the sun wasn't very high, I got my box and kind of slipped over toward the door on the other side of the room. A hundred fifty or two hundred yards away was a little draw; you went through it and then you hit the creek and a lot of brush. I seen they was back in there cooking and busy and I opened the door and boy! I made it down across that prairie flying. They didn't know where I went. They thought I was still in there. About two or three miles across country a man lived called Jeff Thornton that I knowed. He had a wife and two kids and I went there. I told Jeff I was leaving and he said, "Well, stay all night and in the morning you can pull out."

I didn't have a copper cent in the world, and not a thing to eat. So I stayed all night, and in the morning I had bacon and biscuits and gravy for breakfast. Then I pulled out. It was eighteen or nineteen miles to Thurber, Thurber Junction. That was where the railroad was, due north. I set out and as I left Jeff 's house about two hundred yards away, there was a field there where the wind had blowed the sand up against the wire fence until there was just this one wire sticking out of the top. I walked up there and looked right straight east. The sun had just cleared the horizon. It was clear and cool and the sun was like a ball of fire. I stood there and looked at that sun, and I said, "Now that is something I'll never forget."

That was the first day of June, 1903. From that day on, although I may never think about that year for 364 days, when I get up of a morning on the first of June, that is the first thing that comes into my mind. It's never missed me one time.

That was just old brush country that they cleared out for farming. Raised nothing but cotton and corn. In the spring of the year, February and March, the wind would blow and blow, until you couldn't see four hundred yards in that sandy country. It would blow for a month or six weeks. And there was some brush in the fence that had helped catch the dirt and piled it up as it swept out of the fields. In some places later on them fields would be bare down to the hard ground.

Maybe that land shouldn't have been farmed, but they had to. All of it was thataway. That's the way they made their crops. Then when planting time come, that wind would quit blowing, you see. They didn't know that land would blow away in them days.

So I pulled out with my little shoe box under my arm. Jeff had told me where to hit the road, so I hit that road, an old wagon road, and I went right north. I never seen anybody. It was a Sunday and there was very few houses out in there. When I got to Thurber, that was a big coal mining town, it was two miles over to the junction. We called it Mingus in them days.

There was a train pulled in there at noon and stayed about a half hour while they ate lunch. I was still in Thurber when I seen it pulling into the junction, and I set in to run all the way. I was plumb give out when I got there, and the train was set to leave. I got on it and plopped into a seat. Didn't have a nickel, but I set me down on them cushions, and did that feel good. It was six miles over to Strawn.

The conductor come through and says, "Where's your ticket?"

"I ain't got none."

"You can't ride the train without a ticket."

"Well, I ain't got no money, and I got to get to Cisco. That's where I live."

"You ride to Strawn, then, and get off." And he left. When we stopped in Strawn, I moved back to another coach so if he looked in there he wouldn't see me. We pulled out, and pretty soon here he come. "I thought I told you to get off." So I told him again that I had to get back to Cisco. Well, wouldn't you know, the dirty old rat put me off. Stopped the train and threw me off. I just caught the next car and got up on the platform, and he stopped it again and threw me off again. As the train started up, I went to catch the back of the next car and there he was. He had run through the coach and got to the platform and he kicked at my hands so I couldn't catch ahold. I grabbed up some rocks and throwed at him as the train pulled away. So there I am a mile and a half out of Strawn and fifteen miles from the next town, Ranger. It's about one o'clock then and I hadn't had nothing to eat, so here I go down the middle of them tracks. Just before I got to Ranger, I seen an Irish potato patch off to the side there. Them potatoes was about the size of quail eggs when I dug them up. I took them to the creek, washed them off good and chomped them up like they was candy.

I walked into Ranger at sundown. From there it was twenty-two miles to Cisco: eleven mile to Eastland and eleven more on to Cisco. I was going to catch me a train that night. Out close to the depot there was a lot of wagons, so when dark come, I crawled up into one of them and laid down. I'd walked thirty some odd miles and was pretty beat. I thought when a freight train come along, it would wake me up. About midnight a freight come and I woke up, but I was just so sleepy I couldn't get up. About two o'clock a passenger train was there and all I had to do was walk across the tracks and climb on it, but I was too tired. Come daylight there was no trains, so I pulled out with my bundle down them tracks, twenty-two mile.

I got to Eastland and a freight train overtaken me, but it whooshed on by me like a pay car passing a tramp, and I had to hike all the way. In Cisco, I went to where my people lived, but they had moved, a lady told me, to the other side of town. Cisco was a town of about three thousand people then, so they was a half mile off. When I walked into the house, here come Joe—he was only about two years old—and I grabbed him up and behind him was my mother. I told her I hadn't had nothing to eat since yesterday, so she cooked me some meat and give me some biscuits and gravy and after I'd filled up, I was number one again. She had wrote to the Lights at Stephenville and asked about me. The post office knowed everybody in the country and they got her letter to them. The Lights wrote her back that they was taking care of me, that I had plenty to eat and a good horse to ride, and that satisfied her that I was all right.

The day I walked home from Stephenville, that was the second day of June, 1903. After I got settled down, I says, "Where's Jess?"

"They got him in jail over at Eastland." They fought game roosters all over the country in them days, and Jess was working for a rooster fighter. When he got ready to come home—he was maybe twenty miles away—he picked him out a couple of roosters and took them home with him. They arrested him, fined him twenty dollars or so, and he had to go down there and work it out on the roads and the city streets at fifty cents a day. He had run off one time and they come and got him at the house and took him back. But the funny thing is, they'd put you out on the street, just one prisoner, and they'd pay the man that guarded you three dollars a day! Now where's the sense in that? That's your graft, just graft, even back then. So in a few days, Jess come in.

We had the horses and wagon, Ma and us kids, and we'd go up on the river somewhere or on Battle Creek or a big tank over at Delmar Lake. We'd camp and fish for a week or two and then go to another place. This was while the old man was driving the freight wagon from Cisco to Rising Star. He'd go down one day and come back the next with four horses on a wagon, and he'd haul them groceries to Rising Star because there was no railroad there. He'd haul back something else, or if they didn't have anything, he'd come back empty.

That fall I was living with my married sister over close to Cottonwood. They had said if I come over there, they'd buy me clothes and I could go to school in the winter. They had a four-month school right close. Meantime, my daddy had quit the freight wagon job when cotton picking time come, and they went up to Gunsight, a little town right north of Cisco, and contracted with a guy to pick his whole crop. The family went up there, and they got paid sixty cents a hundred and we boarded ourself, I think.

*Left to right: Jess, Tull, and Joe Newton*

I managed to stick it out with my brother-in-law until about October, I guess it was, and then we got into a fight and I walked off. He was a kind of bossy, overbearing guy and I seen I could never put up with him. I lit out for where the folks was at, it was about twenty mile, and when I got to Gunsight, I asked where they was at, and a man said, "Come out here and I'll show you." He pointed at a mountain two or three mile off north of us, and dug into the side of that mountain was a house. About half of them in the country was like that in them days. It was an old house that had been there probably thirty-odd years, with walls ten feet high and dug back in about ten feet. Where it come out, they'd put a roof on it, and inside they'd drop a partition to make different rooms. Some of them houses that had been built in the 1870s was all in rock, so the walls was rock. The later ones, they'd put lumber walls in them and a comb roof because they was in the dirt. By about the fifteenth of December, we had the man's cotton all picked out, and my daddy had the itch to go to South Texas. My mother wanted to move there too, so he said, "Come on boys, we're heading South."

# 4

# HARDSCRABBLE FARMING
# (1903-1907)

Y eah, we was heading for South Texas, but like with most things Pa did, he wasn't in any hurry to get there. We went down south of there to Comanche and outside of there a little piece, their cotton wasn't all picked yet. Boy!, did they have cotton. It was only the second or third year they had ever raised cotton there, and it was just as white as snow. The old man said, "We ought to stop and pick awhile here," and we agreed. Stayed there maybe ten days and made us some extra money for the trip.

"We left and headed for this new country where there was nothing but wide open spaces."

We was travelling in a wagon, a covered wagon with two horses on it, and a hack with bows on it and a wagon sheet over that pulled by one horse. All our life savings was in that wagon and hack. Of course we all had our bedding and stuff like that, cooking utensils. When you go out working like we did and moving around, you have very little furniture. Mostly our beds was on the floor. Of course, when we settled down and stayed all year at a place to make a crop, why we had bedsteads.

After we left Comanche, we travelled down to San Saba, and some guy asked if we wanted to pick pecans on halves. The old man said yes, so this guy told us to go on over to Lometa and we could pick up all the pecans we wanted. Pecans wasn't worth but five cents the pound. So here we go and camped over there on that river for about a week picking pecans, before we come

47

back to San Saba and hit across west for Brady City. There we camped down on Brady Creek that comes through there. Just looking around, you know, seeing the country.

Then a guy come along and said, "You fellows want a job?"

The old man said yeah, so he told us he was building a ground tank down about fifteen mile away and needed two fellows, one to drive a team and the other to fill the scraper. My daddy and Jess filled that bill. We went down there and they went to digging out that tank. It was just three or four days before Christmas.

"Let's quit and go back up to Brady for Christmas," the old man said, so they collected their pay and we headed back. The old man was getting a dollar and a half a day and Jess was getting a dollar, I think.

Christmas was just like any other day to us, then, because we was driving around in that wagon. There wasn't any celebration to it. We had a camp on a big bluff up there where there was lots of trees, squirrels and even a few turkey. It was a real pretty place, a place where we could live fat. We had traps and caught pole cats and possum and coons and skinned them and made us a little money that way, us kids did.

So on Christmas Day, I had found me a pecan tree that had some huge pecans on it. I got a flour sack and shook them off, had maybe twenty-five pounds of pecans. I said, "I'm going to take these pecans down to Brady City and see if I can find somebody that wants to buy them." Me and Jess, and I guess Tull, headed out with an old dog we had name of Bob. I had the .22 target rifle along with me. It was about two or three mile from where we was into town, and there was somebody camped just this side of Brady Creek right close to town, and Bob went down there. He come back to us from their camp, and in about five minutes he fell over in the road with a fit. He'd got poisoned down there.

We run to town and got some grease and stuff and tried to give it to him, but it was no use. He died. We put a rope around him and dragged him off down in there and buried him, and then I seen two guys come out of that place where I had seen Bob come out of. I was crying, and I went down there and met them, and I went to cussing them. I said, "You bastards, you poisoned my dog." I said, "I'm going to kill you," and I come up with that twenty-two and put it right up to that man's eyes and I started to shoot. But I wanted to tell him what I was going to shoot him for, so I went to talking to him for awhile, and he begged me and begged me—and in a minute or two, I woke up to myself and I let him go. I was just fourteen years old, but that had broke my heart about my dog.

Later I went back and sold my pecans to a man in a restaurant for a dollar and a quarter. Got five cents a pound for them.

After about two weeks on the creek, the old man decided we'd better not go on, that we should go back to Cisco. So we headed up toward Coleman, and that country was settling up, them big pastures there, and they had a lot of pretty white cotton. We picked there again for a few days, and in Coleman me and Jess got us a burro apiece. When we took out again for Cisco, we was riding on them burros. Before we got to Cisco, Jess and me cut across to Cottonwood where we rode around and visited people there that we knowed. The old man and the family, they went on to Cisco and he went to work in the oil mill.

While we was in Cottonwood, Earl Ashbum asked me if I wanted a job and I said, "Yeah. What do you want me to do?"

He said he was clearing land down below there, "grubbing brush," was what they called it, when you cut the brush off at the ground and then take them big old plows and dig out the roots and pile them up. It was the same thing they do in this Uvalde country, but that was all sandy soil there.

He told me he'd give me ten dollars a month and my board, so I went right on with him. That was just before

Christmas, when I turned fifteen. The only way he could pay me was to give me credit at the store so I could buy anything I wanted and charge it to him. So that's what I did for two or three months before trouble come my way.

Earl had an older brother called Burr who was a school teacher and an old smart aleck. It was his brother's place Earl was living on, and one Sunday I was over there when Burr come up. Burr shoved me or slapped me or something, so I cussed him out and threw rocks at him. When Earl come home that night—it was a Sunday—Burr told him to fire me, that he didn't want me on his place. I told Earl what it was all about, and he knew what an old son of a bitch Burr was and told him he damn sure wouldn't fire me. So they had a big ruckus, and Burr told him to move his things and get off there.

Later Burr got somebody else to come and talk to Earl, and this other person got Earl to agree to let me go so Earl could stay on the place. He said that would be the best thing all around, best for Burr and for Earl and even for me. Then Earl come to me and told me he had nothing against me, but that he had to make a crop here and that I could get a job anywhere. I agreed, and so I left. On the way out, I went by the store at Cisco and bought me some clothes and things with an order that Earl give me for what he owed me.

So I headed back for where my family was. The old man had stayed at the oil mill at Cisco until spring. By then they had got all the seed ground and hulls ground and cake done. He run into somebody who had 160 acres of fine, sandy, black ground over there south of Putnam, and about fifty acres of it was hard land with good grass on it and post oak trees. The old man had made a deal with the guy and bought it, I think for six or eight dollars an acre. He had got him a little money, and he went out there and built a big, one-room house out of two by twelves. House was about fourteen foot wide and about twenty-eight foot long. They put a bed in this corner, a bed in that corner, a pallet here and one there, and all at the other end was the kitchen and everything. There was lots of room.

When I come back to Cisco, the old man had moved out there, so I did too, and we went to clearing land, grubbing that land so he could plough it. Doc had never left home, and him and Tully and the old man had cleaned off about twenty acres. As they got it cleaned off, they'd plant cotton and corn on it, and they was selling the wood. He didn't have to pay the man nothing the first year, no interest nor nothing.

They'd saw them post oak trees down and cut them in fourteen inch blocks, then split them up into small sticks that you could burn in a cookstove. Fireplace wood we cut two foot long. It was six miles to Putnam, and we'd load that big wagonbed full—I bet there was a cord in every load—and he got two dollars for the load. You could get near fifty dollars now. So every day, he'd go to Putnam with some of the wood he'd stacked from clearing the land. Doc would drive the team and haul it.

By spring I guess they had about thirty acres, and Pa planted it. Made a good crop, a bale to the acre of cotton, and corn, forty or fifty bushels an acre. Just dry farming, you know. In the fall of the year, he'd go to work at the gin because he could make two dollars a day and that was big money. The kids could pick the crop off anyway, and I think he stayed there from 1903 until 1906. That was the longest he had stayed anywhere in his life.

He always gave my mother money for groceries and stuff. We got what we needed. He never drank up his money. Oh, once in awhile, he'd get ahold of some whiskey and get himself drunk, but he never spent much in his life on whiskey.

In 1906 they decided again that they'd come to South Texas, so he sold the land and got five or six hundred dollars for what he had in it. He sold his interest to Jim Cook, so we always called it the Cook Place after we left there. Then we moved down to Tin Can, and he went over to a little old store owned by Tom Vestel , who also had a gin, and found Tom and worked at the gin all that fall.

One day I come into Cottonwood to my Uncle Henry's place. He was always mean and thought he was better than we was. My daddy said, "Damn him, he always run over me all of his life." He had ten or eleven kids, just like us, and I was going to stay the night there—it was nearly evening—and I went down to the cotton patch, and no one of them would hardly speak to me.

I said, "What in the hell is the matter here?"

Uncle Henry said, "Well, Jess has been talking about Rena, and what he said was a lie. And the next time I see him, I'm going to whip the hell out of him." Rena was one of his kids, and you know how people is about things like that.

"Well," I said, "The next time I see you and I'm with Jess, I'm just going to remind you about how you said you were going to whip him," and I left. I slept in a cotton wagon in town that night, then walked the six miles across to Tin Can where the family was. When I got there, I told Jess all about this. It wasn't long before Jess and I went riding one morning and he said, "Let's go over to Cottonwood and whip the hell out of old Uncle Henry."

I said all right, so here we go. We got to town about one or two o'clock, and the first thing we saw when we got there was Uncle Henry had driven up to the gin with a load of cordwood and was unloading it. Up we rode, Jess on one horse, me on the other, and Jess jumped him up about what he had said. He wanted to deny it, but he couldn't. I reminded him what he had said, and Jess said, "What I said back there before wasn't a lie. It was the truth. Now are you going to whip me?"

About that time Uncle Henry went to throwing them sticks of cordwood at him. He hit the horse and Jess jumped down. I had jumped off mine, and there was a rock on the ground and I hit him right square on the ribs and he doubled up and fell off the load of wood on his head! When he got up, he grabbed him a stick and come after me. If he'd got to me, he would have killed me with that cordwood, that's what he'd have done, he was just that dirty. And me just a fourteen or fifteen year old kid. I had them rocks in my hand and I kept saying to him, "Uncle Henry, I don't want to hit you with this, but you keep coming and I'm going to." But I backed up and give him room—he was just the picture of my daddy, with them old gray whiskers and about fifty years old. He looked so much like my daddy that I couldn't hit him, white whiskers and head all gray.

Jess come on his horse, and I jumped up behind him and out of town we went. Red Carter, the constable, had grabbed my horse. Well, it rightfully belonged to the old man, so when we come on home that night and told them all about the fight, the old man was hotter than a firecracker. The next morning he says to Tully, "You go to Cottonwood and tell Red to give you my horse. If he don't, I'm a-comin' after him." Pretty soon Tully was coming on back and he had the horse.

They was going to get the law on us, sure as the devil. Well, my brother Bud was picking cotton way out north of Sweetwater at a little town named Rochester that had just been opened up to farming two or three years, and nearly all the people down there where we lived had gone out there and gone to farming. So Jess and me went and caught a train to join Bud. It was about a hundred mile. They hunted around, though, and found out where we was at, and one day up drove a buggy and a guy walked out to where me and Bud and some others was picking. It was the sheriff.

"Is Willis Newton around here?"

"I don't know Willis Newton," I told him. "Here's Bud Newton, maybe he can tell you about him. He's his brother, I think."

Bud says, "He was here a day or two ago, but he's gone." But we couldn't put one over on him. He knew I was Willis.

"Well, I guess I'll just take you then. I've got a warrant for your arrest down in Callahan County that was sent out here."

"You can take me alright, but I'm not Willis Newton,"

I said, and we weighed up our cotton and started out to his buggy. At the edge of the cotton patch was a fence, then an open field for about a hundred yards, then another fence and a cornfield. I sized that all up, and I run. He chased me across the cotton, but at the fence he didn't run any further. He went to shooting at me. I had run up to that next fence and stepped over it, just astraddle of it, when he shot again, and I seen the dirt fly right there by the side of my foot. Well, I went to run and couldn't. He had shot me right through that instep with one of them big lead bullets. Broke every bone in that instep, and that was the one I already had cut the heel strings on. My foot was crippled up anyhow.

So he had me. I couldn't walk. My brother cussed him out, but he took me into this little old town and got the doctor to dress my foot. That night they put me in the hotel, and the next day at about two-thirty the train come and they taken me back to jail in Callahan County.

The old man come up to the jail for me, and I had nearly enough money to pay my own fine. It was a twenty-odd dollar fine for that fight, but it was six or seven long months before I walked on that foot, and I stayed around home all that fall while they picked cotton and the old man worked the gin. Then we hooked up about ten days before Christmas and pulled for Uvalde. December of 1906.

*About the first thing I can remember up to the time when we come to South Texas is we had a little farm up in North Texas and my daddy sold it and we left and headed for this new country. There was nothing down here but wide open spaces. We left up there at the end of 1906, I guess it was, the first time we come down here. I was five years old and nearing my sixth birthday, which was in January.*

*This was the time when Willis had got shot in the foot and brought back to jail in Callahan County. When he wrote down there to us, my daddy hooked up the wagon and collected what money we had and went up there and got him. Paid his fine and brought him home. If he hadn't been shot, they probably would have left him to lay it out there. It wouldn't have hurt him. Jess and Doc had been working a goat ranch up at the head of the Llano River near Junction, and they come on in too. Then we was all gathered up, so we went back to Uvalde.*

For the trip south in 1907, we was still using a wagon and hack. Ma drove the hack, the old man drove the wagon. Me and Jess and Bud and Tull, we walked nearly all the way. We had one girl, Ila, and she was eight, I guess. Joe, he was six. They rode in the hack with Ma.

*The first place I remember stopping was in the Santa Anna Mountains in a gap where there was a lot of old, burned wagon wheels that were still there from years before that. Somebody told me there'd been an Indian raid there twenty-five or thirty years ago, so that would make it over a hundred years ago now. We come through Rocksprings, hit the Nueces River, and come down that and camped at the Arnold Crossing near a little town by the name of Camp Wood.*

*The next morning as we broke camp, across the river was a high bluff and down close to the water a man was standing there and he had two spotted dogs. Somehow that stuck in my mind, and I can see it as plain today as I did then. He was looking at us, and I guess he was thinking of coming over there, but we was starting out.*

*I don't remember exactly how long the trip took us, but it must have been a good long month. We wasn't in any hurry. We'd make ten or fifteen mile a day, maybe, and get to a creek where there was good water and grass and my daddy would say we'd stop there. I remember a time or two when we'd get to a creek and if it had rained, the water was up, and we'd have to wait until the next day. Some places where Dad wouldn't know whether it was too high to cross, he'd get out of the wagon and wade across. If it wasn't up over waist deep, we'd go across. Deeper than that, the water was pretty swift, and we'd go off on the side and camp.*

*The wagon was pulled by a two horse team. And we had a buggy with one horse to it. There was wagon tracks around in that country, not any real roads like now, and we went from this town to that town to the next town.*

We come down through Menard to Junction City and was there in town Christmas Day. From there it was about fifteen mile up the river to Seven Hundred Springs, and we all wanted to see that. That's where my grandmother used to have her sheep back in the '70s and '80s. All through that country. Joe can tell you about that water, how it had just washed trenches in the rocks, it had run through there so long.

*When we got to those seven hundred springs at the head of the Llano River, that was the most beautiful sight I ever saw, and I don't think I've ever seen anything like it since. There was a big, long mountain there and it was literally covered with big springs of water shooting out four, five feet from the bank, some of them real big, some little ones. I never seen so many in my life. It was the most beautiful thing you ever saw, all shooting out of the side of that mountain, and that was what made the Llano River. No, I just couldn't imagine anything like that. Nobody couldn't. If you go see it today, there's still some springs there, but not near so many.*

We liked it there, so we stayed four or five days. There wasn't any deer in that country by that time, because they had killed them and hauled them out to sell them. It's only been two or three years since they put a law to that and quit it. There was a guy said if we'd go back to an old road in there and take it four or five miles back, we'd find quite a few deer.

We unloaded everything out of the hack, took some grub, and me and Bud drove back in there. I had a .30-30 Winchester in my hands, and as we was driving, boy!, here come two fawns and a doe just a-sailin', and I said,

"Look! Look at the deer! Look at the deer!" I never thought about my gun, and directly here come a buck, a six or eight-point buck right behind.

Bud hollered, "Shoot him!" and I just cocked the gun and shot straight up. It was a good thing I didn't have it pointed at Bud. I had got so nervous, and I'd never seen a wild deer. We camped there figuring to hunt in the morning. Bud got up early and walked all over that country, never come back until one o'clock. He said he'd seen lots of tracks, but never a deer of any kind. So we went back to the camp.

We pulled out from there after a couple more days and went on to Rocksprings in about three days. We'd just drive about fifteen miles a day. Every time the old man saw a good place, lots of grass for the horses, good water, even if we hadn't gone more than ten mile, he'd say, "Hell, boys. This is a good place. Let's make camp." He was never in a hurry to do anything in his life.

There was getting to be a few fences along in there then, but the roads was rough. They'd wind here and there, cross the river, go half a mile and cross it again, go three hundred yards, and cross it again, right up that Llano River until we come out on the top of the mountains that come into Rocksprings. We stayed the night in Rocksprings and another day or so to look the country over, then headed for Uvalde again. Our chuck was getting low, and after we hit the Nueces River, we camped. Directly here come a big bunch of hogs, weighed about two hundred pounds, all nice and fat, and I said, "God! Here's a good place to stock up on meat."

Them hogs would eat acorns, cedar berries, and everything else. They was wild in them days. I had a .22 target rifle, so I headed out in the brush and shot one right between the eyes. Then I called to the old man, "Pa, come here and show us how to skin this hog." He was from Arkansas, and back there they'd hang them up by the nose and skin them down, smooth as anything. But he was scared to death, scared of the law because we'd killed somebody's hog. But we got him up there, skinned that hog, salted him down and put him in a box we had. Now we had lots of meat. We took that hide and all the insides—we let the dogs eat all they wanted—and cleaned up around there. You could see a few blood sign, but you couldn't see any hog sign. We took all that hide and stuff and put it in a sack and took it with us the next morning. Then way down there somewhere, we throwed it in a big hole of water.

Above Uvalde at the Nineteen Mile Crossing was a pecan grove, had the biggest pecan trees was ever in the United States. We camped there and stayed the next day. The Nueces River was running pretty blue water, and we picked up lots of pecans. When we left, we went on down to about six mile outside Uvalde where there was a windmill and a regular camping place. Freighters camped there, them guys that hauled freight to Rock-springs and all that country. That's where I seen my first deer sign. I said to somebody that there must be deer in this country, and a guy said, "Yeah, but they don't allow no hunting or killing them down around Uvalde." Them big ranchers wouldn't put up with that, wouldn't let anybody hunt them pear flats.

That was nearly all state land up where we had been. Back in the '70s and '80s when they killed them deer out, they took them by the hundreds. I knowed an old man, Josh Wright, lived out there and every winter he'd come to Bandera and they thought nothing in the world of killing them deer. They'd kill them and take just the hind quarters. They'd cut the ribs and forequarters off and take the hind quarters and tenderloins and put salt on them and pack them in the wagons and keep them for months. Now, why, you couldn't keep one for two or three days and it would spoil. It's just a difference in the climate. The weather is different.

*Before we got to Uvalde I seen what they told me was my first car. Something was heading at us on the road and there wasn't anything hooked to it, no horses and no mules. That struck my fancy and my daddy says, "There*

*comes a car." It had wheels like a buggy, with solid tires*
*on it, and was going chug-chug-chug right on along, maybe*
*fifteen miles an hour, I guess.*

From the windmill camp, we come into North Uvalde
on the last day of December 1907. There was a big
wagon yard there owned by Arthur Halbert's daddy, that
we drove into and stayed the night. Arthur was a grown
man himself then. There was more business up there
in North Uvalde in them days than in Uvalde proper.
'Course, the banks and the courthouse was down in
town, but up around the wagonyards where the railroad
come in and the freighters, there was three hotels, two
lumber yards, two or three big stores, a restaurant or
two, blacksmith shop—well, everything you wanted was
up there. And it was built up solid with houses. I guess
there was six or seven hundred people living there and
about two thousand down in greater Uvalde. See, when
the railroad was coming to Uvalde, the deal was that the
town was supposed to donate them so much money.
Well, when the road got close to town, about two mile or
three, they demanded their money, and the town
wouldn't give it to them. So they just circled around and
missed the town by two mile. They called it Sansom then,
not really North Uvalde.

*We got to Uvalde on the first day of January, 1907. As*
*we went through the outskirts of town, I noticed big spots*
*on the houses where there were new wooden shingles, four*
*or five feet across. There had been a big hailstorm a month*
*or two before that had beat holes in the roofs of the houses,*
*killed lots of deer, and even a few cattle. We stopped in*
*Schwartz's wagon yard that night where you could pull in*
*and feed your horses and wood was stacked over there.*
*I think it might have cost fifty cents a night or so to stop*
*there, but if you was buying groceries and stocking up with*
*your supplies at their big store, they didn't charge you*
*anything. That was to get you to stop there.*

The next morning we drove into town and there was a restaurant there called Gillydo's. They was from the East and had come out to run that eating place. Mostly it fed the people that was being brought in there as prospective buyers for parcels of the old Cross S Ranch. Buckingham and Gross had bought it and cut it up. That's where Crystal City started.

Anyway, we drove up to the restaurant, and a fellow named Jackson owned twenty acres outside town that Buckingham and Gross was going to drill a well on, the first water well in that country.

They intended to plant vegetables and show prospects that it was a kind of garden, you see. So Jackson said, "You fellows want a job? They're drilling a well three mile this side of Crystal City and need hands down there." We had a whole bunch of big, old boys, so we pulled out that day in a little, misty rain. Got about six mile down there and hit Homer's Pasture, and everywhere you looked the deer was going in every direction. I never seen so many.

*The next day we went on through town a ways to a pretty creek that we camped by. None of them was polluted in them days, and there was big live oak trees. We stayed there a couple of days to let the horses graze then moved to a little place called La Pryor. Before getting there we had to cross the Nueces River, moving from the east to the west side, and that took awhile. When we made camp that night, my daddy took the horses to the river to water them. As he come back it was real dark and he stepped off into a hole about five feet deep, and he said he thought the horses was coming in on top of him. But they could see it and they stopped.*

*What we learned later was down in that country it got so dry the ground would split wide open and you'd have these deep, deep holes. I've seen them with cow bones and deer bones down in them, where they're eight or ten feet deep to the bottom of them and five to six feet wide and maybe twenty long before it come back together. Just dry old weather cracks. These days I see them two to three feet wide that run for half a mile before they play out, but nothing like they used to be. And if a horse or cow fell in there, you couldn't get him out. By the time you found him, he'd be dead, with nothing to eat and no water is the main thing.*

We never got away from there till nearly twelve o'clock, and it was eight or ten mile before we got to the old Pryor Ranch where there was another windmill, about fourteen mile from Uvalde. We'd come eight or nine mile from where we camped. When we got there, they told us where we could camp. Bud and Doc took the .30-30 and was walking around in the mesquite there and we hear the gun, "Bang!" Bud thought he was some marksman, and when we run down there, he had cut down on a deer and broke both hind legs. Went through above his hocks and the deer fell down. As Doc come walking up, Bud said, "I put him down. Shot him right through the heart."

"Damn funny thing," Doc said, "for a deer's heart to be tucked up in his hind legs like that." They put another bullet in him quick, and we skinned him and that was the first deer meat we had. Ma went to frying. See, we had all that hog lard that we had melted up, I guess two or three gallons of it. That's all they used in them days to cook with was hog fat. We didn't have anything fancy. I haven't eaten any of it for thirty years. It's just as good as anything else, but all that grease isn't good for you, and I've got gall bladder trouble now. I eat bacon three times a week now, but I fry the grease out of it until its real crisp and just breaks up.

The old Pryor Ranch was the only real house from there to Crystal City, but there was a little bitty old house we called the Cross S Ranchhouse on down there. It was a two-room place for some cowboy to stay in. Nobody was living there, so we stayed there a night then went on to a lake about five mile outside Crystal that they called Broke Shoulder Lake. Some cowboy had roped a steer there and his horse throwed him and broke his shoulder.

61

That lake was about three mile from where we was supposed to go to work.

Come morning, I rode the horse and the others drove in the hack, and we went over to the well site and he give every damn one of us a job. That was Pa, Jess, Doc, Tully and me, and I was still pretty crippled in the foot. Jim Dawson hired us, one of the best sons of bitches that ever lived or died. We moved over there and set in, and Bud and me took the hack and went to Carrizo Springs for groceries. You couldn't get supplies in Crystal City. There was just two wooden buildings there then, that old Zavala Hotel and a post office. Everything else was tents. For ten dollars we got all the groceries we could haul back, and as far as meat, all you had to do was kill a deer.

*We was heading for Crystal City because my daddy and the older boys was going to work for a man who was digging water wells. Just before we got to Crystal we turned off and made our camp, and the next day we went to work. It was Doc and Jess and Willis, and my oldest brother, Bud, and of course my Daddy. Tully was about five years older than me, and I think he worked bringing them water to drink from a well that was five or seven miles back in there.*

*That was where Doc got bit by a mad wolf. They'd work on the well until they got tired or it got dark, and then they'd sleep out on the ground there. They had blankets and quilts. It was a moonshiney night, and Doc woke up with something licking his face. He thought it was one of the dogs and pushed it away. In a minute, something bit him, on the forehead.*

*He jumped up and seen it and said, "A mad wolf bit me." It was a coyote. The dogs got up and got to running him through the camps, running him in a kind of a circle. I was sitting there listening, and all of a sudden, a dogfight like you never heard broke out right at the foot of my bed! I went under that cover, and finally the fight broke up and swirled away into the dark. Then my mother come and got me and we got up in the buggy and stayed there* the rest of the night. It was after daylight when everybody came back. They'd caught the wolf two or three times, but never could kill him. Them days there was worlds and worlds of prickly pear as high as your head, and that's where he went.

The wolf bit every dog we had, so after breakfast they caught each dog, tied them to a tree, and got an iron red hot and burned the spot where they'd been bit. That was the only remedy we knew of. It worked pretty good, but still one of them went mad in two or three weeks and went to slobbering and biting, and they had to kill it.

Then there was Doc. They had to go to Uvalde in a wagon and send him to Austin. That was the only place you could get treated. So off he went and took them shots in the stomach with what he said was an awful big needle. He was sixteen or seventeen years old.

Doc had to stay there two weeks. He never got up there for seven or eight days, and then he took that hydrophobic treatment—whenever Doc would get right hot, he'd just slobber at the mouth, all of his life. He'd shake his head and say, "My damn head hurts," and he'd slobber a little and shake his head. All of his life. He had common sense, but Doc had no judgment about doing anything, no more than a child. See, that's how he got into trouble stealing the cotton that I'll tell you about later on. He used no judgment. He couldn't make money selling twenty-dollar gold pieces at half price, if you give him a barrel full of them. And I think some of that was caused by the wolf bite.

Doc wrote us a letter when he'd be back there in Uvalde, and we went up there and got him, because there wasn't any railroad went to Crystal City.

While we was there, some fellows came and bought the Cross S Ranch. You'd call them real estate men now, but we called them "traders." Story was that the Cross S had been sold once in the past by an old couple that lived on it when there was drought and the cattle died off, and

63

a salesman come along and they sold the whole ranch to him for a Singer sewing machine! That was the story. I don't know how much these traders had to give for it in 1906 when they bought it, but it was a big ranch, probably fifteen miles each way. The Nueces River ran right down through the middle of it. They planned to break it up into small chunks and advertise it to northern buyers.

That was Buckingham and Gross had bought it out, and they'd sell you anywhere from five acres on up to whatever you wanted. They had made themselves a kind of a bus out of an old car. Had a top on it, and they built seats along the sides, inside. It would haul ten or a dozen people. They'd meet the trains up there, them people coming in to look at the land, and they'd take them out to see the country. They had surveyed out a good straight road and wouldn't let the wagons run on it. I suppose the reason was that in wet weather, the wagons would cut real deep ruts.

# 5

## TANGLING WITH THE LAW
## (1907-1908)

W
e was working at what they called the
Jackson Switch three mile out of Crystal City. Jim
Dawson had made a deal for a water well with Buckingham and Gross, but it was just verbal. They'd pay him
as he went down, a dollar a foot for a thousand feet. So
he drilled his thousand feet, and they didn't have no
water. Well, he closed down there, and they wouldn't
come to pay him. They owed him five or six hundred
dollars, and he owed us. So we said if we ever caught
Mr. Buckingham in Crystal City, why we'd get it out of
him, and one day somebody said he was in town. Me and
Bud and Jess and Doc and Jim Dawson, we went down
there and we was going to grab the gentleman, and as we
passed the Zavala Hotel I said, "There he sits, right in
there."

"No, no, that's not him."

"It damn well is," I told them, but we went on and
later somebody told us he was up at the hotel. "I told you
he was sitting right there," but when we got back he had
done got wind of it and was gone. We never did get hold
of Mr. Buckingham.

*They worked there at Crystal City digging that water*
*well until fall. Since we had been there the time before,*
*they had run the railroad from Uvalde down to Crystal City*
*and Carrizo Springs, Asherton, and then across to San*

*Antone. It wasn't Chinamen that built the road then. It was just common American laborers. All the heavy work was done with horses and teams, with slips to haul the dirt off with. Crystal City was growing in other ways too. It was pretty well laid out in blocks, and that land outfit I told you about had built its own hotel. We settled down on a block that belonged to somebody we knew, cleared the brush and trees off it, set up our tents, and lived there for, oh, must have been a year.*

*My daddy and the older boys went to work for the same man that had been running the well rig the last time we was down there. Jess spent most of his time over at Big Wells because there was a family named Davis that had some boys his age and two or three girls. He was over there going to dances and getting into fights. Since the railroad had gone through, that was an easy way to get around to all the dances, you see. Jess was fourteen years older than I was, and Willis was twelve years older. They was twenty-two and twenty years old at that time.*

Sometime in July the old man said he was going to go back and run the gin, the same one he'd left the fall before. They wasn't drilling no more wells and we didn't have work. But he had a six months job waiting for him, and he went back to it.

*We headed back up north so my daddy could work at the gin stand in Tin Can. About the time we got to Brownwood or so, the four older boys, Jess and Bud and Doc and Willis, they turned off and went somewheres else. Willis had got to where he could walk and he was off somewhere. No telling where he was. My mother and daddy and Tull and Ila and me headed on to where he had a job. We stayed there through the ginning season. That was the first time I went to school. I was eight or nine years old.*

*Jess was a big, stout fellow when he was young, and he enjoyed life the most of any of us. Didn't care if he had fifty cents or fifty dollars in his pocket. He lived the same* way. If he had the fifty dollars and you wanted it, you could have all of it. If you had it, he wanted some of yours, and you were more likely to have it than he was! [laughs]. He was pretty helter skelter all the time, just working long enough to get him a little money, then heading off somewheres to spend it. He was the first one of us that always had horses on his mind, then Tully turned out to be that same way, and finally I got like that too.

The first pitching horse I ever rode was one that Jess tricked me onto. He come up by me one morning when I was walking along and asked me where I was going. I said into town, and he said, "Come on up here behind me." Well, I didn't want to do that, and as it turned out, this morning was the first time that old horse had been rode. Jess had just got on him and wore him down a little.

"Give me your hand," he said, and reached down for me, "and then jump straight up in the air. When you get behind me, hold around my waist." So here I go, and when I hit the horse's back, he got his head down and went to pitching. Jess had thought he could hold his head up, but between holding onto me and trying to stay on himself, he couldn't. We flew this way and that, and I was way down on the horse's side and Jess would pull me back up. We stayed on somehow, and finally rode him into town.

We didn't live in a tent all the time, but we rented a house around there. I don't know what you had to pay for a house. We finally bought one, though. One Sunday I had gone with some other kids over to the far side of town, it was a mile or two, and we was fixing to play some ball. Then the older boys came there, Jess and some other boys, and they had the fine idea of getting us to fight with each other. We didn't want to do it. We was all friends, but they made us and tied one of our hands behind our back and had us to fight.

Just in the middle of all this, we seen some smoke from across town and Jess said, "Why, hell. That's our house." The big boys took off on horseback, and we run. By the time we got there, it was burned to the ground, and they hadn't saved anything. My mother had thought I was *upstairs asleep, and they spent what time they had trying to get up there through the windows. We never bought a house no more. Just rented.*

Bud and Doc and Jess and me went to San Angelo, and Jess went to work for Booger Red's Wild West Show. He took pitching horses all over the country, and Jess hired out to him riding broncs. Then me and Bud and Doc come over close to Ballinger to where a guy had some land he wanted to clear. Bud had some horses and worked for the man a week or so, at three or four dollars a day for him and his team, and we had us a stake. We went on up above Sweetwater to Hamlin, and got a job cutting the heads off maize for a dollar a day, and stayed there about a week.

Then Doc decided he'd go back and work with the old man at the gin stand, so he saddled up and left me and Bud. He was going to run the boiler, you see, an old steam engine, and my daddy was on the gin stand. It was about September, and Bud and I went on up to Wichita Falls and Vernon and went to picking cotton. Cotton had just begun to open up there. We had our wagon and a cooking outfit, and we'd get sixty to seventy-five cents a hundred and we'd stay five days or a week, while there was good cotton, then move on to another place where there was good cotton. We was there two or three weeks and I decided I'd go back to Crystal City. Jim Dawson still owed me a little money, and when I got there another guy had come in there and was going to drill that well deeper. They had put up a big rig there, but hadn't done anything about it and didn't look as though they was fixing to. So I left there and went to Aransas Pass and stayed a couple of months with my half brother, Jim Johnson. That was in the fall of 1907. When I finally left Jim's, it was in January 1908.

My daddy, when he had got done running the gin, had rented him a farm over there. That was at Tin Can, in Eastland County, where we had always run them gins. So he made a crop there on what we called the Kneeves

Place. I come on back home in 1908. I said to Doc, "Let's go back down to Crystal City and do some hunting and trapping this winter down on the Nueces River." So we went to Cisco and caught a freight train to Fort Worth, then caught the Katy over to Taylor, Texas, then come on down to San Antone riding the I&GN. Riding freight trains. We had us a little money, and from there we come out west to Uvalde, then down to Crystal. That old well was still a-sittin' there. The boss there hadn't never done a thing with it.

We bought us a tent and cooking outfit and went down on the river to what we called the Rock Water Hole. There was a big bluff there and we stretched our tent, had a cot apiece and all our camping stuff. I had a Winchester and Doc had an old six-shooter. I killed all the game.

We was over at this camp one night and Doc and Mark Thompson had got hold of some cider or something, and whenever he got a swallow of anything, Doc didn't have much sense. He went to firing that old pistol and shot that old boss right here in the arm. The bullet just followed right on under the hide up to his elbow, about six inches along his arm, but didn't break it. They went to town and got a doctor, who just split the place and took the bullet out. It was well in two weeks.

Everybody knowed Doc had a pistol, but I didn't have no pistol. But the old boss went and swore out a warrant for me and Doc for carrying pistols. And I never had no more pistol than we've got a Gatling gun in here right now. Never had one. But they charged both of us. Didn't want to charge Doc without me. We was over at John Thompson's tents at the rig because they'd decided they'd "shoot" that well and see if they could bust it down in there like they shoot oil wells. So we was there and a guy come up and said they wanted me and Doc to come down to the telephone office in town.

I told Doc, "That's a lie. It's a damn trap," but we decided we'd better go on down there. Doc took his pistol and left it under the pillow of one of the tents that was there at the rig, and I kept my Winchester. When we got to town, the sheriff come and said, "I got to arrest you boys for carrying pistols."

"I ain't got no pistol. Never had none. I just got this Winchester." It was against the law to carry a pistol, but not a Winchester. I think they got that law all over the United States.

"Will you let me have the Winchester?"

"Yeah, but it's not mine. I borrowed it from such-and-such a boy here in town. He's not using it and I've had it for a month or two," and I gave it to him.

"Well, somebody's swore out a charge against you boys for carrying pistols," and I just looked at him and laughed. He took us down by the telephone office and put an old drover with one eye to watching me. I knowed this drover, old Joe, just like I know you. So the sheriff went in and I told Joe, "I got to go to the toilet." They was outside houses, you see, so me and him went walking down there, and as we went I said, "Joe, we'll both go up there to it, and when you go in there, I'll jump out and slam the door to. Then when you get out, just run like hell shooting straight up after me."

He said all right. So I slammed the door on him and turned the old latch. He took two or three minutes to kick the latch off and waited until I got a good run. Then he went to shooting, just as I was hitting the brush down there. Boy! I was gone, but Doc was sitting in that office and he heard the racket and knowed what was happening. He knowed I was out of there. So he made a run, but he went right the same way I did. He'd have got away, but some more guys had run down there and was looking for me, and he run right into two of them and they grabbed him. That was Doc's luck.

I circled around there and went back to Thompson's tent where we'd left the pistol, and there was a horse tied out there. I slipped in the back of the tent and got Doc's pistol, then walked out. It was getting pretty late, and I started out from there on a new road that had been put in. There I seen two guys go across the road on a horse.

They seen me leave Thompson's camp and they had circled and was going to cut me off. Thought I was coming down the road. So instead I went down through the brush behind them and there they sat waiting for me. One had a Winchester and the other a pistol. Old Ewell Burleson and some other old rat. I slipped up close and put the pistol on them and said, "Drop them guns."

"Oh, Willis. What's the matter? We're looking for an old buck. We're looking for an old buck."

"Well, I'm the buck," I told them. "Drop them." They did, and then I come up and told them, "You dirty old lousy cowards. Running around here. I've never done nothing, never had no pistol of my own, now I tell you what you two damn rats can do. You get them guns and go back to Crystal City and tell that sheriff I'm not going to go to jail for something I didn't do." So back they went and told everybody there that they just had to beg and beg and do everything else to keep me from killing them. It was about night then, and I knew what I was going to do. I could hit the woods and build me a fire and sleep anywhere I wanted to.

Meantime they took Doc and went to the Batesville jail with him. They put a log chain around his legs, around his boots and chained him to the buggy. As they went along, he eased his boots off and put the boots back on and he was unchained. As they got close to Batesville—the road wound all around through thick mesquite—he just fell out in the mesquite and prickly pear and was gone in half a second. Before they could get out, he was done gone. Then, just sure as Judgment!, he took the road all the way back! The same road that they had come on to Batesville, the main road, he was walking right down it in broad open daylight with his coat over his head. It was raining just a little and he had took it off to cover up with.

He had got to within five or six mile of the camp where we was staying. He was coming back looking for me, but they rode down on him and grabbed him and said, "All right, Willis. We got you." They hadn't gone with the sheriff and they thought it was me. "By God! It's Doc. How come you're here?" And they took him over to that old well and turned him over to somebody to hold while they went to Crystal City to look for me.

They took Doc back to Batesville jail then, and I went to Eagle Pass and stayed awhile and come back. They said they was going to turn Doc out, but they didn't. So I went down to El Paso and stayed there two or three weeks or a month, and even then when I come back, they hadn't turned him out. I looked Jim Dawson up and he said Doc was in that old jail on the bottom floor with just some padlocks. He said, "I'll get you some hacksaws if you want to turn him loose. You can saw them locks off."

"You get them." I'd hung around there two months or more waiting to see if they would turn Doc out. At night, I'd build me a fire and make a little ring of brush about me, then lay down where my head was under the poles. There was coyote wolves, thousands and thousands of them in that country. I'd get up of a morning and you could see where they'd come so close all night and went around looking at you. If it was a right warm night and I didn't have to build a fire, I'd go to them feed troughs where they fed cattle and they all bedded down. I'd get under one of them big troughs and go to sleep. Them cattle's the finest company in the world, all night getting up and down, up and down, up and down.

One night I come by a fellow's house where I knowed the boy that worked there. I asked him to get me something to eat and he said, "I'll have to ask old so-and-so," the owner of the place. I knowed the owner too, and I guess he didn't want to give me anything because he was afraid, but eventually he fixed up some chuck and sent it out to me. The boy I'd asked to go in there said the man told me I could stay out in the barn, but I was too smart for that. Instead I went on some two or three mile and made me a fire and put up for the night. Then sure enough, he went and snitched on me. Told an old deputy over in town that I was at his barn, and I found out later that they searched it, but of course I wasn't there.

Jim Dawson had got me some hacksaw blades, so one night—it was as bright as day with the moon shining—I slipped up to the jail. It sat right out in the middle of a square. I'd say it was about eleven o'clock, and the dogs was barking and crossing the street, so I got down on my all fours like a dog and here I went across that street too. I could hear Doc breathing in there and I called low to him, "Doc, Doc, Doc," and he jumped up.

I told him I had a saw and was going to cut him out and he says, "Hell, I've got a key for my cell that I stoled off of them. I'll throw it out to you." Then I went around to the front and started in on the padlock there. It took me about thirty or forty minutes to cut it through, and then I went in and unlocked his door and out we came. He'd been in there for about two months.

We come out of Batesville and into a pasture, and as we got up on a fence to go over it, I looked close at him. Hadn't had time until then. He had these black chin whiskers and I said, "God damn! You sure look just like Buffalo Bill!" We walked from there to south of the old Pryor Ranch and went down to the Nueces River and laid down and slept all day. Late that night, we got moving again until we hit a fence line. There was no La Pryor then, but we headed west of there about four mile to where Jim Dawson's brother, Claude, had taken up eighty acres of school land and was living on it. Jim was drilling a well north of there. When I had started over there to get Doc out of jail, Claude's wife had said, "If you bring Doc back, I'll cook you a cake."

We come walking in the next day and I asked her, "Where's the cake?" She laughed and went in and made it. Then we went on to Jim's rig. There had been some people that lived over there and they had a nice big tent all fixed up just like a house. I think there was one bed in there, and lots of other stuff. They left and took everything but that tent. It was about two mile from where Jim was drilling, so we'd go to his place and eat at night, then go back to that tent and stay. We hid out

73

around there and in the surrounding woods while they hunted and hunted for us.

One day we come up on a big tank there where about six of them old deputies was swimming. It was an old, high tank, and long, maybe two or three hundred yards. They had swum from the dam to the other end and there laid all their clothes. I told Doc, "Let's go get them." That would have been the best thing in the world. We could have gotten everything they had and left them there naked! But as we went around that big old dam, one of them was swimming back and was nearly there. That blowed us, or we'd have really had them.

Well, they stayed around there three or four days. One night we went over to Jim's camp to get something to eat, and it was a good warm night. You could lay down and sleep anywhere you wanted to. As we started back to that tent, something just struck me. It's saved my life three or four times, and I said, "Doc, you know those guys are still all around here. They're liable to find that tent, and they can tell somebody's been sleeping in there. Let's just don't go back. Let's go over in the woods and bed down."

The next day when we went to Jim's, he said, "You know, them guys found out where you was sleeping and they laid out on you. All five of them, last night, to kill you." And they would have too. They wouldn't have tried to arrest us. They'd have shot us, they were just that dirty, that old sheriff and the kick he had with him. And we didn't have a gun then. The old sheriff said he knowed we was staying around there, and he had told Jim that if we'd get out of there and go home, he wouldn't bother us. But as long as we were around there, he had to hunt us.

That settled it. We cut out for Uvalde. We made it to the house where we lived and stayed there about a month, I guess, until one night we was over at old man Runnels' house visiting his boys, and the first thing we know, there was the sheriff and his deputies come to arrest us. They had sent a warrant up from Batesville for us.

Well, Doc had got typhoid fever, and he was sick as a bear. They handcuffed and shackled me and handcuffed Doc, and we was standing around there and I was kicking them shackles as a guy come by. He could see we was just young boys, and he said, "My God. What have you done?"

"Oh, they got this big bad sheriff down in South Texas and he says somebody's accused us of carrying a pistol. He's taking us about five hundred miles back down there and putting us in jail for it."

"Is that all? For a pistol? I thought you had murdered somebody." He said that with that old sheriff standing there listening, and he made some remarks about him being a coward and walked off.

I had me a piece of a hacksaw blade right here in my shirt and I intended to cut them shackles off and tie a string around me to keep my britches closed so he couldn't see. Then I was going to hit them mesquites on him.

But by the time we got to the jail in Batesville, I was so sick I couldn't see. Typhoid fever had hit me. I knowed I couldn't run, couldn't do anything, and I didn't even have the strength to try sawing the chain. I just laid there and burned up. There happened to be a good doctor down there that helped me. Doc never got down like I did. He was so strong, like a bull all his life, but I had a tough spell of it, I tell you. It must have been about three weeks. Finally I got the fever off a bit, and was getting along all right, and you know when you get up after you haven't had anything to eat, you'll eat anything. You don't know any better. But you sure can't eat grease when you've had typhoid fever for a long time, and they brought me four or five greasy strips of bacon for my breakfast and I ate every bit of it. The next day I was burning up with fever. It give me a backset.

For another ten days or two weeks, I didn't know nothing, but still they kept me in that jail. Finally I was so sick, they took me upstairs and let a guy stay with

me every night. I come to once and there was a light right
there in my eyes. I reached over and put it out, and didn't
know anything more after I had done that. But he run
down and told them that I was trying to put the light out
to get away, and here I couldn't even walk. It didn't
matter. They rushed me back down to the jail that night.
I didn't even know they done it. Then in a night or two I
woke up and thought that I'd never felt better in my life.
I sat up on my bed and talked to myself, and Doc was
listening from the next cell. I said, "Here I am but twenty
years old, and got to die." Then I fell off on that floor.

Sometime in the night, it blowed up one of them
quick showers from the west. It was so hot all the
windows and doors was open and water blowed in there.
I woke up in the night with them picking me up from
water three inches deep. The old steel floor had held the
water, and the cool, wet water brought me back to life.

They put me on the bed and got me some dry quilts,
and I began to come to. I got a little better and was careful
not to eat no grease. I told them I couldn't eat grease and
eggs and stuff, not for a month after this fever. It had
settled in my legs and I couldn't walk. My head had
burned up with that fever, and I didn't have no more hair
than you've seen on newborn babies. Jess had had
typhoid at home a long time ago, and I remembered about
that and was careful to eat just what I thought would be
alright.

What I didn't know was that we was already convicted. See, I had taken my backset just a day or so
before they was to take us up before the judge. If I'd
knowed what was happening or had any sense, they
couldn't have convicted us. But I was with Doc, you
know, and I was crazy. They told us to plead guilty and
he did, so I pled guilty with him. Then I just puked and
puked and puked and fell out, and they had to carry me
out of the court. That's when I blacked out for about two
weeks and died before I come to life in that water.

They fined us and added to the fine the four or five
hundred dollars that the sheriff had used to go up to get

us. We either had to lay it out at three dollars a day, or pay it. So we laid there ninety-three days.

About two weeks before our time was up, they come in there on a Saturday and said, "Well, boys, we're going to turn you loose." We didn't have a cent to our name, so there was several of them there that each give us a silver dollar when they turned us out. They give us about ten or twelve dollars. Different people. Not the old sheriff. He never give us nothing. There was a mail hack went from there to Uvalde every day during the week, but it had already gone for the day and on Sunday, it didn't go. It was three or four o'clock in the afternoon, and we'd have had to stay around there until Monday to catch the hack, so I says, "Let's get out." Here we go up the little old road cut out for the mail route. I couldn't walk over a quarter or half a mile, and I had to sit down and rest. Then I'd get up and walk more, and my legs would give out. I was just dead.

We must have walked two or three mile that night to where there was an old ranch house and a windmill. We got us water there and laid down to sleep by the road. It was in July or maybe August. Come morning, we started and I'd walk a piece and have to lay down. Walk a piece and lay down. We walked about half way to Uvalde and it was twelve or one o'clock, with no water. I said to Doc, "I can't go no further." And I got into the shade under some mesquites.

"I'll go to Uvalde and get some water," he said. "Don't try to go any further and you can hold out, maybe."

It was a wonder I hadn't took another backset, but I'd been well a little too long for that. Doc walked plumb in to Uvalde to a house that's down on the road into town and told them what he wanted. They give him a gallon of water and a lot of chuck. I had told him I'd be right in the road, and after he was gone for some time, I inched up the way a little further, and there I laid until about ten or maybe eleven o'clock when he got back. Boy! That water! I drank and drank and didn't want to eat too much. We kept back some of what we had, and the next morning we had a little water and the rest of the chuck, then lit out and got into Uvalde I guess about twelve o'clock and got us something to eat there before we headed over to the depot.

We caught a freight out that night and Doc would have to help me into them box cars and help me out. My legs was so weak I couldn't get up on them, and then I couldn't jump out or I'd fall all over the country. Finally we made it back home. The old man was living at the Kneeves Place. He'd made a good crop that year. It was 1908, and he'd planted it in June. For twenty years he'd been trying to make a bale to the acre planting in June. That year he did it. We stayed around there and picked for him and for other people. I made a little money at trading by buying a cotton patch off a guy where the plants had plenty of bolls, but he didn't think it would ever open. I give fifteen dollars for it and picked me a hundred twenty-five worth of cotton out of it. Well, God! I was getting up in the money with over a hundred dollars! And another place I went and made some money, picking cotton all fall, so I had me something over two hundred dollars. First time I'd ever had over a hundred dollars in my life.

# 6

## MISCARRIAGE OF JUSTICE
## (1909-1910)

"I got up there and told the whole
story just how it was, but they
had a jury fixed to convict me."

About this time, the old man had made his last
cotton crop up there in that country. He got ready to
leave to go back to Crystal City. It was a little while before
Christmas. Well, he owed Eck Huntington a debt over
there at a little old store. And before he pulled out he
said, "Doc, you pick this cotton that's left here and sell
it and pay Eck Huntington the twenty dollars and you
can have the rest of it." I went over there and helped him,
and we picked about six or seven hundred pound and
had it piled up in the field because we had no way to take
it to town. I was living over at Rising Star and I'd bought
me a mare for a hundred dollars and a buggy that I'd paid
twenty-five down on. I had until the next fall to pay it out.
And then I had seventy or eighty dollars left. There was
an old boy over there, Lindsay Basham, who was a
gambler, a poker player. Well, I had this horse and buggy
and we'd ride all over the country and play poker. He
knowed all the poker players and we'd go hunt them up.
Go down to Brownwood, go over to Cross Plains, and go
out in the brush and play poker. Brush poker. Them
farmers played poker all over out there. They'd hitch
their horses to a limb and let them stand there all night.
I wasn't playing but I was staking him, see, and whatever
he'd win, I got fifty percent of it. We'd been gone a week
and come back to Rising Star. I was living with him,
staying at his house.

When we pulled in there about night, some of his kinfolks had come in. They didn't have a very big house, so he says, "Skinny, I've got a lot of my folks here, why don't you run down and stay at the hotel tonight." I was known as nothing but Skinny till I left Texas. When I was thirty years old, I weighed 138 pounds and was twenty-nine inches around the waist.

Anyway, I left my horse and buggy at his house and walked down to the hotel. One of the boys took me up to a room and I went to bed. The next morning a little after sunup, somebody knocked at my door and it was Doc. He had cotton all over him. I said, "What the hell have you been doing?"

"I loaded that cotton over there of the old man's and brought it to sell it. But I filled my wagon up out of old Tobe Roberts' cotton at his gin and drove it down to this gin down here."

Doc had went over to this neighbor and told him that I had left that cotton there and wanted to borrow his team to haul it. Doc was pretty young, about seventeen. He figured he'd say it was for me. He figured if he said it was for himself the man wouldn't let him have the team, but he said it was for me because I was older and knowed the man better.

The man let him have the team, so then he went over and put the six hundred pounds of our cotton in there and went over to Rising Star and drove up to the gin. There was a man named Tobe Roberts that buys remnant cotton and he had a lot of cotton houses plumb full. Doc could see all that cotton in the gin, so he just drove up to it and got in there and loaded his wagon full. Separated a few hundred pounds or so to add to the six hundred. Well, there's another gin in town, so then he just drove from this one down there to sell it.

I told him, "Doc, don't *ever* do that no more because you're going to get caught." But just like I said, he never used no judgment ever since he was bit by that mad wolf. So we started down and the gin was right across over there. There was a lot of bales of cotton sitting around on wagons, and Doc had done took his mules loose and tied them to the hind wheel and fed them some hay. And there was old Tobe Roberts standing right there by his wagon looking at it. I said, "Yeah, there's Roberts now. He's found out you got that cotton out of him."

Doc had left a lot of cotton on the brakeblock as he drove away, and Tobe Roberts said he just trailed him all the way from the other gin by the cotton. Tobe said later that he didn't know how much cotton he lost. Well, I know how much he lost. He lost just about half a bale. And that wasn't a penitentiary offense, what they sent us both to the penitentiary for. But we didn't know how to fight it out or what to do.

Penitentiary offense would be a theft over fifty dollars or burglary. To be burglary, you got to break in. And even with what he had altogether, his and Tobe Roberts', Doc had only fifty-one dollars worth. If he'd had a dollar and five cents less, it wouldn't have been a penitentiary offense even then.

So I says to Doc, "I'll go over here and see what's the matter. You go out here to the schoolhouse and get in that old toilet, and I'll come and let you know what rank you got." So I walked on over to the gin. It was kind of cool that morning and I stood around and talked to everybody. I knowed everybody there.

And while I was standing there, somebody run in and hollered, "Whose bale of cotton is this that's out here to go next?" I knowed what he was talking about. They thought it was my cotton, see, but I paid no more attention to him than if he wasn't there. So I stood around there ten or fifteen minutes, and then walked back over to town to eat my breakfast. But I seen everybody was staring around there and I couldn't get away from there to go tell Doc without somebody seeing me. Then this old constable went all around out there looking for tracks, and Doc was in this outhouse and seen him a-goin'. So he took to the woods.

Pretty soon they come on back there and this old constable named Johnson come up to me and said, "Well,

Skinny, I got a warrant for you."

"What for?"

"For stealing that cotton over there."

I says, "Well, go on over there at the hotel and ask Ben Lester where I was at. I was in the hotel last night."

Ben told him, "Yeah, Doc come up here looking for Skinny this morning and I sent him up to the room and they come back down."

Then old Constable Johnson says, "Where's Doc?"

"I don't know. He was here awhile ago. I don't know where he went." Doc had seen this old Johnson a-comin' up the road looking for his tracks. When he passed the schoolhouse, Doc hit the brush and left.

So they talked to Ben and he told them, "Skinny never went out of here. He come in here about ten o'clock and went to bed." Well, they arrested me because they just thought I'd tell where Doc was and all. That's all they arrested me for.

Some old boy around there, he was a tough fighter and everything and always into something, he got around and said to me, "Why don't you whip old Tobe Roberts? He's the one that had you arrested."

Well, I didn't have no better sense—just twenty-one years old—and I hauled away and hit Roberts in the jaw and knocked him down and kicked him a time or two. So that made them mad at me. I never hurt him, but they sure enough took me. Hauled me off and kept me around there all day, and they had nothing against me. They hadn't decided whether to take me to jail or anything. So finally they give me a trial.

And they didn't have a witness in the world except an old louse, a guy that had murdered another guy but he got off when he claimed he didn't do it. They got him to swear that when he come to town that morning he seen me standing by that wagon. That's all they had against me. And me and Doc had a pair of boots that the same man in Rising Star had made. There wasn't a half a number difference in our tracks. Same inch-and-three-quarter heel, made on the same last. And it hadn't rained in two months. They proved it. It was old sandy country. And the bootman that made our boots was right there all day and I talked to him. He was a friend of mine and everything else. I knowed him a long time.

They set me a bond at three thousand dollars. So in about an hour, in come Al Irvin, the sheriff from the next county, and he had him a stick and he measured my foot and he said, "That's it, Skinny. I want you. That's your track." Doc and this old boy named Red Rains had burglarized a post office over at Cross Plains about ten mile from there a night or two before that. I guess Doc had left a print there and it was just like mine—high heel, inch-and-three-quarter heel.

That was in Callahan County and this was in Eastland County. They knowed they had nothing against me in Eastland, so they thought they could send me to the penitentiary for this post office job and they said, "You can have him, Irvin." So he took me and drove me in an old car over to Baird. It was just the first automobile that ole sheriff had ever got. It took nearly all night [laughs], even though it was just twenty-five miles to Baird. Got in there about two o'clock.

They put me in jail and I got Rawl Ely, that guy that was teaching school when I went that nine months. He was a lawyer. I told him the whole thing and he says, "Well, there's nothing to it."

So the next day Al Irvin come up and said, "Skinny, we're going to send you back to Eastland. We don't want you. They arrested Red Rains down in Cisco last night, and he told us all about it. Said you had nothing to do with it, wasn't there, that it was him and Doc." So they sends me back to Eastland and I had a three-thousand dollar bond against me there. My lawyer wrote out a writ of habeas corpus and we took it to a district judge named Blanton at Abilene and I stayed there about a month before I could get the writ. I just told them all about it, how I went to the hotel, how Doc come up there looking for me, how I went over to the gin—so the little old judge looked at the evidence and he said, "Well, they swore one way over there and Skinny swore the other. If Skinny hadn't took the stand, I'd have turned him loose, but there's a contradiction so we'll have to have a trial. I'll set his bond at three hundred dollars."

They took me back over to Eastland again, and my brother-in-law come over there and made my bond and I went out and worked until the court met sometime around the first of July, I guess. They have a grand jury first and then a court. Me and Booger Boggs—they had a case against him too—we come in and stayed around there all week. Stayed there until the next Sunday and then we met the sheriff, Pat Kilburn. He said, "Boog, there's no need for you and Skinny to hang around here. The grand jury ain't got nothin' agin either of you. So go on if you want to." So me and Boog pulled out that Sunday night.

And after we had gone, he went down and told that grand jury that me and Boog had gone and that I'd skipped my bond! And that grand jury indicted me!

We got away down east, down in there around Arkansas, and monkeyed around, and Booger he left and went back to Cisco. I went over to Fort Worth and then down to Cleburne and then I got arrested for riding a freight train. They called it "vagrancy" them days, you know. Didn't have no job, a-ridin' a freight train, and I got arrested. They took and fined me $26.50, and they took me out on them county roads, and I had to work it out at fifty cents a day. I tried to run and get away but they caught me. And they buckled a pick right around your legs. And it was three foot thataway and three foot thisaway, and sharp on each end. And with that on my legs, I had to buck "wheelers," them big old scrapers them days, horses and mules pulled them. They had a big handle to pull them down and hauled lots of dirt. They called them "wheelers." I buckled them wheelers fifty days with that! They never took it off me no time. I slept with it on. When I'd buck the wheeler, that pick was so long my foot come up as high as my waist. And I done that for fifty days, twelve hours a day.

*Willis Newton*

Well, I knowed a girl back there in Eastland that I was going with. I wrote her letters. Just as soon as the letters went in there from me, why they told that old sheriff. But hell, they had told me to leave, or I wouldn't a-been writing back. So Sheriff Kilburn let me stay there. He knowed where I was just a week after I was on that road, which was the first letter I wrote back. He let me stay there fifty days, till I just had three more to do and then he come and got me. They took me back to Eastland and put me in that jail, and the old judge raised my bond three thousand dollars because they told him I'd run.

Boy, I was hot! I told everybody the truth. Told them just what the sheriff had done, told my lawyer. I tried to get a preacher to listen to me, but them dirty, low down rats, all they'd say was, "Oh, you're just mad at society." So I cussed every jailer and sheriff and everybody else. We tried to break jail and then they said, "Skinny, if you don't settle down here, we're going to put you in the penitentiary." I says, "How in the hell can you put me in the penitentiary when I ain't done nothing and every one of you knows it?"

So I laid there six months waiting for a trial. Then it come to trial and they had the man who swore that Doc had come and got his mules and said he and I was going to use them to haul cotton. And another feller that I'd knowed all my life, Jim Head, swore that he come down to that gin early that morning, that he passed there before, just at daylight, and that I was a-tyin' them mules to the hind wheels of the wagon. All lies. All lies.

That boot man got up and swore both my boot tracks and Doc's was down there in the sand, and it hadn't rained there in two months! He said that Doc's boots and mine was the same size but the reason he could tell them apart was that there was more tacks in mine than in his! He was the star witness agin me.

Well, if I'd had the boots, I could have killed him right there, but I didn't have the boots. I'd wore them out or traded them off or something. Anyway, they all got up there and nailed me to the cross.

Then I got up there and told the whole story just how it was, but they had a jury fixed to convict me. When they run out of a jury panel, why they'd go outside and pick them up, and there was an old boy around there, that was all he done. They went and got him and put him on my jury. They convicted me and give me two years in the penitentiary. Then they tried me for burglary. To be a burglary, you've got to break in, and that gin was wide open, but they tried me for that.

So I took the case to the higher court, but I had stayed in there three months before I got this bond and then I had stayed in there six more while we took this to the higher court and they reversed my case. They said that mule man, the one Doc got the mules from, he couldn't testify against me because I wasn't there. So they threw his evidence out. Well, every six months they had court, so I had to stay in there another six months until they met again. So I stayed in there a year over that appeal. They ruled out everybody's testimony but the bootman.

Nobody would testify against me that they had up there the first time and the boot man had moved out to New Mexico and he wasn't there. He hadn't come. So the judge put my case off until Monday of the next week and said, "Now if this bootman, this man from New Mexico, ain't here next Monday, I'm going to dismiss this case." And wouldn't you know it, Monday morning that son of a bitch was there.

When they put Jim Head on the stand that had swore I was there that morning at daylight and tied the mules, this time he said he didn't see me and the judge wouldn't let them use him for any other evidence. Then another witness they had said he hadn't seen me, and the judge overruled him too. Said they couldn't use him. All Tobe Roberts knowed was that he'd lost the cotton. But when they got to the boot man, he told his boot track story. That was the only witness they had against me. They never asked if I had ever been in Rising Star or was ever seen in Rising Star, nothing about the cotton—just the boot tracks. That was all the evidence. My lawyer said, "Hell, nobody's ever seen you in Rising Star. I ain't going to use no witnesses." And he let it go to the jury.

They stayed out two days and nights and then they called for me Saturday at dinner. The judge was from Abilene and he always went home for the weekend about four o'clock on the train. He called for the jury and they said, no, they was a hung jury. So he told them he was going home at four o'clock and if they didn't bring in a verdict by then, they would be locked up until Monday morning. He said they should have been able to decide this case long ago. That was just the same as telling them that I ought to have been turned loose. When I went back to the jail, I was told there was nine for turning me loose and three for convicting me, and just as we got to the jail, the phone rang and they told them to bring me back. My attorney said, "Well, they've turned you loose, Skinny. Them three has turned over." So we went back there and wouldn't you know the other nine of them turned over and they give me two years!

So I had to appeal it again and there's another seven or eight or nine months. And finally they come back and affirmed my case on that lone boot track. I never was seen there in Rising Star or nothing. They just swore my boot track was over there in that old dry sand by where that cotton was stole. And they affirmed my case and give me two years in the penitentiary.

My brother-in-law come down there when my case was affirmed, and every juror signed my petition for a pardon. I hadn't done it and they all knowed it. The judge wrote the governor a letter and said since they had caught my brother, they found out I wasn't guilty, but even if I was, I'd served more than a prison sentence and I should be pardoned. I'd already stayed in that Eastland jail twenty-two months and twenty-six days. The cell was six feet by eight feet, just as long as the bed. Then there was a little corridor fourteen feet by eight feet, and that's where we all exercised, in that corridor.

I guess everyone that swore a lie agin me, they all wrote letters for me to get out. They took it to the governor and he said, "Well, I'll have to let him serve a year before I can pardon him." Governor Colquitt. So I went to Rusk Penitentiary, in the Walls.

# 7

## LIVING AND DYING IN THE TEXAS PEN

"They valued mules twice as much as they did human life. Mules cost money, and convicts was free."

When they caught Doc, I was still in Eastland jail. I'd done been convicted a second time, and they put him up on the stand and he told them that he had six or seven hundred pound of cotton from the old man's crop and he took it down there and he just stopped at Tobe Roberts' gin and filled it up. He knowed he had between six to seven hundred pound and with all that he took from Tobe he only had fifty-one dollars worth. So Doc really stole only about thirty dollars worth of cotton. But I be damned if they didn't give him two years too.

Tobe Roberts, he got up and said he didn't know how much he lost because he had ten or fifteen bales in there and he couldn't tell how much was gone. Well, they give Tobe back the whole bale and give Doc the two years, for a misdemeanor. He wouldn't appeal it! They'd have throwed that case out, but he wouldn't appeal it. He said, "Hell, I won't stay in this jail. I'll go to the penitentiary and I won't be there two weeks." He just went on to the penitentiary and run away after he was there two, three weeks. He was gone. They was working them out there in the woods cutting logs, and they went to throw a tree and throwed it right toward the guard, him and another old boy, and then they was gone.

So they affirmed my case and sent me to the penitentiary for two years, at Huntsville. When they caught Doc after he escaped and brought him back, they brought him to Rusk where I was at. Some old law had tried to arrest him out in West Texas and he told the old night watchman, "I'm the law myself." He said, "Give me that gun." The watchman was looking for an old boy, Tig Lawlor, that went with him. He had heard Tig was around there. Doc said, "I'm a marshal. Give me your gun. I know where Tig is." The ignorant old watchman give him the gun and then they put a charge agin Doc for robbery. They said Doc took his gun away from him, and they give him five year for that. That's the reason I was trying to get him outta jail. We was gonna run away, which I haven't told you about yet. They was fixing to give him a trial, but we got two more years apiece. Then they took him back up there and give him five years anyhow. For nothing.

I had served eleven months when Doc and I broke out together one night. One thing that helped us was there'd been a fire there before and there was old copper wire laying around there, and it was soft. I already had a key, and I looked at it and bent that wire up just like the thickness of that door key. Then I took a file out and went around to that door. The other trustee who worked over there, he had that key and I seen what his was like and made another just like it.

That's how I could unlock Doc's cell. They had brought him back over there to the pen and was gonna take him back and try him somewheres else. But we cut the bars and went over the wall of the penitentiary and run. During the daytime I had got a hacksaw and there was bars in the windows. And I snuck up there during the day and cut two of them bars. And at night they had school, but I worked on the row at night. Everybody took care of a row. There was so many cells on a row. I was all over the place anytime I wanted to. I was never locked up. So after we come in then, I had that key for Doc's cell.

I went and unlocked Doc's cell. He scooted right down to my cell and we just jumped up in that window and pulled them bars up and went through them and nobody seen us. I had a rope made that I brought in there, a short one. We run out and there was an iron gate. We climbed up on it and then we could reach the walls. We got up on there and hooked that hook back down there and climbed down it and dropped off to the ground. There wasn't any guard around because it was night time. They took all the guards off the wall at night. Nobody seen us go out of there. When they come locking up time, we was gone. When they went to count up the rows, they had to count everybody and was three men short. They looked around and it was old Skinny and Doc and another old boy named Elkins that we was raised with in Callahan County at Cottonwood.

We broke into a store the next night to get some clothes, and they got after us. They seen we'd broke in that store and they knowed it was us. We caught a freight train that come by the next day, but the sheriff was on that freight train and seen us. So the train stopped, and a brakeman run up and said, "You boys better look out. The sheriff's back there in that caboose looking for you fellas."

So here we went. We hit them woods because we knowed it'd only be a little while until they had them dogs out there from the Walls. That wasn't but ten or twelve miles away. We went on down to a house, and there was an old shotgun there, but just two shells. Directly we heard them dogs coming and run on down a fence and through it. There were about seven or eight guards on horses. We got to a little creek, and I said, "Don't stop, boys! Come on to this creek!" Doc stayed ahead all the way and I was next. Old Elkins got scared and climbed a tree, but me and Doc went on down and jumped into the creek and here come them dogs. There was a big old pine tree that had fell down and we run right to this pine tree and them dogs come for it, about seven or eight of them in a row. They was just even with me and I give them both barrels and dogs went in every direction, yelling and screaming and falling over and howling.

Well, when we shot the guards stopped. They knowed we had a gun then, so we went on down the creek where they couldn't see us. We followed it three or four miles and turned around and come back up it about a mile and a half and got hold of a limb and come out on a tree. By then they had got some more dogs and they run us down that creek but we had backtracked and they didn't stop where we got out. They went on down to where we had been. We had went so far back, they never did find another track.

From there we cut across to the river bottom. We knowed everybody in the country was looking for us. We found an old horse and here we went, but my hat blowed off, and when I went back to get it in that field, some of them guards seen us. If my hat hadn't blowed off, we'd been in the bushes and they'd never seen us. So we had to jump off the horse and hit the brush again. They went down and circled us, got ahead of us, and when Doc run out of the brush—he was ahead of me—he run right on them and they caught him. Since they had him, I come on out.

One of them old guards—oh, he was so tough—he run up with his pistol and was going to knock me in the head, but the sheriff grabbed him and said, "Don't you touch them boys. They're my prisoners. I'm after them." He took charge of us right there because we burglarized that store in his county, but the old guard, he wanted to beat us up so bad, and he would have, too, because we had killed them dogs. God Almighty! that was murder to them to kill them old hounds.

They was bringing us back that night and the people all over that country knowed we was in there. About dark, we come out and there was a crowd there. An old man piped up and said, "Boy, sheriff, I'm certainly glad you got them. I'm certainly glad you got them. I can sleep tonight."

And some woman come out and looked and said, "My God! It's just some beardless boys!" [laughs].

Not only that, they had caught us with the stolen

clothes on. So they took us back there and tried us and give us two more years. They strung them out, so that made me four. Doc, they give five years. Then they transferred me down on a farm out of Sugar Land. I stayed there until I done thirty months, then my mother went and talked to Governor Colquitt and he told her he'd give me a pardon.

They wouldn't let you go to the governor's office, but I knowed how people done. I wrote to her and she come to see me and I told her just what to do. I said, "You go in there, and don't ask to go in and see him. They got a man on the door. You just sit down like you're waiting for somebody, and when he gets away from that door, just run and go in." She did, and when the guy got a little away, she hit the door. Then they couldn't put her out, so she talked to the governor awhile and told him all about my case.

He said, "I'll turn him out pretty soon."

She said, "No, I'm going to stay right in this office. I've got a cotton crop to pick, and he's a good cotton picker and I need him to pick my cotton. I'm a widow woman." Her and my father were separated at that time. She said, "I'm going to stay right here."

He told her to go home, that he'd give me a pardon in two weeks. That was Governor O.B. Colquitt. He's the man that civilized the Texas Penitentiary. They was beating them to death down there, stomping their heads off, stomping their guts out, until he got to be governor. Just knock you down and kill you in the field. He went down to the penitentiary when he got elected and they had them old "bats" with a steel handle on them, with a piece of leather on it five or six inches wide and thick. Six foot long, and they'd just lay you down and give you that. He went down on every one of them farms as soon as he got elected and told them to bring the bats in. He had a man with him to cut every one of them up.

He said, "The first time I ever hear of a man being hit in this penitentiary, you're gone! And if ever I hear you're cussing and abusing them, you're gone!" So they cut it out. Then he passed all them new laws, you see. Oh, it was bloodthirsty. They built that railroad thirty-six miles from Rusk to Palestine with convict labor, and they say there's a man in every hundred yards of it. There's two or three hundred buried along there. Cemeteries, cemeteries—just to build thirty-six miles of railroad. They worked them to death, fed them nothing, knocked them in the head, did anything they wanted to.

On them old Texas prison farms when I was down there, they didn't have a doctor but they had a mule doctor. He doctored us convicts. They valued the mules twice as much as they did human life. Mules cost money, and convicts was free.

That was in 1900 and on up to about 1914 or '15 when Governor Colquitt civilized it. He made it better. But they still in some places had them horse doctors, and they doctored the convicts and the mules. They called him a doctor, but he was just a vet. He knowed how to give you pills or calamine or castor oil, but that was about all. No surgery or nothing.

If you broke a leg or needed surgery, they just wrapped it up and if you lived, alright. If you didn't, it was alright too. They didn't care. If they got fevers and things, they didn't know what to do. I remember down there in 1914 there was an old boy got bit by a snake. He just swelled up all over. Nowadays anybody could cure a snakebite, but they got this old horse doctor over there and he said, "Well, I've got to operate on him." They took him in there to a little old house over there and stuck a knife in him and entrails and everything else just blowed out. The old horse doctor said, "Push them back in there and sew him up. He'll die." And he did too.

It was the most brutal thing, the Texas penitentiary was. Until when Governor Colquitt went in. That's when I got out. I got that pardon and went to West Texas and went back to picking cotton when I got out of there.

# 8

# THE FIRST TRAIN ROBBERY
# (1914)

> "Why should I worry about robbing the train? I had tried to go and live right, but they wouldn't let me."

In September 1914 I went out around Matador in Motley County. I was in Fort Worth and I met an old boy named Blue that had been there in prison with me and just got out. Blue was his first name; I couldn't tell you his last one. I had got out a little ahead of him, but I went up to Ardmore, Oklahoma, looking for my brother, Bud. He was working for an oil company and I couldn't find him. I come on back down to Fort Worth and met Blue and we shipped out together to pick cotton. The cotton farmers used to come to Fort Worth and pay your way on the train out to their farms. They take you out and give you a job picking cotton, but you're supposed to pay your own way back.

Anyway, I was working out there and me and a girl had got stuck on each other. Old man Ross and his old lady had other married kids, but Vella was their baby. She was about nineteen then. I was picking six hundred pounds a day and was doing okay before they found out I was a convict. I'd hired on with old man Ross and I'd go out there and pick two, three, four hundred pounds on Sunday, if I was where he couldn't see me. He didn't want me to pick on Sunday. He was a religious man, I guess.

Old Ross had a renter down there about half a mile away in a house. So I made a deal with him to make a cotton crop on halves, and the next year I was going to go and "bach" down there. They thought there was nobody in the world like me. I was such a worker, and whenever kinfolks would come, or anybody come, they'd tell them about me. What a good worker I was, what a fine boy I was.

One Sunday evening I was out in the lot monkeying around there, and I seen two guys coming and they rode up to the fence. It was old Blue and another boy that was working for Ross' son. I got around and said, "Blue, for God's sake don't tell him I've been to the penitentiary. I'm here, and getting along all right, and I want to make a crop here." But he had done told him already.

So they left. Course that other guy goes on back and tells Ross' son all about me. And the Rosses, they had been up to Quitaque, a little town above there, to see one of their son-in-laws. They come back about an hour before sundown. The old man and old lady went to the cow hut to milk, and I went in and me and Vella was cooking supper. I looked out the door and seen a horse coming at a lope across the prairie right from where this son lived, and I said, "Oh-oh." He rode up to the log fence, and I seen who he was. They talked to him about three or four minutes, and here come that old lady in. They was Germans. She came in the house and says, "Come here, Vella!" and took her off in one of the other rooms and I hear [whispers] "psss . . . psss . . . psss." I could see Vella had got her walking papers from the old lady, but we went on and had supper and I stayed that night.

Next day they didn't do a thing but load Vella in a hack and take her up to that son-in-law's about six miles and leave her up there. The day after that it was foggy and rainy and damp and I couldn't pick cotton. It was up north where she was at, and I got the old man's horse and rode off to the west. But I guess I was in too big of a hurry to get there, and I turned back north too quick and they was watching me. I loped that little horse nearly all the way to Quitaque, and when I got there and got down and went in the house, I looked out the gate and that old man and old lady was coming to the gate with a hack with two little mules on it in a long lope. She run in and grabbed Vella.

I never said a word. I just walked out and got on my horse and went back. I thought it over and figured I'd just better hook up. So the next morning I said, "Well, Mr. Ross, I guess I'll leave. It's getting to be bad weather." They just begged me to stay. They didn't have a cotton picker and they probably had twenty-five bales in the field. I was picking him two bales a week, I guess, and they begged and begged and begged me. "No," I said. "I can't do it. I got to take off," and I left. Later I sent Vella a letter and she wrote me one and told me they was trying to make her marry some old boy above there and she didn't want to. But she said if I left, she guessed she'd have to.

When I pulled out, I went to a little town about thirty miles away by the name of Spur. It used to be owned by the old Spur Ranch, but they sold it out and made a town. There was cotton all over. Over there I run into Red Johnson from Cisco. We had run around together in Cisco after our family moved there. I had knowed Red ten or fifteen years.

He was out there picking cotton and shooting craps. We monkeyed around there and went out and picked cotton a few days, and then it turned rainy and bad weather. It was getting late in the fall. There was an evangelist there, a man with two little girls about thirteen and fifteen, and a boy about twelve and a woman. They was out of some Baptist institution at Weatherford. They'd get on the streets and sing and take up money. Every morning they'd get out about ten o'clock and then about two and then again about seven. I had saved me up about eighty-five dollars from picking cotton, and it was all silver dollars and I'd throw them two or three dollars every time they sung. I stayed around there about a week and my money had got down to thirty dollars, so I said to Red, "Let's go down to South Texas and rob a train."

He said, "Alright." I was just kidding with him and thought he was kidding too. But we cut out and went back up to a town above there, up around Matador, and run into an old boy one evening who said, "You fellows play any poker?" It was getting late in the evening and I was staying at the hotel and Red had a room over in a rooming house.

I said, "Yeah, I'm a poker player."

"Come over to my room and we'll play." So I went over to his room and we commenced to playing. I couldn't catch nothing. When we started I had about thirty dollars and he'd beat me and pick it up. He was sitting on the bed, and he'd put the money under his knee. He had his own money there and then he put mine there too. So, just about the time he's getting ready to win the last dollar I had, I raised up his knee and I took it all. I said, "You dirty so-and-so. I know you been cheating me all this time. I was just letting it go so I'd have a good excuse for taking your money. You're cheating, so you can't holler. I'll take these old cards and I'll show them the marks on them." I took the deck, and when he went to jump up, I said, "You raise up there and I'll blow your brains out, you dirty card thief you."

He went to begging then and I let him beg and beg. That's what I wanted him to do, to beg for his money back. Finally I said, "Well, I'm going to give you your money back and keep mine." I knowed just how much I had, so I counted it out and give him the rest back. He never said no more.

I went across to where Red was sleeping and me and him slept till just about daylight. Then we got up, walked out of town, and there was a freight train with a couple of passenger cars on the back. It was called a "mixed train." About two miles out was a stockyard and a water tank. We went to the stockyards and got breakfast and stayed there until that train come in in the morning. We caught that freight train to the main line, then got on that for Fort Worth. From there we caught a Katy train and rode into San Antone. Up in Fort Worth, I had bought me a big, old thumb buster .45 Colt pistol, an old single action, for ten dollars. That's the only gun I had, so we come here to Sabinal, close to Uvalde, and went down to a wagon yard in town and I was looking around and there's a .30-30 Winchester laying in some man's wagon. Red grabbed that and I had a pistol, so we was set.

We went over to Uvalde and stayed there a few days in the brush. "I want a Winchester too," I said. "Tonight Number Nine passenger train comes through at eleven o'clock and we can ride it as far as Cline and rob it. But first let's break into that store in Uvalde and get me a Winchester and some shells, and get you some more shells too." That was about two weeks before Christmas. I knowed there was nobody there, so we went down and we kicked into that old store in Uvalde and I got me a new .30-30 and three boxes of shells. We'd got back to the train in time to ride it over to Cline, but when I looked at my shells and went to load the Winchester, they was all automatic shells; they wouldn't work in the gun I had.

We had to go back to that store and go into it again and exchange and get us some good shells [laughs]. This time we went in through the window, the back window. By the time we got back to the tracks, Number Nine was gone and we couldn't ride it to Cline. I said, "Let's take out across the woods here, and cut across the Nueces River and then go up that way."

So here we went. We had a big black overcoat each, and we went over there about three or four miles out of Uvalde and laid down and went to sleep. Next day we got up and went on and hit the Nueces River and went on. About five or six o'clock it was rainy and misty, and we crossed the river up there and saw a ranchhouse. I said, "Red, go over there and see if you can get us something to eat," and directly here he comes with a sack full of pork and biscuits and stuff. A whole sack of it. And he had a big, wide-brimmed, white hat on, and a brand new pair of boots in his hands. I said, "Where'd you get them from?"

99

"I got them outta the house. They just fit too, the hat and boots do."

"You shouldn't have got them, Red," I told him.

"Hell," he said, "I needed them and they just fit too." Then we took out and hit the west fork of the Nueces River and went on up it about two miles from that ranchhouse. It was drizzling rain and we could hear some hounds running up in there. It was getting dark, so we built up a big fire by a bluff that we could get under that night, and then it could rain all it wanted to.

After a little bit I heard someone coming on a horse. He was right close to us and I told Red, "I'll get behind this tree and you tell him that you were with some hunters and had got lost." So here the man rode up. Red had burglarized his house and had his hat and boots on! And of course I had all of his pork and biscuits sitting over there in a sack too. Red told him he was with some hunters, way over there, and got lost and was going to stay there until daylight. I could see the man look at his boots and look at his hat, and look at his boots and look at his hat. Finally he rode away.

I said, "Damn, don't you know that he knowed them boots and hat was his just by looking at them. We got to get away from here."

So we took out, went up the river about four miles, then cut out from there. We broke us down a lot of bushes and things and made a bed with one of them big overcoats under us and the other on top. It wasn't very cold. At daylight we got up and the wind had blowed up from the north and cleared everything off bright and clear. We went on up the river another four, five, or six miles. I kept telling Red, "We got to get out of this man's country, because he'll be looking for you."

About five or six miles from where we'd been, we run on an old log house where there'd been some campers. There was an old Dutch oven and a skillet sitting there with about an inch of grease in it. No bread, nothing else but only that grease. There was quail everywhere and we'd go out there and get down low and get a bunch of them together and shoot two or three heads off with his .30-30 at one time. We killed about fifteen or twenty quail and I went to cleaning them and we really had a quail fry—cooked them in that grease. We stayed there all day. Had quail for supper and quail for breakfast.

The next morning we got up and I said, "We just keep right up this river." We went on about six or eight miles to the double water hole, and there was a house. Nobody there. There was two cots in it upstairs, and there was everything there—flour, sugar, coffee, salt. Everything but grease. We went over by the river where we'd seen some tracks and I said, "Come on, Red. There's some big live oaks over there. If there's any hogs in this country, they're up there in them live oaks." We went off and run into a bunch of hogs. One was a good fat one—about 150 pounds—and Red blowed him down. We skinned him, brought him back, and rendered him all up but his hams. Those we kept. We got us a full gallon of lard, and boy, then we was set. We went to shooting deer. They was all over in that country. We'd kill us one or two of them big bucks every day, and we'd hang him up right where we killed him. Just leave him there. We stayed there two weeks. We had buck meat, we had plenty of whatever, except our flour run out.

So just after Christmas we had two big bucks hanging up that we had killed and a man, a woman, and two little kids drove up in a wagon. He said he was a railroad man out of San Antone and that his mother-in-law lived over there in Cline, right down the little creek there at Cline. Well, we give them the two deer and told him we was going to Uvalde. We didn't say we was going to Cline too. I said to Red, "We can follow his wagon tracks and go down and find where he lives and get us some flour and come back and stay another week or two." We was doing all right. We did that, followed the tracks and came to the house, but there was an old lady there, his mother-in-law, so we didn't get no flour. We went on over there and monkeyed around the depot and stayed in the brush so nobody would see us.

The Number Nine train come in there about eleven-thirty and got water. I said, "Let's rob that train tonight."

Well, when it got late in the evening, we went down there to the depot and they had a little freight house there. In them days, they brought lots of stuff in by freight. Wasn't many trucks, you know. We kicked into that freight house and there was a big ham in there. We took that out and cut us a chunk and went out there in the woods. Boy, we cooked ham until we fell out.

I said, "What are we going to do, Red?"

He said, "We're going to rob that train tonight."

"Alright." So we got our big overcoats and took the linings out and Red—he was as redheaded as a pecker-wood—he wrapped his head so nothing but his eyes was showing and I put mine across my lower face. So when Number Nine come in that night, we hit the back of it.

The old brakeman said, "Hey! You can't get on there!"

I said, "Like hell we can't," and I jabbed that pistol in his belly. Well, when I did that, we could've *had* the train then if we wanted it. We went in and the first car was a special car behind. The superintendent of the Southern Pacific Railroad, old man Watkins, was in there and another old tall slim fellow. Watkins was the first, and we robbed him. He had a pocket book that thick! Had a pass to every railroad in the United States. We thought he had a wad of money in there, but he had forty dollars was all. Then that other slim fellow down there was standing on his head trying to crawl under that bench, his heels kicking up yonder. We went and got him. I took just a little off of him. Then we went on down through them Pullman cars. We'd never been in a Pullman car and didn't know there's a berth upstairs too. We just got the ones on the bottom and went through two of them. If there was a man and a woman together, we robbed them. If there was just a woman by herself, we didn't bother her. We just put the curtain back down.

We rode the train nearly to Spofford. When we come through the first car, we didn't know there was a drawing room in there with a rich old Mexican and his daughter.

THE FIRST TRAIN ROBBERY

They had several thousand in money, and fifteen thousand in jewelry in a little bag. They was in a compartment car and we didn't know nothing about that. We thought it was a privy I guess, and we passed them up. When we got close to Spofford, we pulled the cord and stopped the train and got off. Then we hit them prickly pear flats.

The reason I know they had all that jewelry in there was it come out in the paper. That old man give them other folks that didn't have no money or any way of getting money, he give them a lot of money because we had missed him and his daughter.

So, my mother lived in Crystal City. We cut across them prickly pear flats and walked all the next day and that night about ten miles, I guess. Laid up in them pears. There wasn't no houses across that country. The next evening we got up about an hour before sundown and walked all night for twenty or thirty miles. The moon was shining way across there. The next day we laid up until nearly three in the evening. Then we went and killed us a big beef steer and cut a chunk off and got some water from a creek there and we cooked enough chuck to carry us on to Crystal City.

We went off in there and stayed all night again. The next day, why, I'd been through there a hundred times and I knowed just how to go, we walked into Crystal City at night and went to my mother's. Nobody seen us come into Crystal City.

All together we had got just forty-seven hundred and some dollars off the train. We divided it up fifty-fifty. That was the most money either one of us had ever had. The date of that train robbery was the last day of December 1914, and that's the first time I ever violated the law, a federal law. It didn't worry me, though. Why should I worry about robbing the train? I'd been down in that penitentiary four and a half years already for nothing. By then, I didn't care if I broke the law or not. I had tried to go and live right, but they wouldn't let me. So when I left there, I'd made up my mind to get me a big pistol. I

103

didn't care. I was going to do what I wanted to.

Red stayed around there two or three days and he left. His folks lived in Durant, Oklahoma. So he pulled out and went back up there, and after two or three weeks I took out and went to Arkansas to visit some of my kinfolks. Then I went to Oklahoma and travelled around for two or three months, and in the spring I guess, I come back to Crystal City.

# 9

## ON TRIAL FOR MURDER AND MAYHEM (1916-1917)

"They just wanted a victim . . . .
And we was as innocent as
a baby."

I stayed there in Crystal City all that summer, and I got into a fight with a guy. Somebody come to the house and told me there was a guy down there, old Charlie Simms, was going to kill my brother, Jess. Me and him had had a fight before that. I got my pistol and went on down there to the livery barn that this fellow Steadham run. Simms was there and he had a pistol in his boot. He reached for it and I just pushed mine in his belly. He hollered, "Don't shoot! Don't shoot! Let's just fight it out."

I said, "Alright, just give Steadham here your gun and I'll give him mine. I'll take you down and whip the devil out of you." So he gave him his gun and I give him mine. I took him by the arm and we started down the road. Told everybody, "Stay here. If we need you we'll call."

We went on down and he turned in the dark and wouldn't go any further. He wanted to be where somebody could pull me off him. Yeah. So we started to fighting, and he bit me. When he done that I just reached down and got his hand and throwed it in my jaw teeth. His forefinger, and I come down on it. And he went to screaming bloody murder and I just ground it and ground it and ground it. When I did turn it loose, it just fell down right away.

I'd bit the whole finger off. There was just a little

gristle holding it. I bit the thing plumb in two. They had to cut it off that night, a doctor did.

So we got arrested for fighting and carrying pistols. They had a trial the next day. He was in with a clique, you know, and they turned him loose. I still had another charge against me for carrying a pistol. In a few days, the sheriff come over. He drove around but never did come up and arrest me. I knowed if I stayed there I'd have to go to trial.

So one morning, well, the train come up here so I got up and waved to that train, caught it, and left there. They could have put me in the penitentiary for biting his finger off, but they never thought of that. Didn't have sense enough. If I'd had $250 for a lawyer, I'd a-went downtown and killed him, but I thought just the best thing was to get on out of town, so I left. That ended my fight.

And that's when I left there and went on north and went to picking cotton out at Bronte, fifteen or twenty miles north of San Angelo. I picked all around Sweetwater and then went on down to Bronte and that's where I was picking at the time that them boys robbed the bank at Marble Falls. They robbed that bank there and killed the cashier. Well, I was picking up at Bronte, 350 miles from there with fifty other people. I was picking the day that boy was killed. I cashed a check at the bank that day. That's 350 miles from Marble Falls and I didn't have no automobile either.

So here they come and arrested me and O.C. Wells. We was up at Snyder, looking around and picking cotton, monkeying around over the country, prowling around. And we got arrested—just on suspicion—and put in jail. There had been a post office safe blowed over there at Sweetwater, so this old sheriff said, "I got two fellows arrested over here at Snyder. Old Skinny Newton and O.C. Wells." He knowed who we was. "Come over and see them."

So here they come that night and took us right to Sweetwater. I had nine $5 gold pieces in my pocket that

I'd got over at San Angelo. We'd been over there at the fair, and I got them from a young teller in the bank there. I knowed who the teller was. But you see, there was a thousand in gold taken out of that bank in Marble Falls where they had killed the boy, and because I had those gold pieces, by God, I was the guy that killed him. They just wanted a victim.

In a few days, here come a bunch from Marble Falls over to identify me. There was a little boy who had been out at the camp of the robbers eating with them for a couple of days, and they brought him. He said, "No, Daddy, that's not the man." And the man said, "Don't say that, son. You haven't seen him good." All of them went downstairs about an hour or two and then they come back. They said, "Now, son, have a good look at him again." And he said, "Yes, Daddy, that's them." See, they had took him off and told him to identify us.

Well, God Almighty, they handcuffed us and took us to jail at Austin where they kept us six weeks. My brother come from Houston to see me and see what he could do. I said, "You can't do nothing. We haven't done nothing. We haven't robbed no bank." So he went on back. I didn't know what to do.

So after six weeks, the Texas Rangers come and took us back to Burnet. That's the county seat. When we got within ten or fifteen miles of there, we met people in droves and droves. Every school had let out and people was in buggies and afoot. Everybody in Burnet had come to meet us.

That was in 1917, the last of January and the first of February. The bank had been robbed just a few months, two or three months, I think, before they got us. In 1916, I guess.

So, God Almighty, I never seen such wild people in my life. They kept the Texas Rangers there to keep them from mobbing us. If that crowd had gotten to us, they'd just took us out there and hung us to a tree, that's what they'd done. Or shot us to death. And we was as innocent as a baby. They wouldn't get our witnesses, wouldn't pay any attention to us. For seven weeks we was there. Claimed they had twenty-five people that could identify us, that we'd killed a boy robbing a bank. I told them where I was at, and O.C. told them where he was at. We had the proof. I told them about the check I cashed with my handwriting on it, and everybody in that town around there knowed Will Reed—I was going by the name of Will Reed—who was such a cotton picker. But they never paid no attention to us.

Well, they indicted us for murder in the first degree. But there was a girl who lived over north of there in Lampasas, I think. And she seen in the paper where they indicted us for first degree, and she said to a guy she was going with, "My God, they'll hang them, and my brother's done that."

So he come and told them what she said, but they paid him no mind. They had us, you see, and they wanted to hang somebody. One of the robbers had had a red sweater and a white hat on. Well, they put that sweater and hat on me and then had the people come in and identify me. Hell! they didn't identify *me*. They identified the hat and the sweater. "That's him. That's him." They had twenty-five people done that.

Then they took us over to the courthouse to set our trial. The streets was packed. So O.C. says, "Judge, can I make a little talk?"

And he said, "Say what you want to."

O.C. told him the whole story—where I was at, where he was at, what he was doing. O.C. was pretty smart, pretty well educated, and he told the judge and the judge listened at him. Where I'd cashed the checks, and where he endorsed the checks, and where he cashed them.

The whole courtroom got still. He talked with the judge for twenty minutes, I guess. We was ordered back to jail and in about a half hour the judge and sheriff come over and the judge said, "You boys tell this sheriff where all your witnesses are, and their names. If they ain't here when the trial comes and if they're in the state of Texas, I'll see why they ain't here."

Well, that old sheriff got his heart right. We give him the names and in two weeks when the trial come, we had two passenger car loads of witnesses down there. And even then they kept us and all of them two days before they turned us loose!

And you know, then they went right and arrested two other old boys and give one of them life and the other fifty years! And the *same people* that identified us identified them! If they'd had a good lawyer, they couldn't have convicted them, but they didn't have no lawyer, didn't have no money. Had spent all the money by the time they got caught.

When I got through with that trial in Burnet, they still had me charged with carrying a pistol down in Crystal City where I'd had the fight and bit old Simms's finger off, and they called the sheriff and he come up there and took me to Batesville. That was the county seat of Uvalde County back then. Then I had to stay in jail there about two or three weeks. County court was every three months and I couldn't make bond. Sheriff was a fine, likable fellow. When they took me up, they had twelve men in front of us for a jury. They said, "Hey, now, Skinny. You can pick your jury."

I said, "Just give me the first six. They're all good men." There was a dozen of them and I said to give me the first six. I didn't want to pick no jury. So Simms got up and told them that he'd grabbed my gun and took it away from me and give it to so-and-so. I just got up and told them how it happened. The jury went in this room and come and said "Not guilty." I went out of the courthouse and there was two of them jury come out there and says, "Skinny, next time a guy comes by you and says he's going to kill your brother and you don't get your pistol and go down there and kill him," they said, "we're *going* to put you in jail. So why didn't you kill him?"

I said, "Well, he was just a dirty old coward. I hated to kill him."

From Crystal City I went all over the country, around

down to Houston and did things all that winter, down to Humble and worked for an oil company, and for the first time in my life I made three dollars a day. I thought I was going to get rich. I worked there about three months and still didn't have no more money than when I was picking cotton for six bits a hundred.

So I went back to Uvalde and then to San Angelo and found O.C. Wells again. We prowled around stealing something or looking to steal something. Did some gambling. O.C. was a pretty good poker player and I was pretty good too, at that time. I had me a looking glass that I would set down. I'd lay my coat down and put this looking glass up in there, a little piece about an inch and half square. I'd put it in the coat sleeve and every time I'd deal a card I could read them as fast as I'd deal them. Every time I dealed, I knew what everybody had. It was pretty hard to beat me [laughs].

O.C. was in trouble from before. He had some stuff hid under a stockyards out at Abilene. When he was out there one day, there was a nigger had found the stuff and was getting it. O.C. had a pistol and he shot close to him, but it hit a board or something and glanced his arm or leg. He didn't really shoot him. But the nigger run into town and told the law that there was a man had this stuff hid and he'd seen it and the man had shot him. So the law run out there, and before O.C. could get away, they caught him. Never proved the stuff he had was stolen. They had nothing against him, but there was this piece in the paper about him shooting at the nigger.

Well, about that same time as the robbery at Marble Falls, there had been a guy stuck up a grocery store at Coleman. The owner knocked the gun up with a broom, and when he did it went off and killed him, killed the owner. As the guy run out of the store, the owner's old wife come in and she said she just seen the guy's back as he went out at the door.

Alright. That Coleman law come and got O.C. The old woman said she couldn't identify him, but they put him in jail and kept him anyway. Finally them laws went and told the old woman, "We know he's the man that killed your husband, and if you don't identify him, we got to turn him loose." Well, then she went back to the jail and identified O.C. as the man.

So they tried him and gave him the death sentence. It was terrible. Old O.C. showed them where he had robbed a store fifty or sixty mile away from there that night, what was taken and everything. They got that merchant from over there and he swore that that was the way it happened. When they took the case to the Court of Appeals, they had got some more witnesses to swear O.C. was around Coleman, and they electrocuted that poor devil right in Huntsville. Under Dan Moody, they did that.

I'll tell you how justice works. Dan Moody was tough, and yet he commuted one of the most cold-blooded cases that ever happened during his administration. These two old boys from Oklahoma come down to Fort Worth and went to rob a bank messenger. And one of them just shot him! Then they grabbed the money and run. When they caught them, they tried the first one and somebody swore it was the other one that had shot, so they give the first one a life sentence. Then they tried the other one and give him death. The sentence was affirmed, and the day before his execution, Dan Moody said "his hands was clean" of it. That article's in the newspaper. He'd wiped his hands of it. That evening the man's mother and sister—which was a good looking woman some twenty years old—come down and went and talked to Dan Moody. They was in his chamber an hour or two. They had the old boy's head shaved and had him all fixed up, and Dan Moody called in and said, "I commute his sentence"

After that, the guy stayed down there eight or ten years in prison, and was paroled and pardoned, a free man and gone. That's the way justice is handled. They electrocuted O.C. Wells for nothing, and there's a man that cold-blood murdered a bank messenger, and they commute his sentence!

Anyway, when I was working around Houston, I knowed a guy I'll call Wilcox. It was about May, I guess, and he and another fella named Harry Smith had broken into a store way up there somewhere and had a lot of clothes to sell and didn't know where to sell them. I knowed an old Jew that was a fence. So Wilcox and Smith went and got some clothes and give them to me and said, "We got a lot more planted up there under a little house a ways from the depot."

I took and sold the clothes they give me to that Jew. I guess about seventy-five dollars worth. I went back and turned it over to them and they give me twenty dollars. They said, "We're going back and get the others." But there was this guy there I had let know. He was a friend of mine and I thought he was alright, but he was a stool pigeon. He went right and told the law, and here I had give him a suit!

So the law followed me right up and grabbed me and arrested me. So when Wilcox and Smith found out the law had me, right away they just left the country. I still knowed where them other clothes was at. I hadn't burglarized the store, but I had sold this man the stuff and I knowed the stuff was hot. They got me and took me to Austin County where it had happened. That was in the early spring—must have been May 1917—and the sheriff was old man Palm and his boy was the deputy. Good old German people. So I talked to old man Palm and said, "I think I can find them other clothes that those men stole. If you'll see that store man and guarantee to give me just two years, I'll find the rest of them clothes that they got and the man won't lose so much." The sentence for selling hot clothes was two to ten years, so two was a bargain. They had me dead to rights for it. He went and talked to the district attorney and then said, "Yes, if you can find the rest of them clothes for that man, I'll see that you only get two years."

"Alright. You take me over to New Ulm," a little town over there about fifteen miles away. And we got there and I said, "Now, they said they was under a little house

112

down below the depot." There was a house there alright. I went on and crawled under and looked and finally I could see them bundles way back in there. I says, "Here they are!" They sent somebody under to drag them out and that store man was tickled to death.

So we got them clothes and he took me into a little old bar there—it was wet in them days—and he bought me two or three glasses of beer and we stood around and talked to everybody an hour or so. All them old cars, they wasn't enclosed. They was open, you know, like a buggy. Old man Palm set in the back and his son was driving. As we had went on over, I had picked me a good place, a thick place, to jump out as as we come back.

I was playing asleep. I was handcuffed and holding to the top of this old car so I had a good brace. As we went down this hill we were doing about fifteen or twenty on this old, sandy road. There was no paved roads in them days. About halfway down, where he couldn't stop so quick, I flung myself down over the side and out I went. Old Palm grabbed me by the coattail and pulled my coat over my head and drug me a little piece, but my coat tore in two. Well, that let me free. I jumped up and the fence was over there, so I hit over that fence and down through them woods I went.

Palm and his boy got the car stopped and they went to shooting, but they was just shooting up in the trees. Bullets was falling all around, but they was just hitting the trees. I kept running and didn't stop. I guess they didn't really try to shoot me. Finally I lost them. I knowed they was going to have everybody in that country after me. I went about a mile or two straight, and then I turned back. It was old woods and I knowed they wouldn't be looking for me there. I heard them running up and down and I heard them talking and everything, and I heard them going the other way. I laid there until dark and then after that I heard running and rattling until two or three in the morning.

I cut across for about four miles to the Katy railroad track. When I got to the track, I found this big, old iron spike and I laid one hand of the handcuff where the little links went together on the railroad track and I hit them a few licks and broke them cuffs. That was about the next morning.

I walked in the brush then and I was going over to a town called Fayetteville where I could catch me a train the next night. I walked on through the brush and I run up on a little log house. Since I hadn't had nothing to eat, I slipped around and I seen that there was nobody there. I went in and there laid six eggs. Boy, I pocketed them, because I was going to get me a can and go down to the creek and get some water and come back and boil them. Just as I come out of the door with them eggs, I met an old woman and she seen the eggs and she took them away from me [laughs]. I let her have them because they was her eggs and I didn't want to start no disturbance. She might go hunting the law then, but this way she just thought I was some tramp, you know.

Then a man come by going to Flatonia in an automobile. I waved to him and he stopped and picked me up. So we went to Flatonia and that was over on the Southern Pacific. So I got off a mile before we got to town. About four o'clock a freight come along and I got it and rode over to Luling. I knowed Jim Dawson was running a sawmill over there on the Guadalupe River about fifteen miles. I was going up the sidewalk in town there about dark, and I seen an old law. I could tell them by just looking at them, so I walked on up to a corner and turned the corner into this other street, and, boy, I was gone like a cyclone.

I took out on a little dirt road across from the town close to where Jim Dawson was working the mill. He was the same man who was drilling water wells before. We had drilled the first water wells with Jim down at Crystal City. Now seven or eight or ten years later, he had this mill. I walked half the night out on that little road. It was warm and I laid down and went to sleep. The next day I cut across and went to Dawson's camp.

But I made a mistake, because I wrote back to

Houston to a woman I knew there because my pistol was
at her house. See, when I got arrested, I didn't have no
pistol, because I had left it at her house. She got that
pistol to send to me and her old man found out. So as
soon as she mailed that pistol and he knowed where she
mailed it, he goes and tells the law there and they notify
the law over at Luling to watch the post office for me to
get that pistol.

I was too smart to go over there myself. There was
this old boy working for Jim and I asked him to go over
there for me and ask for my mail. He could go over there
and back in two hours. Well, four hours come and he
didn't come back, and I knowed something was wrong.
Every time I heard anything—this was right on the bank
of the Guadalupe River—every time I heard anything I
went out and looked. Directly I heard a car coming. I
run out the door and looked up the road and there was
this car coming forward just lickity-lick-lickety-lick, all
with big white hats.

It was brushy and I just run out the door and down
to the river. It was running pretty high, about four to five
feet above its natural run. I took out down that river
about three hundred yards and I met about eight more
guys coming up the river. They had figured I'd run down
the river. They jerked their pistols and hollered, "Stop!,"
and I stopped. They was all around me grabbing at me
before I know it. And there was a bluff and I ran to that
bluff and off that bluff I went on my head in that river
and one shot at me and hit me in the bottom of the shoe
sole. It didn't quite go in. It just stung me a little on the
foot. And I hit the water hard, hollering, "Your broke my
leg! You broke my leg!" and I wallered and made like I
could hardly get to the other side. There was a bank
there about ten feet high with this old grape vine coming
down it. I was stumbling up the bank and they hollered,
"Don't shoot any more. His leg is broke." I climbed up
the vine and they said, "When you get to the top, you just
sit down over there."

Well, when I got on top, there was a ditch. I squirmed

around until I got about four or five feet from that ditch. "Sit down over there and stay there!" they said.

The river was up pretty high and none of them was coming across with their clothes on. I got within about a few feet of the ditch and in it I went. They couldn't see me now, and they just rained bullets through them trees and I just went right on through the ditch. I cut out across a field and went way on up the road about two miles and then I turned back. That's what I'd always do, and they'd think I was going the other way. I whipped back and come back over to about half a mile or a quarter from where I'd swum the river. I went up a ditch and there was a bunch of bushes up this ditch and they thought I was going across the country. I just laid around in them bushes until the next day. They believed then that I was gone.

I went back over to Jim's camp that night. He give me something to eat and give me some chuck, and I come on out and cut across the woods and walked across to Kingsbury on the Southern Pacific railroad. A long freight train come by and going up them hills it run real slow. I run along and grabbed it and got on, in a coal car or something. Went to San Antone and got out and walked around San Antone. All the trains that went west stopped out there at the I&GN crossing. There was a lot of woods out there. I stayed in them woods until night then headed on out to Uvalde.

# 10

## IN THE TEXAS PEN AND OUT—AGAIN (1917)

"I've seen them hang them old boys up there . . . and whip them until they just fall out lifeless. . . . They don't need an excuse to punish you, you know."

I stayed around Uvalde quite a long time, about two or three weeks or so. My mother had moved over to Sabinal from Uvalde. My daddy was not living with her at this time. He was up in Oklahoma. They was separated. She was living here, he was living there. Doc had a place up there and I think my daddy was living on it.

Well, there was a store in Uvalde and I wanted to get me some guns, so I kicked into this store one night and got me a few. I gave Jess some of them. I was going to jump into the mail car of Number Nine going west and rob it. I laid down there in an old lumber yard and waited for it and went to sleep. I dreamed that I caught that train and jumped in that car and they caught me. Well, now the train was coming and that was fresh on my mind, so I just wouldn't get on it.

I went over and put my Winchester under an old house and caught a train over to Sabinal and stayed with my mother a few days. I was fixing to leave then, and I had done walked out of the house when Jess said, "Say, come back here and give me a bill of sale for these guns." I wrote how much he give for them and I wrote a bill of sale, and spent about thirty minutes in there I guess, and when I walked out of the house, boy, the law was all over the place. There wasn't a getaway. They was front, back

117

and everywhere.

They got me there and took me back to Fayetteville where they had caught me before for the clothes and I had made the deal to get two years. So I laid in jail about six weeks before court come, and I went up there to plead guilty and there was a little kid in there with me for stealing a razor. They'd seen him leave a house with this razor and went down and caught him. A little old kid about sixteen years old. So he went up and pled guilty in front of me and they give that kid four years! For stealing a razor. They called it burglary. Just breaking into the house was called burglary, if you stole anything.

So I called the sheriff over, the one I'd made a deal with when I got the clothes back for him, and I said, "Listen, sheriff. You go over there and tell that county attorney and that jury to just give me two years, that you want me to have a two-year sentence." So he went over and talked to the county attorney and he said yeah. So when they got me up, I pled guilty. The judge told the jury, he said, "I'm satisfied to give this man here a two-year sentence and I'm going to ask you to give him that."

So they went out and wrote out a verdict that said two years. Old Judge Kitchell, he said, "Skinny, you're a fortunate man. You just got off with two years, with your reputation." I never said a word.

So I went in again for them two years. They took me to the Eastland Farm to serve them and I went down there and served until about Christmas.

While I was down there I escaped once. Me and an old boy that was working in the barn, we slipped out when the guard was out of the room. We slipped out the side window, went out there about half a mile, and caught a horse. We thought we'd ride this horse about half a mile or a mile, then get off of him up a tree and they couldn't trail us. But it was cloudy weather and when we got on the horse, our scent was still in the air. Them dogs trailed us right on the horse! We got to a tree, and we swung up on a limb and never touched the tree. There was moss all over it, and they couldn't see you up in there. We got in there and thought we was alright. If we'd circled that horse around before we went there in different ways, we'd have had them. The dogs run under the tree and across the road on the other side. "Bow-wow-wow," and then they stopped.

The dogs had lost the scent. And them old guards they all come up behind them on the horses and old Captain Jones says, "Well, I guess somebody come along this road and they caught them a buggy or something, or horseback or a wagon and they went up this road. Let's go this way."

So they headed off, but the wind was blowing right straight up that road the way they was going, and when they got about a hundred yards away, our scent went to the ground. Them dirty old dogs smelled it and they come back to that tree just "yaw-groww-yaw," about fifteen of them. I knowed they was going to shoot us down out of there, so I just hit that tree and come on down and all them dogs was around and I come off in the middle of them like a fox coming off a tree. They nailed me. Boy, they chewed me and chewed me and chewed my legs. When they come at me, I'd throw my arms thisaway, sideways, and they'd bite on that. Well, they chewed on me there for . . . they thought they was going to make me scream, but I never opened my mouth.

The guards, the captain, all of them was right there. And the other old boy I was with, he was too slow coming down and somebody said, "Shoot him out!" and as they shot, he slipped and it hit right over his head, and then he just fell out. Them dogs was chewing on me, but when he dropped down there, they jumped him, or some of them did, and he went to screaming and begging and the captain made the dogs stop. The reason they let them chew me so much was I wouldn't open my mouth. I never said a word.

So they took us and run us all the way back to the house. I'd lag and that old captain would whip me with his bridle reins every once in awhile. I'd keep trotting, and he'd whip me all the way, about two miles along to

119

the house, just reach around and hit me across the head. The guard said, "Keep up, Skinny," and I just kept trotting, kept trotting.

That's when the dogs chewed my legs. I got scars all over them now. I got dew poison in there. We went to picking cotton while my legs was still sore, and that made big running sores all over my legs.

About a month or two after that, this guy that escaped with me got into something and Captain Jones was cussing him about something. He said, "You goddamn big coward. You screamed like a baby when you jumped out of that tree, and old Skinny never said a word." So that captain was my friend from that day on. I went to picking cotton again and it wasn't long until he put me in the building. My legs was sore and he put me in there patching cotton sacks. And there was an old boy on the farm by the name of Bruce Willis. When we was hoeing in the fields, he could hoe lots of rows. I was never too strong, and he'd just carry the lead row, and he'd work a lot of us to death. We had to keep up with that lead man, see. As lead picker, he was picking five hundred and something a day. The captain thought that was great—Bruce Willis, the cotton picker. One day I said to him, "Captain, how about little old Skinny go pick some cotton?" I wanted to get out there in the patch with him.

"You couldn't keep up with the pull-dews." The pull-dews was a squad that couldn't pick no real cotton. The head squad would leave rows here and pieces there and pull-dews would pick them out. So I said, "Well, I can drag a sack anyhow. I can keep up and drag a sack." He never said anything.

The next day when they called out the Number One Squad, he said, "Old Skinny!" I went out there and they put me with the pull-dew squad. We went on there and picked an hour, hour and a half. Come in to weigh up and all the rest of them had about twenty pounds. I had nearly fifty or sixty pounds. Old Jones just sat down and said, "Where in hell did you steal that cotton at, Old Skinny?"

"Out of them burrs, just like that little row."

He said, "Aw, you didn't pick that much cotton."

The guard said, "Yes, he did. He picked every boll that's in there." So we picked on and I got hundred-fifty, two hundred pounds easy, on the pull-dew squad.

Next morning, the Number One Squad come out and he said, "Old Skinny!" Then he said, "Boss Higgins, you got another man." And we hit the cotton patch. Captain Jones come on out when we got there and Mr. Bruce is the lead row man on everybody. He says, "Give Old Skinny the lead row!" and he says, "The rest of you goddamn so-and-so's better keep up with him." So I hit that row, and if I didn't carry them! If I didn't carry that Bruce Willis! He took out after me, but he couldn't hold a shovel to me. The next day he says, "Skinny, let's hold them down a little, let's hold them down."

I said, "When we was hoeing that cotton last spring, you wouldn't hold them down. You just pick your cotton and I'll pick mine." I carried them like that for three or four days or a week picking six hundred every day. Because I could pick more than I could carry, half the time he'd make them carry my sack. I made a believer out of that Bruce Willis.

I was such a good cotton picker because I was natural. Natural. I was just fast with my hands. My brother, Jess, if he could get a hundred-fifty a day, why, he was lucky, and he worked just as hard as me or harder. And I'd pick five hundred or six hundred. He just couldn't do it [laughs]. I could keep cotton going in my sack all the time.

About this time I put together a deal to get myself out of prison, but it didn't work. There was another guy, Ike, that was a trusty that worked in a shoe shop outside, him and a nigger. And there was another old boy we called Sweetwater in there that was about to get out. He would do anything. So we made it up, me and Ike, to ask Sweetwater if he'd go to Humble and get a pistol off my brother, tell him that I wanted a pistol, and then bring it back and hide it under this shoe shop. Then the old boy who worked there, the trusty, he would just go and get it and put it in his shirt and bring it in from there.

So Sweetwater went down to Houston and seen my brother. I had said, "Don't tell him what I want it for. Just tell him I want a pistol, that I'm going to get out of the penitentiary before long." Well, my brother give him an old .45 thumb buster. He brought it back in two or three nights and slipped around there and put it under this house. The next day Ike gets it out from under the house and shows it to this nigger!

Nigger says to him, "You better not take that in there." But old Ike he didn't have no better sense. He brought it on in and give it to another guy, not to me. The nigger run and told, and the first thing we know there was shotguns and everything else in there, and they went right to the guy who had the pistol. And the guard said, "You better come up with that pistol."

The guy said, "It's right here under my bed."

Well, they went out and in two or three days they arrested Sweetwater, the boy who went and got the pistol from my brother. He told them that I sent him to get the pistol. They never connected it to me until then, three days later.

So they called me in and they was doing what they called "swinging you up." They had a long board about two foot wide with holes through it and they'd put your hand right up there through one of them holes and strap it tight, then put the other one through another hole and strap it so they was about two foot apart. Then they'd pull you up in the air with that, high enough to where your toes wasn't quite off the floor, but nearly one foot would be. You could catch a little with the other. That was the punishment for most any little thing. Twice I got into that kind of trouble.

The second time I hung in the chains was about a month after that, I guess. Me and Stone Innis, we was racing each other picking the cotton and was about neck and neck. In fact, it didn't do any good for me to beat him or him to beat me, and we was picking more than we had to anyway, but we was racing, and one day when we weighed up, I left about six or seven pound of cotton in my sack, then rolled it up and stuck it under my arm. While we was going back to the rows to pick again, Captain Mac come riding up. He was the field captain, and he seen that wad in my sack. "Come here, Old Skinny. What you got in there?"

I told him I was just trying to beat Stone. I said, "Captain Mac, you know I don't have to steal cotton. I'm picking way more than I'm supposed to." But the old rat slung me up anyhow for about three-fourths of an hour. I got my foot on a clod of dirt, so I was all right for awhile, but when he went off, that clod broke and you know I was really swinging. The dog sergeant, he was standing there watching, and he liked me. They was all for me. Awhile after Captain Mac had rode off, the sergeant told them to turn me down, and my thumbs right there on each one of them was numb for ten years. And sometimes there's a little numbness right there in my right hand yet, and that's been forty or fifty years ago. Them straps rub and cut the circulation off my thumbs.

My brother, Doc, he was down there so long, he hung there for hours and hours and hours. He was always into something, and he never used any judgment. He'd cuss them out no matter who it was. He was down there for ten year, and to the day he died he hardly had any feeling in the thumbs. I guess they must have hung him up two to three hundred times, maybe five hundred. Lots of times for six hours at a stretch.

Doc was a kind of a bullheaded guy and stout as a mule. He'd tell anybody to go to hell, you see, and that was right up their alley. They'd just as soon punish you as be decent to you. They'd rather hang you up all night than you sleep in a bed. They didn't care how tough you got, because you couldn't do anything about it. And that kind of thing affected Doc all of his life.

I've seen them hang them old boys up there and throw water at them and whip them and beat them until they just fall out lifeless. Then they just take them down, let them fall on the floor and throw water all over them to bring them to life. They don't need an excuse to punish you, you know. After they get it in for you, if you do any little thing, or even if somebody says you done something, they stomp on you. It's just like when you get out as an ex-convict. Whether you done anything or not, they're after you. So I started working my mind fast, what to do, how to get out of this.

Now remember that Governor Jim Ferguson was in office at that time, and if you just got fifty or a hundred dollars and give it to one of the captains, they could just send your name in to Ferguson and write your letter and you were pardoned right now! They had kind of a "system" going, see. Finally I said to the assistant captain, "Send for Captain Mac. Tell him I want to tell him something." The captain came out and I said, "Now, Captain Mac, I want to tell you what I told Sweetwater to tell my brother. He said he got that pistol from my brother, but I don't believe he got it from there. He didn't bring it in here to me. He brought it to somebody else," and Mac knowed that. I says, "I told Sweetwater to go to my brother and tell him if he could get me two hundred fifty dollars cash, that I could get a pardon, that I knowed a way to get a pardon with it."

He stood there and said, "Why didn't you tell me that before?" Of course he knowed the deal that was going down with Ferguson. He knowed the route.

About three months after that, I got hold of about fifteen dollars. I had hurt my knee and I was hopping around. I gave Captain Mac the fifteen dollars and he give me a job as assistant building attendant. There was nothing to do. Twenty minutes work. We had to have somebody clean up the building we lived in after everybody went out. The head attendant made me his assistant and I never done nothing. Just cleaned up the building when everybody went out, like a janitor. Sweeping the floors, and cleaning the spittoons and all like that. They had them spittoons all over the house. You had no other place to spit. Oh, it was pitiful in them days, them buildings they kept you in. Old wooden buildings with the old bunks hanging up there, smelled. Now they got modern buildings all there now. Before, they was just old wooden shack buildings. Now I see they put criminals in jail and feed them this and that and preach to them and make them reading rooms and give them picture shows. Hell, they ought to have been in there when I was and they'd have found out the difference. Looks to me like they're kind of babying a lot of these prisoners.

They was brutal in that Texas penitentiary in them days, even after Governor Colquitt. They couldn't whip you, they'd stopped whipping, but I've seen them out in that cotton patch, old boys that couldn't pick very much cotton, the guards would run their horse over there on him and knock him down. And about the time he'd get up, they'd run back over him again till he couldn't get up, and then the guard would just ride off.

Once, early on when I was in there, Captain Mac rode up to where me and Stone Innis was partners together. We picked three rows and the rest just picked one. Well, Mac rode up one day and Boss Lloyd was our guard. Stone and me had just got five or six steps behind the rest of them cause we got to talking. I went in there with a bad reputation, partly because Doc had give them so much trouble, you know.

So this day he started after us, Captain Mac did with the horse, and Boss Lloyd said, "By God, hold up there. That's two of the best men I've got on this squad. They're picking three rows and the rest of the men are picking one." Mac stopped then and rode off the other way. He was going to run over us with his horse and Boss Lloyd stopped him. We never had another run-in with him.

Me and Stone could do anything and do it good. We were both Lloyd's buddies and he'd do anything for us. He said to us one day about this gun business, he said, "Skinny, was you going to get that gun? You fellas going to come out here and stick me up?"

And I said, "Boss Lloyd, we'd fight a son of a bitch if we knowed he was going to bother you. Nobody's going to stick you up as long as me and Stone's in your squad, cause you're a friend and we know it. I didn't have the gun, but if the rest went out, I'd of went with them."

When I was at Imperial Farm, the first time I was in the penitentiary, I picked more cotton than anybody on the farm that fall. They put on the books how much each man picked. They didn't make you pick a certain amount each day, but they could look at you and tell about how much you could pick. They put you out by squads. Number One Squad, Number Two Squad, Number Three Squad, Number Four Squad—that's the way they went. I was the high man. That was because I wanted to show them the kind of cotton picker I was. But down there at Eastland I didn't. I didn't see any purpose in working that hard. Lots of them picked hard there because they didn't know any better. But I knowed better by then.

On Eastland Farm, if you could get a rabbit and take it in, they'd cook it for you. A rabbit was a treat there, fresh meat. Old Stone and me was picking cotton together and this rabbit jumped up and Stone took him up thataway and he circled and come back. Stone was six foot three and weighed about a hundred eighty-five pounds, and could run like a mule. I seen this rabbit come between these two cotton rows, and I squatted down. It was high cotton, and Stone couldn't see me. Just about the time I nailed the rabbit coming down that row, Stone hit me flying just like a horse. He run into me blind. One knee hit me in the side of the head, and the other hit me in the side, and that twisted me. I was squatted down and my feet was sort of stuck in that old dirt and that twisted my knee. Slipped the knee joint and tore them ligaments right up and down my knee joint.

We had no doctors down there in the penitentiary. They said there was nothing the matter with my knee. It was a year and a half before I could walk on it, then it never bothered me any more until about five year ago I was taking a bath and my foot slipped in the tub and I wrenched it again. Now it never will get well. It's as bad now as when I hurt it five years ago. I've got to watch, if

I ever hurt it again I'll be on crutches. I've got to be so particular, and that's the reason I don't walk very good protecting that knee.

For breakfast at the penitentiary they'd give you hog jaw. They bought hog jaw, wagon loads of them. They'd take them old hog jaws and lay them down on a board and take a knife and cut. Maybe this strip would be one-fourth of an inch thin, and the next one would be one-half an inch, and the next one would be an inch. Then they'd throw it in a big kettle and cook it. Maybe there'd be a little streak of lean once in awhile. Then they'd take them and put them in a big pan, and of a morning they'd give you breakfast. Sometimes they'd give us corn bread, but usually they give us biscuits for breakfast. They'd come out with them hog jaws in a pan and they used a spoon to give it to you. Then spoonfuls of molasses—hog jaws and molasses and bread for breakfast. For dinner they'd have something else. Beans cooked up some way and cornbread all crumbled up. They used a can and just dipped it up and give it to you. You never come in to dinner on weekdays because it was too far to walk. They just brought the chuck out there in them old boxes and fed you on what we called the "turnrows." That's where they drive between each cut of cotton.

That's what they fed you. But I'll tell you one thing, you ate it all! And you enjoyed it. Because that's all you got. That was dinner. Then in the evening they give you just as near to nothing as they could find. Hash or something they'd throwed together like the rest of them hog jaws they'd made that morning and put in something else and gummed it up and come around with a big spoonful for your plate. And you ate it and enjoyed it, because you was starved to death all the time. You was hungry all the time. They didn't give you all you could eat of that kind of stuff, even. They'd just give you so much.

Any kind of meat you caught or anything, just give it to the cook and he had to cook it. "This is for old Skinny and Stone." That was orders from the captain, the head man. We'd  catch them rabbits during the day, then they'd cook them for us at night. There wasn't enough rabbits for everybody. There was a hundred and some of us, so you couldn't divide it up. If you did, you didn't have any. And that rabbit tasted good! You know, a cottontail rabbit's good anytime, but, boy! that fried rabbit's delicious. So we was always looking for rabbits. No rabbit ever had a chance when he was jumped up by them squads. If one didn't get him, the other one would [laughs].

The whole time I was in Eastland, I kept thinking of ways to get out. When Jim Ferguson was governor, it was pretty easy to get a pardon if you had the money and could get it to Ferguson. But I could never get the money. Then Ferguson got impeached and William P. Hobby, the Lieutenant Governor, got the job and things changed. But one day I was talking to this old boy, another prisoner that was a smart guy about writing, and he said, "I can write any signature you can give me. I can just look at it." We picked out different signatures, and he could write them. He was in there for stealing something, but I mean he could write like a forger.

I said, "Would you sign some letters for me if I can get you some signatures?"

He said, "All you want." So I got hold of a little money and I talked to him and said, "Write me up a petition to get a pardon from the penitentiary. Write it up and head it and all and leave room for sixty or seventy signatures down there.

I give him a couple of dollars and he fixed it up just like it was real. When I got that, I talked to them prisoners. You see, we used to write them companies and they'd send you something to sell, and you send them the money back. I gathered my signatures on the petition by telling them old boys, "I'm getting up a pretty good list to send to the company and I'll get a lot of stuff back and we'll divide it up." I got about ten or fifteen and then further down some would sign it again till I got me sixty signatures on it, just like they was citizens, you know, from the county signing to give me a parole.

Then I wrote to the old judge. Would he recommend me for a pardon? I knowed he wouldn't. So Judge Kitchell wrote back a nasty letter and told me how fortunate I was to have gotten them two years, and that he couldn't recommend me for parole. Well, then I had his letterhead, and I had his signature, and I had his envelope with his name on it. So I took his old letter out of there and got this forger to write me a recommendation on good bonded paper. He looked at the signature and wrote it a few times, and he wrote the judge's name on it as good as the judge did! Well, I just doubled that up and put it in this envelope where it had been torn open.

Now that I had that, I wrote to Sheriff Palm and he wrote me back and said, "Well, Skinny, it won't take you long. I let you get off easy." I knowed he wouldn't recommend me for a pardon, but he was a good old man. But now, you see, I've got Palm's letter, his signature on it, and my forger out front goes to work with his bonded paper and writes me a recommendation from the sheriff, and it was "genuine." Then I put that back in the envelope with his name on it.

Next he sits down and writes me one to the parole board from the man who run the store—I knowed the man's name—and asked them to pardon me. Said that I wasn't really to blame for the crime, and through me he had recovered nearly all of his stuff, that he had lost very little. That was a good letter! We didn't have to have his signature, because they wouldn't know the difference about his signature anyway. Now I had me what looked like a perfect petition.

When that was all ready, I sent it to the Board of Pardons and then I got some money and sent it to my mother. I asked a guard if he would mail it for me. I was in his squad and he was a good guy. Well, I wrote her a letter and told her what to do, not to come here, but to go to Austin. See, she'd already got me a pardon before, and she knowed how to go to them old governors then. I said, "Don't go to the governor's office. Go to the governor's mansion and see his wife." So she went over and seen Hobby's wife and told her she was a widow woman and I was in the penitentiary.

The wife said, "You go back over there to the governor and tell the governor I said to give that boy a pardon." I was about twenty-seven years old at that time. My mother went back, just walked in on them and told them what to do.

She went over and talked to the governor, and the governor said, "Well, I'll have to go through the Board of Pardons." But you see, the guard had done mailed my petition in by then, and I'd been down there in the penitentary about nine months. So the Board of Pardons said when half of my time was up, they'd recommend me for a pardon. That was good enough. She went on home, and in eleven months I got a full pardon from Governor Hobby.

See, they never investigated them letters. They didn't write to the sheriff or check them signatures at all. So meantime the Board of Pardons was making a trip around through the prison. And they come in there in the building where I was and I asked them and they said, "Yes, Skinny, we gave you your pardon, but we had to let you do half your time on account of you being a second timer. If you hadn't been a second timer, with the good petition you had, we'd have turned you out as soon as we got it." Well, I thanked them nicely anyhow.

Well, it takes two weeks to get it, even after it's there. So a couple of weeks come and out I went.

*When World War I broke out in 1917, both Jess and Tull was taken in the first draft. They took men from twenty-one to thirty-one, and Jess was exactly thirty-one, Tull twenty-one, so in they go. They was both sent to Camp Travis at San Antone. All that was was tents off by Fort Sam Houston. They trained them there a short time and then Tull was sent overseas. They held Jess back even though he wanted to go with Tull. Later he was shipped to New York City, but he fell or something there and hurt his back and he was discharged there.*

130

# 11

## BREAKING INTO THE BANK BUSINESS (1918)

> "He said, 'Skinny, do you want to get in on a bank robbery? . . . I didn't hesitate. Hell, if you hesitate you're liable to get in trouble."

**W**hen I got my pardon and they turned me out I wore a thirty-inch pants in the waist and a thirty-eight coat, and they give me a suit with a forty-two inch pants and a forty-six coat. They don't care if it fits or not. They just give you any old thing. So there was a guy over in the little town where we used to catch the train and if your prison suit didn't fit you, you could trade off for something else. Well, I went over there to this merchant and I traded this suit for one good pair of pants. They give you a citizen shirt, hat and shoes, but I already had citizen shoes, 'cause you could wear them there at the farm. You didn't have to wear convict brogues.

At the prison we wore clothes made out of old white cotton ducking. You didn't wear stripes unless you got in trouble and was put in third grade. They called it a punishment, third grade, and I got in third grade the first time I was there and I wore stripes about three months. Then you got to build yourself out. It took me just two weeks to build myself out when I went to picking cotton down there. The captain came along and told me I was doing fine, to get white clothes. I said, "Well, captain, I'll put white clothes on, but I want to stay at the building where I'm at, where the stripes is at." He says, "You can stay over there." He called them guys over there the striped . . . so-and-so's.

When I got out and went over to Houston where my oldest brother Bud was at, I just had that pair of pants and good shoes and that shirt I had on and an old ace deuce hat and no underwear. Bud had worked for an oil company there for nearly twenty-five years.

I stayed around there two or three days and couldn't get a job, and then I met another old boy and I said, "Let's go up the road here and get us some clothes." So we caught a freight train and went up about sixty miles above there, and that night we went into town and broke into a store. We went in there and dressed ourselves up in just what we needed in good clothes. We put our old things in a bag so we could take them out with us. It was good and light in the store, so we picked us some more good clothes and filled a suitcase full and some extra pants and stuff.

Then we caught a freight train coming through there about three or four o'clock in the morning and come back to Humble. I monkeyed around down there and I didn't have no money, but I knowed a guy that run a tailor shop. So I went down there and sold him about six or eight pair of brand new pants. And some constable figured somebody in the oil field might have done the break-in, and he come around looking in them stores. He went to that tailor shop, and there was them eight new pair of pants hanging there. He asked the tailor where he got them, and he told him he bought them off of me. The constable identified them as stuff coming out of that store up there.

Meantime I'd been getting papers together to get Doc a pardon like I'd done for myself. I went over to a town near to the county seat. Big Bend was where Doc was convicted the last time, for taking a guard's gun away from him. They made it highway robbery. If he'd been tried, he couldn't have been convicted, but Doc never could do nothing but plead guilty. So at noon time they went out to dinner and I went into the judge's office and I got ahold of some stationery and an envelope. And I done the sheriff and the county attorney the same way. So I done got all them wrote up into good recommenda-

tions and was fixing to get a petition and I had this stuff.
Then I had a letter wrote from old man Neal Espert, the
head of the Invincible Oil Company  my brother had
worked for for years, saying that if Doc got out he'd give
him a job at any time,  that my brother had worked for
him for years, see.

But when I got jumped up over that burglary I had to
leave the country.  And I never got the pardon through,
so  Doc was still in.

I left and went up to West Texas in the fall of the year.
There I met up with first one guy and then another and
we went up to Oklahoma.  Then I picked up with Stone
Innis, who was with me at Eastland but had escaped.  I
met him up there in the country that fall,  and we was
monkeying around all winter nearly.  We went out to
around Mineral Wells, me and Stone, and we burglarized
some stores.  We took the stuff out to the section crews
that worked for the railroad, the extra crews. There'd be
maybe one to two hundred Mexicans in these camps.
We'd take these clothes, these suits and pants, and turn
them over just as fast as we could sell them.  Them
Mexicans wouldn't snitch on anybody.  For pants we got
two dollars or so, and suits eight or ten dollars.

We was up there above Denison one night and we was
busted.  There was a little town, Bells, right out of
Denison about fifteen miles and we located us a good
store.  We went over there and it was cold.  The ground
was froze hard as a rock and ice was all over everything.
We didn't know there was a night watchman there.  So
we went on in the back window, got in, and I said, "I'm
going to pull off this overcoat and leave it right here on
this box till we come back out."  We went on in there and
we was sacking them up, getting all sizes.  It was light
and shiny and you could get any size you wanted. We was
getting us a lot of stuff ready together when all of a
sudden a flashlight went in at the back door.

I said, "There's a nighthack, Stone!"  Boy!, he run to
the front of the store and just leaped through one of them
big glass windows.  When I got there, there was nothing

for me to do but crawl through the window. All the glass was out. The old nighthack run around the side of the building and the moon was shining bright as day. I went thisaway and Stone went thataway. And that nighthack carried a little pistol and them bullets was hitting the ground, boom! boom!

Stone went on down there and now a bunch of dogs was after him. He hit a cotton patch. I went the other way and they was chasing Stone instead of me. So there goes Stone and the dogs and the nighthack. Did they run him! That nighthack was a young fella, and he'd reload his gun and shoot at him again. Never did hit him. But you could hear the bullets hitting the hard ground.

A bunch of dogs got after me, too, but they didn't bother me. Just as we'd went in at the door of the store, I'd said to Stone, "If we get separated we'll meet at the little house." There was a little house about three miles down from the track where we'd been waiting for dark to come. That's all that saved me. They run Stone through that cotton patch and finally Stone got away. Well, I got to the little house first and I was froze to death! Oh, it was cold. See, I didn't have my overcoat. I had left it there at the store. Stone had his. Finally I heard something—rattle, rattle, rattle—Stone was coming down the track. Directly he come in. He was carrying his overcoat. He was a young, husky bull, and I never was so strong. I said, "Boy!, give me that overcoat." Well, we didn't have a thing in the world, not a match or nothing to make a fire with. We had to walk to keep warm. And he give me his overcoat and we walked to daylight. I never was so cold in my life as when he give me that overcoat. And all I could do was keep walking to keep warm with that overcoat.

We went on down and went to Denison. Got in there at the edge of town and went into a restaurant to get something to eat. While we were sitting there, I noticed Bud Russell, the transfer agent, the man who transferred prisoners all over the country. He'd put chains around their neck, put them in rows, you know, and he carried the chains with him and when he'd get a prisoner, he'd make them carry the chains. We was sitting down there eating and Stone was escaped and I was wanted down there in Humble and all at once old Bud Russell come in there and two, three prisoners with him. He come in there and he threw all them chains right down at my and Stone's feet, and I said, "My God, that's Bud Russell." He knowed us both well. But he was so busy getting them prisoners back in the back to eat that I just tried to get out of there before he'd notice. And out of there we went and escaped Bud right there. He didn't see us! He had his back to me and didn't see my face. He sure knew both of us was wanted. If he'd seen us, he'd of grabbed us right there.

Then we took on out and went on down to Ranger. I'd been selling even before I seen Stone, so I had about $475-$500 in my pocket. We ran into an ex-convict out there and he knowed Stone was escaped. My brother-in-law lived out there and I went to his house for a couple hours and Stone and this ex-con was monkeying around there and that guy goes and snitched and told that Stone was escaped from the penitentiary and gets a twenty-five dollar reward. When I come back, they had Stone arrested. Of course I was wanted for that clothing store burglary north of Humble, so I blowed town.

And that's the last time I ever seen Stone Innis. He went back to the penitentiary and then got out, and him and some old boys that turned him out went back and killed a guard. They got away and that's the last I ever heard of Stone. I seen a lot of guys in the penitentiary, six, eight, ten years after, and they said they never heard of Stone Innis anymore.

So I went on out west and met up with old Red Johnson, the same boy I had robbed my first train with down here in Cline. Me and him went on out there around Abilene, and we burglarized a store over there and we had this big, long, black overcoat. I met some other old boys there in Abilene, the bank robber Frank I gave the key to and let out of the penitentiary, and there was another bank robber with him, his partner, and a third old boy. We went off and talked, and because I'd done him that big favor Frank said, "Skinny, do you want to get in on a bank robbery?"

I said, "Anytime. Just let me in on one. I been accused of robbing them all over Texas and never robbed one yet. But I'd like to rob one." I told Red to wait for me at Abilene and I'd be back in a day or two. So I left with Frank and went down to rob the bank in Winters, Texas, because we had a tip from old man Boyd, the detective for the Banker's Association, who had told Frank that there was a safe in there you could blow. Frank was supposed to give him some money if they got it. We blowed the vault door and went in, but after we had blowed the drum door, there was a round safe that we couldn't blow. We monkeyed around inside there and found about thirty-five hundred dollars in liberty bonds and took them.

So we come on out and we had to go back to Abilene on a dirt, sandy road. During the job we had got no rank—no police—after us, but the wind blowed the sand and you couldn't hardly tell one road from another and we got on the wrong one. We hadn't gone but a mile or two and the driver says we were on the wrong road, that we missed it back yonder. Frank said, "Hell, go on. Don't go back."

"This is an awful damn road, the way this sand is piling up."

"Well, go ahead!" We went about three miles and got in that sand, and we had a Hudson car that the clutch was easy to burn out. He was pulling in and out of that sand and the clutch burned up and there we was, way up in them hills close to Buffalo Gap. We couldn't do anything but leave the car. So we got out and took to them mountains that day. So the next morning, about nine, ten, or eleven o'clock somebody found that car. These guys and Frank had been down in this town playing oil men a few days before and everybody had seen them, but of course I hadn't been down there.

They knowed we was in them hills, but they wouldn't come up there in the daytime. Just circled round on the roads. We had went way across the mountain and I said, "We better hide till tonight."

Frank says, "No, let's get closer to Buffalo Gap and go in there at night and steal a car." They had seen us on that mountain that day but they was scared to come in there because we was bank robbers! They thought we was tough people. They didn't know there was an old cotton picker in there.

So, about dark, nine or ten o'clock, we walked into Buffalo Gap. We went and found a Ford car out in a little old barn where they used to keep their buggies and cows. That was where they kept their Ford cars now. We pushed it out and started cranking it and couldn't get it to start. Directly a car drove by with four guys in it and they all had big hats. They didn't go but about a hundred yards and they stopped. We was all around that car and I said, "Boys, that's the law. Let's get away from here!"

Frank said, "No, the hell with them." That was the tough man talking.

So I said, "Well, I'm gonna get to where I can get away. They're coming back. What are you gonna do? Stand there and wait for them to arrest you?" So me and one of these old boys, named Slim Edgarton, just took out in the dark. The other guy, Al, Frank's partner, stayed there, and them laws came back and Frank went to shooting and they shot Al down. Then old Frank run and hit the brush. That was the last we seen of Frank.

So we went on out in the brush. I told Slim the only way to get away was to separate. I says, "I'll go my way and you go your way. Abilene is down yonder there, but don't go into town 'till tomorrow night, and then catch you a freight train." That's what I was going to do. He never done that, though. Instead, when daylight come he went up to a farmer's house and told him he wanted something to eat and a place to sleep. The farmer fed him and put him to sleep and went and got the law and they got him out of bed!

I went over about two miles to where I knowed a guy, and he took me to Abilene that night. So I went and hunted Red up, and I said, "Red, I'm in a jam and I need to leave the country. Do you want to come with me?" And he said yeah.

So a freight train come in that morning. It was about three o'clock in the morning and we caught it and rode it to a little town called Eskota, a little coal chute just this side of Sweetwater. When me and Red got there, it was just daylight, and I said, "We got to get off this train and get in the mesquites and lay all day and night. Then we'll catch another train at night because they'll be watching these trains." But an old brakeman had seen us after we got off that train and he was suspicious and he went and told the law.

We went on down there, oh, about a quarter or a half a mile, it was pretty cold, through thick mesquite, and made ourselves a fire and laid down and went to sleep. We was going to sleep there all day and go back and catch a train out west that night. Well, we was sleeping and the first thing I knowed they was grabbing at us, pistols was at our sides and Winchesters. They was hollering, "Put 'em up. Put 'em up. Search 'em. Search 'em."

But see now, I'd stole that big black overcoat about forty miles away from the bank robbery, so I knowed I had a dead alibi on them. I'd gotten away so quick from the car and had never been seen in Winters and the others had been. When I got that guy to take me to Abilene, I was there that night or early the next morning. I could prove that. If I could do that, I couldn't have been in on that bank robbery. But they grabbed us. And I said, "What the hell have you got us for?" So I told them I was somebody and I told them Red was somebody. But one of them, a sheriff from Sweetwater says, "That's old Skinny Newton." I was already knowed all over that country.

So they took us over to Sweetwater and put us in jail for about three hours and here come the sheriff. See, they'd killed that fellow Al at the car and caught Slim at that farm, and they said me and Red was the others. They had to have four guys, you see. They'd killed one and caught the other and now they had me and Red. Frank, he had just walked off. He had gone to Abilene and caught a passenger train and they'd quit looking for him, especially now they got Red in his place.

They brought us back over to Abilene and there we had them big, long overcoats with wooly collars. They took us over to the Ballinger jail that night and put us in there. I told the sheriff where me and Red was at, and he went over there and checked my alibi and Red's alibi. Now he knows Red's not there at the robbery and he knows I can't be there if I'm with Red that night staying the whole night with him. Red had been around there all day playing poker. He had the perfect alibi and he was the perfect alibi for me! I could show you now from the piece in the paper where the evidence showed that me and Red wasn't there. I had made such a quick getaway knowing somebody over there and that gave me a perfect alibi.

But they had started thinking about that store. We'd sold about five hundred dollars worth of clothes out of this store, you know, before then, but we still had them big overcoats. So then they got to talking about that big store that had been burglarized about thirty or forty miles away. As soon as we got in jail, they had this old potbelly stove, an old heating stove in the cell. Slim, the guy they caught at the farm, you know, he was in there with us. "There's plenty of coal, and plenty of wood and stuff," the sheriff says. "Make a fire." I jerked Red over there and said, "Start that fire right quick," and I went to tearing and cutting overcoats. I tore them all to pieces and we crammed them in that stove. In an hour's time we had them overcoats burned up.

A couple of days later they come up there and said, "Say, Skinny, you and Red bring them overcoats out here. We want to look them over."

I said, "Hell, Red got cold during the night and I woke up and he done made a fire and burnt them coats up."

They took Red out and looked at his clothes to see if he had anything stolen on him. When the deputy asked if he should bring me out too, the sheriff said, "Hell, don't bring Skinny out. If he had any of them, he'd burn them up too." If they'd got them overcoats, they'd of connected us with that store burglary down there. That would have killed us.

They held us anyhow. One day the sheriff's wife come up to our cell. She had a boy in the army in San Antone in some kind of trouble. She needed money. I had deposited four hundred dollars in the bank in Ranger where my brother-in-law lived. And I had a hundred or so with me. She says "Skinny, if you give me five hundred dollars I'll turn you boys out of this jail."

I said, "how?"

"I'll just unlock the door and let you go. My boy's in trouble, and I need some money."

I said, "No. That would get you in trouble if you turned us out that door. I'll tell you what I can do. I can get four hundred if you mail a letter for me. You don't have to turn us out. Just you come up right slow if you hear the sheriff saying anything about hearing any racket up here."

She said, "Alright," and when she said that we was halfway out. I wrote a letter and she got me a check and I re-fixed it and sent it down to my brother-in-law in Ranger. He went down to the bank there and I had told him to come to the jail at Abilene at twelve o'clock when the sheriff wouldn't be here. There was a big crowd coming up here everyday at twelve o'clock. People was coming from all over town, all over the country, to see us bankrobbers! We was right new. So I told my brother-in-law you be right there and she'll let you up. I told her he was a tall, slim, curly-headed fellow.

So he got the money and brought it in twenty-dollar bills. He come up there with that big crowd and we was talking and he just slipped me the money through the bars. The sheriff had a little boy six years old and he seen him slip me something.

The funny thing is, we could have gotten out the night before, but I said, "No, I'd told that woman I'd give her that four hundred and I'm going to give it to her. I'm not going out tonight. We can go tomorrow night and they won't find us. My brother-in-law will be here with that money at noon, and I'm going to give it to that woman, because she come up here and offered to turn us out at the door." They'd have put her in the penitentiary if she'd done that, and I wouldn't let her do it.

So we done had a hole fixed and covered up where we could go up through the ceiling, and then go to the top of the building and down. The ceiling was steel, but it had been there so long the bolts it was fastened with had come loose, and we could prize it and just pull that steel down until there was only the wood. The ceiling was made out of wood two by fours. So we tore a piece of flat iron off the end of the cot about twenty inches long and we built a fire in that stove and heated it and held it against the wood there until we had a hole. Then we could turn that steel back up, and nobody could see the hole.

We stayed there that whole day and had it fixed and that night the sheriff come up. The boy, the woman's son, had told the sheriff what he'd seen. The sheriff said, "My little boy here said that somebody handed you something through the bars."

I said, "There's half a dozen people handing things through the bars, cigarettes and such."

"Oh," he said, "That's what it was." And that cured it. The next day we was ready to go, but the wife had come up there the day after my brother-in-law had brought the money and said, "Have you boys got any money left?"

"No," I said. "We don't have a dollar."

Then she said, "You had a hundred dollars downstairs and the sheriff done spent it. He says they want to come after you from down in East Texas. He's got a wire here to hold you." The sheriff would have turned us loose if it hadn't been for that, but they wanted us back in East Texas. So that night she gave us a twenty-dollar bill back from the money I had give her.

About twelve o'clock I guess it was, Red had said he wasn't going to go, so I went out first. It was an old, tall jail about two stories and then they had a story on top. Why, it was forty feet high! So, I went out first and here comes Slim. Red wasn't supposed to come, but directly here he come. He couldn't stand it. There we were up in the ceiling of the building and it was about ten feet to a hole that went out the top, and there was no way to get to it. We wasn't tall enough to get to it and it came into a dome and you couldn't climb the walls. Well, we kicked around up there, and there was a ladder I guess had laid up there forty or fifty years, that they had used up there, about eight foot long. But it was rickety and dry.

I said to Red and Slim, "Pick that ladder up and put it up into that hole and you get on each side of it and hold it and I'll get on it and climb out." I was the lightest. So they held it and I got on the ladder and climbed out. We had brought us a bunch of blankets up from the bottom in the cells to make us a rope to go down the wall. I noticed when I picked them up—we had done tied them together—there was an awful weak-looking blanket there, but I figured it would hold. So when I got to the top, they give me the ladder out and I laid it crossways over that hole and tied the blanket to it and let it down and it was strong enough so Slim climbed up and come out and Red climbed up and come out. We tied the blankets around a chimney thing, and let it down the wall.

The moon was shining bright as day. It was still as death. It was after midnight. I'm going to be the first one down that blanket, so I swung on off it and got about half way and there's that little old rotten blanket. It was about eight foot long, and it went to tearing. Well, it was bright so I could see the ground, so I just turned all loose, but I kept it kinda in my hand and slid, took my weight off it and when I hit the next blanket down there, I caught a little and slid and then dropped to the ground, to keep from breaking that thing. If it would of broke with me up there, I was fifteen feet from the ground.

I called up quiet to them, I said, "That little blanket's rotten. Pull it up there and take it out. It's long enough anyway." They pulled it back up there and taken it out. I ran out and sat behind a telegraph pole about thirty yards away across the other street. There was nobody guarding. I knowed the sheriff was in there asleep. I sat there and never felt better! I don't think there was a time in my life that I felt better than I did right then. Sitting back there looking at that bright moon and them coming down. I was home free! So Slim he come down and then Red come down. Well, they come over to where I was at and they said, "We got to walk out of town."

And I said, "No, we won't walk out of town. You said you could drive a car, any kind of car. You just come with me." We went up the street about four or five blocks out to the edge of town and the first garage we went into, there was a nearly new Ford with the key in it. We was all husky and strong, so we just backed that thing out, then pushed it down that alley and down the road a couple hundred yards and got in there and turned that key and zoom! here we went.

I said, "I know a guy in San Angelo where we can fill it up with gas and that'll carry us to San Antone." When we got over there, the road was changed. They was building a new road, and we had to detour. There was all of them tractors, with gas, oil and everything. We was about ten miles out of Ballinger. I said, "There's no use in stopping at San Angelo. There's a can. Get you all the gas and oil you want." We got two ten-gallon cans of gas and put it in there and two or three gallons of oil, and boy!, we went right on to San Angelo and from there we took out south and the first town was Eldorado, about forty miles. Just at daylight that sun was coming up and we was going through Eldorado and I said, "Red, get back there in the back and lay down so if anybody sees us they can't see but two of us."

Going through town I looked back there and old Red's

head was sticking up. I said, "That red head is just as bright as the sun. Get it down there!"

But as we was driving, it turns out they had a murder trial in Junction and they had moved it to Ozona. Now this was Sunday and all the laws was going from Junction so they'd be there in Ozona for the trial Monday. The road was winding around through them pastures and things, and here they come in cars with them big hats. So that scared old Red. But I said, "Just keep going." They had never got the reports, you see. It was only about nine o'clock and they'd left Junction before it had passed around. They didn't know we was anybody. So we drove by them waving, "Hi. Hi." There was about five or six cars loaded with the laws and everybody else, and we just went on around them and went on.

After we passed them, I said, "Now, boys, we've got to take to the brush. It's not far to the Llano River bottom over yonder. Speed her up, and we'll get over there before they can get to this next town." We got out in this thick brush. All that country, there was nothing cleared off in them days. I said, "Turn right in there, Slim, and we'll go right in at this plank gate and we'll go down in this brush about three to four hundred yards and hide the car and then one can come back up here and watch the road."

We got some brush to cover the car and we brushed the ground there and nobody could tell anyone had come in. We went on down there and I sent Red back up there to watch. I said, "You stay up there about two hours and then I'll come up there. Don't go to sleep, and if anybody comes through that gate, you come to us." So Red stayed up there two hours while I went to sleep. Then I said to Slim, "I got a little sleep so I'll stay up there three hours. You sleep and then you come and stay three hours and that will be about time to get out of here. It'll be getting dark."

So we watched that gate, one of us all day, but nobody never showed up. People passed on that road, but nobody looked at that gate. We waited until about eight

144

o'clock that night. A report had got out that we was west of San Angelo and that's where they was looking. We was going the other way. The next day the San Angelo newspaper come out saying that the biggest manhunt ever had been looking for Skinny Newton and his partners, and we'd been seen forty miles west of San Angelo. And there we was forty miles over the other side heading the other way!

We come in through Junction and them other little towns, Kerrville, and come into San Antone just about daylight. Well, Slim says, "I know where I can sell this car." That's where he lived, in San Antone, so we come on in there and come to his home and got something to eat.

I told him we were pulling out. He wanted to get back to Tulsa, Oklahoma, just as soon as he could. He told us where we could find him, and he left. He had said, "I'm going to sell this car, and I'll leave the money here with my mother. I can sell it for $250."

I said, "Well, just leave us seventy-five apiece and you keep a hundred." So Red and me come back in there in about three days and Slim done sold it and was gone. The mother, she gave us seventy-five dollars apiece. We monkeyed around, and then went out to Uvalde.

I said, "We can go down to a store that I burglarized, a good store down there in Waelder, Texas. A freight train comes in there about two o'clock and we can get the store and ride that freight train into San Antone and go on through to Spofford, where there's one of them Mexican gangs, I guess two hundred men, and we can sell everything we get."

So we went on down to Waelder that night and broke into that store. In them days, they had that fine silk. There'd be about five hundred yards in the store and people made their clothes, women's clothes, out of it. So we got a big suitcase, and we packed all that silk in it. We'd sell it for fifty cents a yard as fast as we could get it out, and it cost two or three dollars a yard in them days. Then we got a lot of suits and pants and rolled them up in two big rolls. Then we took another big suitcase and we filled it with good, readymade women's clothes and dresses. It was a first class store. They had them in them little towns in them days. So we planned to carry them two big bundles of clothes and when the freight train come in, we'd put them in a box car. Break the seal, put the clothes in the box car, wrap the seal back on it, and they couldn't see it. Then when we got to where we wanted to get off, we'd go back there and break the seal and throw our stuff out and nobody would ever know it was in there.

While we was in the store, we opened the cash register and got about ninety dollars out of it. I went back in there and there was a little bitty old safe about three feet high. I got down there and got hold of the combination and got hold of the handle to see if they'd left it on the day combination like they do on them old vaults.

And open she come! Well, there was just a little duster in there. I come back to Red and I said, "I got the outside door of that safe open, and there's just a little thin door. Go over to the blacksmith shop and get one of them sledge hammers and come back and hit that a few licks and it'll fly open." We'd done been in the smithy's shop before and got a bar to open the window. He went back and grabbed a sledge hammer and come in there and I stayed outside. Old Red was just like a mule, and he hit that thing and blammy! "Clang!" I heard that door fly open. I stood there and directly I heard money rattle, rattle, rattle, and here come Red out of there with a big sack full of hard silver money in each hand.

He said, "Here. Here. Take it!"

I said, "What is it?"

"Mu-mu-money! And I got all my pockets full of greenbacks."

I took them two sacks of silver out there and said, "Just get them two suitcases and let's leave these rolls of suits here." So we just left the two rolls of suits there and took them two suitcases, the one of silk and one with the dresses. We went over to catch the freight train. It

146

was bright as day, and we counted and counted and there was twenty-seven hundred dollars in greenbacks. And there was still them two sacks with all that silver. We didn't even count that. So when the freight train come in, we got down in the end in a refrigerator car. When we got half way to San Antone, he said, "Here's another roll in my side pocket." He got that out. We had a flashlight so we counted it and there was four hundred more.

When we got to San Antone, we got off that train and there was a little restaurant over there and we walked right over to that restaurant, set them old suitcases down just like we was traveling. Got something to eat, and there was a taxi cab standing there. We got in the cab and rode to the other side of town. About halfway we said we wanted to get off here. So we got off there and we walked about four blocks and we got another taxi cab.

I said, "Take us out to the crossing of the Southern Pacific." There was a lot of Mexicans down in that lower country. Lots of houses there, so we went down and peddled about two hundred dollars worth of that stuff. That night, we caught a freight train and went on into Uvalde.

We hung around there two or three days and I give my sister all them dresses and all that silk and stuff while we laid around. Then me and Red come on back and I told him, "I want to get some nitroglycerine." We was going to take it to Oklahoma with us to blow some banks. That's what it's made for, is to blow banks.

We went to New Braunfels and I told him, "I'll tell you where there's a house. You go to Brownwood and walk up the Santa Fe railroad track about half a mile and you'll see a little lumber house out there. Wait till night, pull that lock off, and go in there. When you open it up, it'll have a light in it. There's two gallon cans in there. Just take you a quart bottle and get it full. Get a good strong quart bottle."

I'd been there and got some "grease" before.

Well, Red had been married, and his little old woman had quit him. She lived up at Denison, Texas, so while he was up there getting the grease and coming back, I waited for him in New Braunfels. But in place of coming back, he went over to Denison. He had that money that we'd got down there out of that store, and he thought he could get her back. So he went up there and walked out in the country about eight or ten miles where they lived. But they had done read in the paper where he broke jail in Winters, you know, when we went out the roof. He stayed out there till nearly night, and I guess he couldn't get her to go with him, and he started back to town.

As soon as he left, her daddy went straight to the first telephone, called, and told them Red was there and that he was the one who broke jail in that Winters bank robbery. 'Course Red had told them he wasn't guilty, but they thought he was. And, boy!, before he got to town they come in on him on every side, and that's the last time I seen Red till down in the Smackover, Arkansas, oilfields in '22.

That grease I sent him for, he never got it! He got arrested. He was going to come back and get it, but he never got back. I waited there at New Braunfels a solid week and it was three or four or five months after that before I ever knowed what happened to him. I thought he just took that money and took out and went back to Oklahoma or around. But he got arrested. Later I was down in Denison that winter, and Frank Holliday was down there too and he was telling about it, about Red getting caught. I said, "Well, that was my partner, Red." That was the first time I knowed he was arrested.

Several years later, I was down there when I was in the oil business and run into old Red. He was working on some oil rig, driving some teams and things like that. He never did rob any more banks. Never did.

After that I went up to Durant, Oklahoma, where I met up with a fellow who said to me, "You want to get in on a bank robbery?"

I said, "Yeah," so he introduced me to these two guys who was getting ready to stick up a bank, and I was in.

One was a tall, slim boy named Charlie Rankins and

148

the other guy—he never did tell me who the other guy was, and they never knew who I was—nobody told them my name. Charlie lived out in the country a few miles in Valiant, a little town down there, and the other guy lived over at Hugo, Oklahoma. They had some horses and furnished me a horse, so we planned up the Boswell bank in Oklahoma back this side of Hugo about fifteen or twenty miles. When you went through the town, the last building was the bank and it was just brush from there on. But there was some trees around there where they tied horses.

We went over there to Boswell one day and tied the horses. Nobody in the country had got to know me, so I went in as though to get change and in come Charlie Rankins and the other feller. Just as they come in, the cashier come to the window to give me change, so I put it on him and we catted everybody up right there. There was several people in there. The other guy and Charlie run around behind and sacked up the money, and I kept the front at the counter and watched the door. Charlie got the money out of the safe and out of the cash drawers too, ten thousand and something dollars. Then we just went on out and told nobody to come out of the bank. We got our horses and hit the brush. As we did, we were still looking back and nobody had ever come out of that bank.

Charlie was raised up in that country, I guess, and the other fellow was too, and we headed across that South Boggy, a little river they called Boggy. We followed the river and I told them to get me as close to Hugo as they could. We stopped and divided the money and I give them my horse and saddle and I said, "Now you fellows go on. I'm going into Hugo tonight and get me a train and get out of here." They wasn't looking for nobody to catch a train. Me especially. I knew a passenger train left there sometime after ten o'clock, so I stayed out there in the brush till dark. They took all the hard money and give me green money for mine, so I just put it around my waist and some in my pocket and you couldn't tell I had it in my pockets or anything. I had my coat on. It was the fall of the year. So ten o'clock come around, I walked in there and bought me a ticket to Ardmore and got on that passenger train. When I got to Ardmore I had clear sailing.

Well, about two or three weeks or a month after that, old Charlie got arrested for this bank robbery. They found a lot of that money rolled up down there at his house, that silver, and the Hugo police had him in jail. About a week or two after he was arrested, I went over there because I wanted to get in with Charlie to see what to do. I knowed an old Indian, a stool pigeon from the penitentiary, so I went around there and talked to him about bank robberies and stuff and I said, "Yeah, these around here would be good banks, I guess, to stick up."

So he went and told the law that I was Skinny Newton from Texas and they better watch me or I might try to rob some of them banks. When I went down to the depot that night to catch a train, the law was waiting for me. They grabbed me and put me in jail, which was just what I wanted. So then I got to talk to Charlie and I said, "Is there anything I can do? Can I come in and turn you out, or what can I do?"

"No, hell," he said, "I don't think they got enough dope on me to put me in the penitentiary. I'm going to make bond in two or three weeks. I'm going to stay here a couple or three weeks longer and then I'm going to make bond." I think they had set his bond at twenty or twenty-five thousand dollars.

They kept me there three or four days and just wouldn't turn me loose. They could keep you in jail just as long as they wanted to, then. And I had to go get a lawyer and pay $250 to get out of jail. Later on I found out they sent Charlie to the penitentiary at McAlester for twenty-five years. I never did see him again, but I heard guys that knowed him down there in McAlester.

I got right around four thousand dollars out of the robbery, but I didn't have it on me when I came back to Hugo. I had come down to San Antone and put six or seven hundred in the bank and I give them lawyers a check on the San Antone bank to get me out. Well, about two months after that I went down to San Antone to draw my money out and they had the law waiting for me. I had wrote a check to get my money and this teller says, "Well, wait a minute." And he took it and went back there and I seen him talking to somebody and I knowed then they was going to arrest me. So I just walked off and went down to Uvalde and give a little lawyer a check for all my money, and he went up there the next day and got it. I never did know what they wanted to arrest me for, but that's what they was fixing to do. They arrested for nothing in them days and just keep you for good luck! Yeah. They'd do anything they wanted to do with you.

The bank at Boswell was the very first bank I ever really robbed, to get any money out of it. That was a daylight stickup. But I didn't hesitate. Hell, if you hesitate you're liable to get in trouble. You go to do anything like that, you better do it. That's what I always said, "Let's go boys," and I took the lead and we never stopped for nothing.

The bank robbery at Winters, Texas, with Frank the old bank robber was my first night job. We never got but thirty-five hundred in Liberty Bonds from there, though, and they killed that one old boy there alongside the car. So I never got nothing out of that. He had the bonds in his pocket, the one who got killed.

*Willis with two coyotes*

# 12

## DISSENSION IN THE GANG (1919)

> "If anybody ever told after we
> robbed a bank, we was
> supposed to kill him. . . .
> I didn't believe in killing then,
> and now I know it stronger."

It was the second day of May 1919 when I hit Tulsa at midnight one night on that train from Muskogee. I went down the street and stayed at the old Colorado Hotel, and I'll never forget it. I had some change in my pocket then and I had a pocketbook with two or three hundred in it and at night when I'd go to bed, I'd take it out of my pocket and put it in my pillow.

So I went on and stayed all night and got up the next morning and went to eat my breakfast. I kinda had a habit of hitting my hip pocket, and when I did there was no pocketbook! Hell, it was nine or ten o'clock then, so I busted back to that Colorado Hotel and as it happened I'd got in late and they had already made up the bed. I said to the woman, "Have you changed the bed in such and such a room?" And she said yes. I went on in there, hit the pillow, and there was my pocketbook! See, they just patted the pillows and didn't change them. I would of never got my money if it hadn't been for that.

Well, I got hold of an old boy there called Slim. Went out to his part of town and got me a room. We monkeyed around there and got together with Frank—he's the old bank robber I turned out of the penitentiary and did the night job at Winters with. We had a little Dago with us from down in Henryetta. That little Dago had some people that lived up in Kansas in a mining town. That's right when all them Victory Bonds arrived. That was the last sale of bonds. And everybody bought them by the pocketfuls. They paid more interest than the other bonds did, the Liberty and Victory Bonds.

So he said he knowed a little town up there and knowed some Dagos lived there right close. Them Dagos sticks together. So we went down to their house and ate dinner at the edge of town, about a quarter of a mile from the bank. Sat around there all day, in a nice Buick car. Then he borrowed two shotguns off them Dagos that night. Me and Frank Holliday went over to this town and stayed all night, and Slim and the Dago went over to another town and stayed all night, and Sunday night we go over to rob the bank at Arma, Kansas.

Well, Slim had been telling me, "Now if you see anybody going around with lights, they'll be waking up people. Lots of times they discover people robbing banks, they'll go from house to house to wake the people up." This was a mining town. Frank stayed on that side of the street and I stayed on this side. The little Dago went in with a pick and there was a concrete vault, but it wasn't over four inches thick. Slim went in and hit a few licks on it and Frank, he was lazy, he hit a few licks on it, and then he says, "Well, we can't get in there." But we give the Dago the pick and he took to it, and the first thing you know, he caved it in. Got a good hole in it. Him and Frank went in there to get the stuff. They didn't have safe deposit boxes. It was just like a post office, just little boxes all along. And they was packed with them Victory Bonds and Liberty Bonds. So they went to getting them out and putting them in that handbag.

Directly at four o'clock the miners started changing shifts and as they went they had lights on their heads. I seen them going, but here come Slim around there and said, "Well, we've got a rank, boys! I seen them going from house to house waking them up."

I said, "No, that's miners going to work with lights on their heads. I watched them go."

But old Frank considered himself the boss, and he said, "We got all the money we'll ever need." So we took out. They never knowed the bank was robbed until eight o'clock the next morning. And it was raining and all muddy roads, and we'd swing out around a little town on our getaway route and get stuck. And we had sixty-five thousand dollars in Liberty Bonds and Victory Bonds. But we'd left $200,000 or more in the vault, and that's where we'd all of been rich, right there.

We come back to Tulsa and cut up the money and bonds, and me and Frank took them bonds to Memphis, where we had a market and sold them for seventy-five cents on the dollar and we had over ten thousand apiece. Then what happened was that the little Dago and Frank and Slim had made a deal if anybody talked about it after we robbed the bank, if one of the guys told anybody else and the others found out, they was supposed to kill him. Slim, he's the one who laid the law down to me.

Slim had took up with a gal named Pearl. Wasn't his wife, just his gal, and they had an old brother-in-law and an old sister-in-law and another old sister, sorry old people, so when Slim got his money, first thing he done, him and her, they went downtown and spent twenty-five hundred dollars for clothes! Slim was a kinda halfway pimp all of his life. Slim bought him twelve shirts, that's when the silk shirts come out at twenty-five dollars a shirt. And I don't know what Pearl bought. Well, they told the sister-in-law and brother-in-law all about it, that they'd robbed a bank, told them where, over in Arma, Kansas. And the sorry old brother-in-law told somebody else. So it wound up Slim had thirty-five hundred left at the sister-in-law's. He had it laying in the tray of a trunk. So the sister-in-law framed this up with her old man and gets Slim and Pearl to go to town. When Slim and Pearl left for town, Pearl set the key up there on a shelf. Then her old man comes in and gets the key, goes to the trunk, unlocks the lock and gets Slim's thirty-five hundred.

Slim comes to me and told me, "I know who got it." So the woman who lived next door said, "I seen a man come in here and get the key and open the door. If you know who he is, I'll identify him." Slim brought him out and she said, "Yes, that's the man."

But they had old Slim in a tight. They said to him, "You are going to have us arrested? What are you going to do about robbing that bank over at Arma? You want us to tell? The money isn't yours anyway, because you got it by robbing that bank." So Slim couldn't do nothing, couldn't say nothing, but he was mad.

About that time, somebody come to Frank and told him that Slim's brother-in-law had stole Slim's money. There was several old timers around there talking about it and they told Frank. So Frank come to me and I told him, "Yeah, that's the truth. That's what he done." Well then Slim left and went to San Antone, and me and Frank and the little Dago, went to Memphis.

Frank says, "I'll tell you what let's do. You call Slim and tell him you got a job. I'll take him out by this river and I'll put him in a hole. He won't tell nobody else." Well, I just didn't want to kill nobody, but Slim's the man who put it on the line to me, Slim did, so he damn sure knowed about it. He lived in San Antone, and I called and told him to meet me in Little Rock, Arkansas. When he met me, I told him we was going to get a whiskey boat over there on the river. The others went over there the day before, down right close to the river and dug him up a nice grave

That night we went to Memphis and I told Slim we was going to listen for boats to come up the river and when we knowed the unloading place, we was going to stick them up and get all that whiskey. That's what Frank told me to say to get him over there. That day, we had all throwed a dollar, even and odd, to see who killed him, and it fell on the Dago. I don't think I'd of killed him if it had fell on me. I don't think I could. I didn't believe in killing then, and now I know it stronger. I knew a guy got killed one time and I could have stopped them from killing him, the people that did it, and I've been sorry ever since that I didn't stop it.

Anyway, we went over there to the river that night. Dago said, "I ain't going to shoot him. I'm going to get me a club, an iron club, and knock him in the head. I don't want to shoot him." There was a big old log up there, we all went up there and sat down on it. Frank he couldn't stand it, he had to get away. He went off in the woods, to take a leak or something. But Slim had got wise. He told me later that night that he had got leery and had his pistol out and had it under his arm. So when the Dago hit at him and just glanced his head, Slim ducked and shot at the Dago and burnt his arm right across there. Well, then Slim just hit the brush in the dark. He didn't try to shoot nobody else. He got over there and hid.

Frank come over to me. He says, "You know him better. You tell him to come back and we won't bother him, and I'll shoot the so-and-so."

I said, "No, you won't. If I tell him to come back, nobody's going to shoot him. We're going to let him go home. We're cut out from him from now on, but he can go about his business."

Frank said alright, so I said, "Come on back, Slim. Anybody tries to hurt you, they're going to get hurt. I'll guarantee you aren't going to get hurt." He hesitated a little, and I said, "Come on back. You ain't going to get hurt now. You're going to be on your way." And he come on back. We stood there and talked awhile, and Frank told him to go on back to Tulsa and get his things and go to California, leave the country.

Slim and me went back to the hotel and slept all night. I told him, I said, "Slim, if it had fell on me, I wouldn't have killed you. But you done all this to yourself. You preached those rules to me."

He said, "I know. I was a damned fool." He was sorry, but he had to leave. So he went to Tulsa and got his things, got his old lady and went on to California and stayed, oh, till that winter.

The rest of us come on back to Tulsa, but before we come back, Frank was renting a house over there in Memphis and Digs Nowlen and Floyd had a drug store. They was dope and whiskey peddlers and I didn't know

157

it. I was going to stay at the biggest hotel. I always stayed in the biggest hotel there was, all of us, all the time. We never went to a rooming house, a cheap hotel, or nothing. We went to the best ones.

Frank says, "Oh, don't stay down there at that old hotel. Go over there and stay at Digs' rooming house. Go over there and stay with the Dago." Digs had a brand new Stutz car, and he was going to Chicago to celebrate on the day that all of the whiskey was sold.

It sounded real good, so I went over. We had that Stutz car and we just picked up gals, piles and piles of them, just get any of them in that Stutz car. It was brand new, you know. And we'd been out late in it two or three days picking up gals, so late this one evening we picked up a pair of good looking gals. We'd take a couple new ones every night to the apartment with us. This was in Memphis, Tennessee, and you could find girls on the streets, anywhere you went. Just get on a street car track of a morning and you could get any of them. All of them would ride with you in them days. So they come and stayed all night with us and the next morning we got up and was fixing to go to breakfast and that old smart alec Frank called us. He had got a tip that someone was going to be after Digs, or something, and he said, "Don't leave the rooming house till I call you again." We told the gals to go on and leave, that we'd pick them up somewhere's else that day, and it wasn't thirty minutes after he called us that the law come!

The house was full of law. They thought Digs had a lot of dope, and they just swarmed him. As it turned out, he didn't have nothing but some whiskey he'd brought from Chicago, but they arrested all of us, me and the Dago, and so we all went to jail.

I've got two $1,000 bills and five $100 bills and, I don't know, a hundred or two in other change in my pocketbook. Back here in my hip pocket. Well, I slipped my hand in my pocketbook and I thought I slipped them thousands and them hundreds and put them in my bosom. But I missed the two thousand-dollar bills! I had the others in my bosom, but the thousands was sticking together and I missed them both.

They took us to jail and searched us. There I am with that money. "God damned bank robber! That's what he is. He's a bank robber." Then they searched me further down and found all this other loose money in my bosom, twenty-seven or twenty-eight hundred. Well, then they knowed I was a bank robber, and I told them my name was so-and-so. They put me in jail and of course I couldn't get a lawyer that day.

That night there come two old policemen from a little town down there in Tennessee where somebody had held them up and robbed the post office one night, two or three months before that. Well, they thought I was a robber and they come in there to look at me and they said, "Yeah, that's him. We heard him talking and we knowed his voice. That's the man who stuck us up." Positively identified me. Now, I know there's no way to keep out of the penitentiary with that kind of identification.

So I said, "No, mister, you're wrong. When did this happen?"

He said, "The twelfth of June."

I said, Well, I still say you're wrong."

"No, we know." The next morning they had lawyers take me down in front of a judge who set my bond at two thousand so I just took these two bills and made a cash bond. Then I left and come back to Oklahoma. The Dago he come back. Frank stayed awhile and he come back. Well, the twelfth of June is when Governor Hobby signed my pardon in Texas and I wasn't discharged from the penitentiary till the twenty-eighth of June. I knowed I had them. So I come home and wrote my mother for that pardon and sent it to my lawyers. It was two or three months before I got my money back, my two-thousand bond money.

We come on back to Oklahoma but we had a problem then. We didn't have Slim, the blabbermouth that we didn't want with us no more. There was just me and the little Dago and the other guy, Frank.

We come back to Memphis, all of us, and from there to Tulsa. The little Dago, he lived down in Henryetta. He went home and Frank stayed in Tulsa, and I come down to Texas. Monkeyed around all summer, just monkeyed around. I didn't do a thing. Just visited down here in San Antone. I slipped down home to Uvalde lots of nights, and stayed down there a day or two. Sat in the house, never went out of the house. I avoided being seen around there if I could.

Then I went back up there to Tulsa sometime in September. We picked up another guy, John, and that made four of us again. So me and Frank, who was supposed to be a tough guy, we went to Michigan, to Detroit. We got up there and bought a car in some other name, you know. Whoever drove the car, whoever handled the car, well, we put it in his name. So the little Dago bought it this time under some name that he made up.

On our way back from Detroit, we found us a bank we could blow. So we went in there one night. I was out behind and the Dago was over on the other side. The other two was in there blowing the bank and these northern lights come up. I knowed of them and I'd seen them before. But they didn't know what northern lights was. So I was standing out behind, the little Dago over yonder. Well, he heard some noise over there somewhere and he got scared, and he hollered, "Get back in there!" There was nobody showed up, and them northern lights was just flashing as bright as day. So he run around and told us, "There's somebody around there," and they done had the safe blowed. They come out with the money and about a thousand of hard silver in a sack and them lights was just a-flashin' across the sky! Off they run to the car with the soft money, these other two fellows, and told Dago and me to bring that heavy sack of silver! The car was about half a mile away.

So little Dago he grabbed it up and here we went. He carried it about three hundred yards, and I carried it about ten steps. He carried it again about a hundred yards and I carried it ten steps. Finally we got to where they was at. They was waiting at the car.

I said, "What in the hell? Them northern lights is all it was about, and you run off and leave us with that? The next time you run off and leave us with hard money, I'm just going to let it lay there."

We drove all that night and the next day, and went into a hotel and stayed all night. Then we come out of there and drove to Terre Haute, Indiana. Some of us got the train and come on back to Oklahoma. The guy that had the car, he drove it on into Tulsa.

Well, we stayed there just a little while and they got to talking between themselves about the Dago getting scared up there, running around telling them there was somebody out there and hollering. So this "bad man," Frank, he said "Well, I don't want him anymore. Let's just cut him out. Get somebody else."

He thought he was the smartest man in the world, just thought he was. When I learned about the business, I saw that he was the silliest man and the biggest coward I ever seen in my life.

So we decided we'd get somebody else. We cut the Dago out and got us a big guy, six foot three and 230 pounds. I'll call his name. Big Sam Shuman that we'd knowed a long time from up there in Tulsa. Well, that made four of us again. Two men could rob them banks, but there was always four of us because we liked to put two men outside to watch while the others worked inside. But since that time I know of fifteen or twenty that's been robbed with just two men.

Now we went back to Michigan. This time Big Sam, he bought the car. So we come on down there in Michigan and found a town that was a mark and we could blow the safe. There was some people that lived right across from the bank upstairs. We come down there that night and I always cut the wires because I could run up and down them telephone poles like a squirrel. I was light, I wasn't scared to death, and I was always ready to go.

I sawed the wires, come down the pole, and then we looked in the back window and Frank said, "There's an old man sleeping in there." I said, "Well, you just raise that window up and I'll get the old man." The window wasn't fastened down so we just oozed it up. Oozed it up, and got it up, and I stepped in and run over and it was an old woman! Seventy-five years old sleeping in the back of that bank. I said, "Oh, lady, we thought you was a man."

"What are you fools doing in here?"

"We're going to rob this bank."

"Ha! Ha! Ha!" she laughed. She said, "You big fools. You can't rob this bank."

I said "You'll find out. You just stay right there in the bed and you won't get hurt," but somebody tried to come out of the back door. They had heard us. And so this guy on guard down there hollered, "Get back in there!" And this idiot Frank with me, he just run out, grabbed his gun and run out, and there was Big Sam, and he just "bloom! bloom!" shot him right center in the chest and down he went.

The other guy come running and I said, "John, come here. Sam's shot." He come on up there and we got ahold of him and John handed idiot Frank his shotgun. We went on carrying Big Sam and when we turned the corner going around the street, we woke these people upstairs there. A man and a woman come out on the porch up there and was just looking and said, "What's the matter? Anybody hurt down there?" And this idiot, he didn't know how to work that automatic shotgun, or he'd have killed them both! He pointed it up there and was trying his best to pull that trigger. He'd have shot them both off that porch! That idiot would.

Well, we took Big Sam down the street, got him across the railroad tracks and laid him down. He said, "Boys, there's nothing I can do. There's no use hauling me away from here. I have to get a doctor somewhere. You boys just take everything and go on, and I'll lay here, give you an hour, then I'll holler and they can find me and get me to a doctor."

We drove off, just took the car and hiked out all night

long and we knowed an old man that lived down in Terre Haute, Indiana. We made it to that old man's place late the next evening. We stayed all night and rested up there. Meantime, when we got away, Big Sam hollered and somebody come out and got him.

We rested up there in Terre Haute a night or two and then we went out and looked for another bank. We found one. So a night or two later we go over there to get it, and there was this man stayed upstairs and none of us knowed it. They went in to get what was in there, and I was the outside man. There was three of us then. So while they was in there working, somebody come out and shot a little pistol out the window and then shut it. I was where he couldn't see me. He couldn't bother nobody where he was, so I never went in and said anything about it. We had a great big handbag, it was mine, and they put everything they got in this handbag. It was pretty heavy.

We had parked on the other side of the bridge, so when they come on out of the bank, I said, "There was somebody upstairs about an hour ago and he shot out the window with a pistol, but I watched and never saw him wander down the steps and I never bothered about him." Boy!, did they snort! They both ran up through them weeds and across the bridge, and down into them weeds again and left me. Here I am with the shotgun and I had the bag.

Well, I just walked. It made me so damn mad, I wanted to die. I just walked. I was an hour getting over there, I guess, and then when I did, if I didn't eat them up! But we got a whole lot of bonds and some money out of that one.

We went on to Terre Haute and took that car down in the bottoms, took five gallons of gasoline with us, poured it all over it, and set it to fire. There really wasn't no use in that. They could find out where it come from anyway with the motor number, but we burned it up. Then we caught the train out, and went on back to Tulsa.

There was a Bankers Association down there, and old

man Boyd had worked for the Association for thirty years. That old devil was always after me. But now he come to Tulsa and we made a deal. He was going to resign his office on January first, and he told us about banks all over Texas with them old, square safes that you could blow. He give us the names of fifteen or twenty, told us where they was at. We give him three thousand dollars and if anything happened, he was going to protect us.

He was the surety man with the Texas Bankers Association, the detective. If a bank was robbed, he was the man to run the robbers down. He's the one who put me and Red Johnson in jail and tried to hang me over there at Ballinger for the Winters robbery. Oh, he was a dirty old rat. I says to Frank, "You tell old man Boyd when you give him this money down there to lay off of me."

So Frank told him, he said, "You lay off Skinny Newton, now. He's my partner."

He says, "I'm sure glad you told me." Said, "Every time anything's done down there, I'd a-put them after Skinny."

So we went down to Dallas, stayed there and monkeyed around and went up north of Dallas and robbed a little bank. I never got much. A few thousand dollars. Finally we went down below Dallas to a little town by the name of Crandall, and there was two banks there. The telephone wires—there was lots of loose wires and you could cut the big cable all at once, but when you cut them loose wires they dropped down and hit the house or something. There was lots of loose wires and it was a bad night. We both told Frank, "There's one bank way over there we can go over to and rob it and not cut them loose wires. Nobody will ever know it."

But of course "bad man Frank" says, "No, no. Cut them loose wires." It was rainy but we had a hard road to go back on. But we had pulled the car out in a cotton patch and it was muddy and slicky out there. It had rained some while we was there, but we figured we could get out.

So I went up there and clipped this wire and that one, and they fell against the building and directly a man jumped up, come to the window and looked out because he heard something fall and he ranked to what we was doing. He hollered and shut the window back down. Well, we knowed we got a rank and there was a lot of them wires ain't cut yet. So we just beat it on back there to the car.

Frank got in the front seat with the other guy, John. John was the driver of the car, and I got in the back seat. Well, the car was slipping and sliding so I just jumped out and went to pushing and pulling and pushing down and pulling it back. And the dirty louse Frank, he looked out and seen me and he come out of there with his pistol and he started to come around and John grabbed his arm and said, "That's Willis!'"

Well, he put his gun back. And I kept pushing and pulling until we got out. He never mentioned it, this "bad man Frank" didn't, who tried to shoot me, but the next time we got together, John said, "Don't you know he like to killed you last night? If I hadn't hollered he would of shot you."

"Well," I said, "that's enough of it for me. We'll drop him right here." Frank had figured there was something wrong, and so he began to talk to me about jumping John, and me going with him. I said, "I got nothing against John. If you want to jump, jump." So I told John. But old Frank was busted and in fact he owed me twenty-five hundred dollars, so John said, "I know where there's another little bank. We can go down there and get it and get maybe ten thousand. That'd give him a little money, his cut. And then let him go if he wants to."

So we went down there to get that little bank when it was raining one night. It wasn't far out of Dallas and we had good roads back. The streets was muddy and so when we got ready to get the wires, the "bad man" started to come along. I said, "No, I'll get the wires, but I want John to come with me." Frank, he didn't like that because I had told him what to do. John said, "To hell

with him, Let him just wait, and if he goes, let him go."
See the "bad man" thought that when he left, I would go
with him. So we come on back after we cut the wires,
and he was standing on the sidewalk in front of the bank
and the clock on the bank says, "bloom! blooey!" and he
just leaped into that mud! Well, sir, I laughed and I
laughed, and he was so mad that he wanted to shoot me.
I laughed and I laughed until I was sick, and John says,
"I was afraid to laugh."

So we got the little bank, got about ten thousand
there, and went on back. Frank he lived in Tulsa. John
and me had an apartment down at Dallas. Then Frank
says, "Well, I'm going on in. I ain't going with John no
more. You come up to Tulsa if you want to and we'll go
that way."

I told him, "Well, you go on ahead. I'll do what I want
to." So Frank left and we stayed together, me and John
did, and went on back to Tulsa. That's when I wrote my
brother Joe the letter to come to us. I wrote him a letter
and told him I had a job for him in Tulsa. That's when
he come up there. He wrote me and told me when he'd
be there, what train. So the train got there about seven
o'clock and I taken with me some girl that worked at the
telephone office. She was a smart little old girl. I'd been
out with her several times. "We'll just park here. I got a
country boy coming up from down in Texas. We're down
here to pick him up."

And there was crowds coming out and somehow I let
him get past me. She looked up and there was that big
hat and them boots, and she said, "Is that him up
yonder?"

I said, "Yeah, that's him," [laughs]. So I jumped out
and run over there and stopped him. And he come on
over. I took her to work, and we went on. So we monkeyed
around there a day or two, and finally I said, "So what
are you doing today?"

He said, "Well, I got to get my saddle and stuff out of
there."

I said, "What did you bring your saddle and hat and

boots for?"

"You said you had me a job."

I said, "Yeah, I got you a job, but it's not that. I got you a job carrying a shotgun. I want you to stay outside while we're robbing banks at night."

*"That was my downfall, right there" [laughs].*

"That was your upfall." So I went over and I give him three $100 bills to go get him some clothes. Boy!, he looked at me and he looked at the three hundred, and he was ready to go back home! He didn't need to rob banks. So he went on and got him a cocked hat and good shoes and clothes. So we started from there and went to Omaha, Nebraska. That's where Joe first started in with us, right there.

*Left to right: Willis and Joe Newton*

*Joe Newton*

# 13

## JOE NEWTON (1914-1919)

*"It just seemed like I was a natural rider. I never touched the horn or anything, and I was never throwed."*

**A**bout the time World War I broke out, my daddy moved us up to Uvalde from Crystal City, and I went to working on and off around there breaking horses. Henry Vanham come and looked me up about working for him on his place that was called the Eight Mile, because it was eight mile outside of town. He was a little short fellow with whiskers and tall boots and driving a Model T. He was a fine old fellow, and him and me went to work repairing the windmills and building fence on his place. Them windmills get to where they won't work and you have to pull up the sucker rods and replace the leathers on the end that have wore out. When that happens, they won't hold the water.

Late the next fall he hired on three other fellows because he was fixing to round up and sell fat cattle, but I worked alone the first fall. We got a dollar a day and keep, was what we got, the four of us that worked his country. At four a.m. we was up, cooked our own breakfast, by daylight we was gone, and it was dark when we got through. Dollar a day and beans, was what we used to say we got, and it was mostly beans, with a little of that old sorghum molasses and some biscuits.

When I got known a little around there, fellows would hire me to break their horses, and you got ten dollars for breaking and gentling a horse. I wouldn't work unless they'd hire my horse too, and I got fifty cents a day for him. It was day work. I'd ride out, work the day, then ride back into town and stay the night. I was really doing all right at that, and just sixteen or seventeen years old.

One time there was a bunch of cattle that come into town headed for a ranch ten or fifteen miles below town, one that we later took to calling the Pecan Plantation. I hired on to help drive the cattle, and when we got them all unloaded, there was 750 head. Up to that time, that was the biggest herd I ever saw. The dust was so thick I couldn't see my horse! I hope to die if that ain't the truth. And when you can't see your horse, you can't hardly ride him, even at a little jig of a trot, because you can't stay with him. You don't know which way he's going.

When we got them to the ranch, the other men went to distributing the cattle out over that country, and the foreman—he was a big, husky man with iron-gray hair—he put me to work on the pens. Along about ten o'clock his wife called from the house did I want any coffee. I said I sure did, so she said to come on up. The men ate at a long table in a screened porch there, so I sat at one end and she gave me coffee and sat there at the other. She was about twenty years younger than her husband and a fine looking woman herself.

Well, she got to talking to me and asking me who I was and where I was from, and I think the reason she did is that she was curious because of what had been in the paper just before that. See, Doc was down in the penitentiary at Huntsville, and he had taken a shotgun away from a guard out in the field and then got up behind him on the guard's horse and went all around through the fields turning loose every work squad they had out there. Must have set two or three hundred men free. Then he took out on that horse across country. There was big headlines in the San Antonio paper about it, and I think her husband must have told her I was a Newton and kin to that convict in the paper.

I hadn't no more than got started on my coffee and I heard the screen door slam. It was her old man. He'd left them cowboys and come on back by himself and there he stood. "Say, kid," he says to me. "What are you doing in here? I put you to work on them pens."

"Yes, sir. I'm just having some coffee."

"Well, you get on out there and get back to it," so I did and she went into the house. I never seen her no more to this day. Then he come up to me out there and he said, "You see them mountains off there, that gap between them?" They was about two or three miles away.

"Yes sir."

"Well, you take your bedroll and ride on over there and make you a camp. I'm going to have you go to work burning prickly pear this winter."

I just told him, "I tell you what I'm going to do. I'm going to roll up my bed and put it on the porch over there. And I'm going to saddle my horse and ride him into town. The next time you come in, you can bring my stuff for me." So there went my job.

About that same time, Jess had been out in West Texas working for that same man. He was just sitting out at the headquarters doing nothing. Drinking coffee. He was coming home for Christmas. They had told him they was restocking the remuda with young horses that never had a rope on them except when they was two year olds and they throwed them in the pasture and castrated them. They was all fat, big stout horses. That's what they used on them big ranches. They was sixty miles square. That was out close to Dryden, which was a town owned by the ranch. There was a store that supplied everything and a little wooden hotel they owned and four or five houses.

Jess told me about this job and at first it didn't interest me, but I knowed an old boy named Shorty Coats and Shorty he said to me, "Let's go out there. It's wide open and not like working in all this mesquite and pear we got around here."

"Do you know what they want us to do?" I said. "He's got all them horses, and the man he's got out there just picks out a few that aren't so bad, but the big, stout ones, the worst ones, he won't ride them. That's what he wants somebody for."

"Oh, hell," Shorty says. "I can ride anything. Any of them. I'll ride mine and then top yours off too and take the pitch out of them." I never had seen him ride even a gentle horse. His family had come down from Odessa and had a little ranch outside Uvalde and he was always busy out there. He was a pretty good old boy and I never had caught him lying, but this time it sounded like he was bragging, and he was just a little fellow and short-legged. Usually the best riders are long-legged.

He stayed after me, and in about three days I agreed to go with him, and we put our saddles and bridles and spurs in tow sacks and caught the train for Dryden. The hands was supposed to be coming into town for supplies and would be camped there. We got into there in the dead of night, about four o'clock in the morning. It was dark as pitch and colder than the dickens.

Sure enough, that was the cow outfit camped there. We had coffee as they went to getting up, and finally the boss got up. He said, "I guess you're the boys Jess sent out here. Now, some of what we've got here is pretty bad horses that we want you boys to ride."

Shorty told him, "That don't make any difference. You just furnish the horses. Bring them out and I'll ride them. I can ride anything you got." You can guess what they thought about him when he was telling them that, because he was such a little short guy. And I didn't know better for sure.

"Well, I'm not quite that good," I told him.

"That's all right. I know who you are. Jess told me last night." Here we thought Jess was back in Uvalde, but he must have left the day before and come out there. And he was over at that hotel.

By then it was daylight, and while the cook was getting breakfast they went and roped our horses out. There'd be one man to help hold your horse until you could saddle him, then they tied him over at the fence until everybody got saddled. Then we'd eat breakfast and after that they'd start riding them one at a time. They'd help to hold him until you got on, and then he was yours until noon that day. It didn't make any difference where he went. If he went twenty miles thataway, he was still yours. Nobody never helped.

I guess there was thirty people lived in that little old town then, and by the time we got finished with breakfast it was along past sunup, and here they was all standing out there. The word had got out that they had some bronc riders coming and they was going to ride them horses. And I tell you, Shorty really put on a show. They got him on a big old brown, rawboned horse, and he was a pitching sonofagun. Shorty sat up there like he was going to Sunday School in a rocking chair! The old horse got about a hundred yards out there and turned sideways to the crowd and you'd see him reach up on the horse's neck as far as he could, up by his ears, and he'd come down with his spurs. The next time he went up, he hit him again, and all this time he was sitting up in the saddle looking back over there at us! Yessir! That was the best ride I ever saw in my life, right there!

It come my turn, and they give me an old, long-legged roan horse. They held him and I mounted him and went off across there. He was jumping ten foot high and thirty foot long, but he was easy rode. I guess that's the reason the wagon boss give him to me. Jess had told him to take it easy with me for awhile to see what I could do on them kind of horses. Well, I done all right.

They had got the supplies the day before, so we saddled up and left out that day. Went on towards the country where they was going to work. Out in that country there was a fellow there helping out because his ranch joined this one on the Pecos River. His name was Babb, Boyd Babb. The Babbs owned that country way back in there, and Boyd was working to see if they had any stray cattle. He'd put them in a trap or something and pick them up later. He was about twenty-eight or thirty years old, something like that, and he had some awful good horses, dun horses, and real cow horses. One day I had been riding one of them pitching horses, and he come down off a hill over there where he'd been watching, and he said, "I thought you said you couldn't ride."

"Well, I didn't know whether I could or not. I seem to

be doing all right here. I've rode a lot of pitching horses, two and three year olds. We broke horses all the time." Nowadays folks put reins on horses and drive them around and around to break them. Back then we had somebody to hold them while we saddled them up, and if he wanted to pitch, why let him go ahead and pitch. That's the way we broke them, and we didn't break nothing real young like they do now, yearlings and like that. I told Babb that I'd try anything they bring out. It didn't make me any difference.

Awhile after that, Shorty had tore up the inside of his hand on the horn of his saddle which had got cut away little by little as we worked, and after some time it had got down to where it was just a metal post sticking up. When his horse pitched hard on him, his hand come down against that horn and sliced it up pretty bad on the palm. The next day they roped out one of the worst dun horses you ever saw. Boy!, he was trying to eat them up. Shorty had showed me his hand before that, so when they called him to come and get this dun, I told him, "When you go down there, just show them your hand and you won't have to ride him. They'll get you a gentle horse."

They were holding the horses in a rope remuda to keep them from running off and I seen Shorty walk down there and show them his hand and they motioned for him to go off thataway. Then I seen Babb walk over to this wagon boss and start talking to him. They both looked toward me, and pretty soon he hollered, "Come get him, Joe." But there was another old boy there name of Joe too, Joe Fowler, out of San Antone, and neither of us Joes moved. The boss called again, "Come and get him, Joe." And this old kid, he said, "I can't ride that damn horse. No use me coming to get him."

"I know you can't ride him. I wasn't talking to you. I'm talking to that other Joe there, that new one." Well, hell, that was me. So I went down there and they had that old horse choked down there and spraddled out, and I went up and stuck my hackamore up towards him, and "Whew!" here he come! [laughs]. I like to run over a *watertrough about a hundred yards off getting away. Oh, that was a bad sonofagun. But a Mexican had ahold of a rope that was on him, and he finally turned him and I outrun him until he got him turned. Then this guy Babb hollered in Spanish to just hang unto him and he'd come out and hold him with his horse. So he come out and when he got there he pulled that horse's head right up and put it over his own horse's neck. Then he took the rope a few turns around his own horn and handed it over to that Mexican on the ground to hold him. He got himself over that horse's head to kind of blindfold him and took an ear in his mouth and went to chewing. Before that he hollered, "When I get hold of his ear, you go ahead and saddle him."*

*I got my saddle up there and throwed it on him. I'd have it back on the root of his tail one time and up too far the next, and directly he'd throw it off. He done that two or three times and finally I got it on. I went to girth it up, and Babb said, "Put it up in front." I pushed it up a little bit, and he said, "Gimme that!" and he set it way up in front, sticking up on his withers. "Now girth it up." and I pulled it up as hard as I could, about three or four heaves with both hands and drawed up a lot more slack. "I think that'll hold it," he said. "Now is there anything you want to do first?"*

*"Yeah, I think I need a drink of water," and I went over to the trough, fixed my leggins up, seen that my spurs was all right. Whew! I really hated to get on that horse. He was pretty but an awful big, stout horse, five or six years old, with a black stripe down his back and them zebra stripes down his legs. Real black mane and tail and black feet. They're good horses, but they're bad horses.*

*I'd stalled it just as long as I could, so I said, "I think I'm ready now." I got around there and got on him, and he stood just as still. Never moved. Course Babb was chewing on that ear. He turned it loose and said, "Now I want to tell you something, kid. I might have over-rated you a little bit. I tell you the truth, I don't know for sure whether you can ride this horse. I believe you can. But I tell you what I'll do. You get your reins fixed up there, and*

*I'll ease this rope off some, and I'll lead him right up this little road. I'm going to let him pitch but I won't let him throw you. If he's about to throw you, I'll pull him up and make him run."*

So that made me feel better that he was kind of on my side, looking out for me. But I told him, "I've got to ride him all afternoon. You can't lead him all day. So you just do that rope up and ease it over here onto my saddle. Then you take him on up this road and let him go." So we started up in a little jig of a trot, and he was the easiest riding horse I ever rode in a trot. But he was still humped up in such a bow that that saddle wasn't touching him only right where it was setting on his withers.

And he was on his tiptoes. And about that time, why, damn! here we went! I looked down to watch his head, you know, because that's the way you've got to ride a pitching horse. You've got to watch his head to stay in motion with him, and I couldn't even see his head, couldn't see nothing but my saddle, and in place of going up and down, it was going sideways. Right in front of me. And I never seen that horse at all as we went pitching up that road.

Then Babb caught up to me when the horse went to running, and got him stopped. So he said, "God damn it, kid. You know what you done?"

"I have no idea."

"You just rode the hardest pitching horse that was ever on this ranch. And I'll swear to that, because I've seen many of them rode right here."

"Well, I don't know nothing about it," I said, and that was the damn truth. I don't know nothing about what happened. I looked down and one of my spurs was way up on my boot, and Babb told me he seen the other one come off back down there. Now how in the hell it got off, I'll never know. I didn't even know I was spurring him or nothing. He was just a-goin' thisaway and thataway so fast I couldn't see the sonofagun.

Well, I rode him the rest of the day and he pitched half a dozen times, but never like that first time. Jess had taught me some when I was young, but I never had too much practice. It just seemed like I was a natural rider. I never touched the horn or anything and I never been throwed. Jess was just the same way. He come out riding any and everything. Now Tull, he was a little different. Jess would get throwed once in awhile because he was liable to jump on something bareback without any spurs or without anything else on, you know. I know several times he got throwed, but it was him that caused that. When he got himself really ready and got on one, why, hell, he never got throwed.

After just a little while, Shorty got a letter from his folks, and his sister was sick again. That little sonofagun just wouldn't stay anywhere very long. He was using that for an excuse. So he left me out there. I got all them horses from then on.

I don't know how long I stayed there, seven or eight months. We had went there in January, right after Christmas, and that fall it had rained about eighteen inches! It washed all the fences down, because all that old ranch was covered with draws and creeks. They called the cow outfit in and split them up and sent them all over that ranch to where they had line riders. "Go stay with him and help fix that fence there."

And I thought, why, hell! When they sent us out there, they said, "We want somebody that can ride these horses." And here they was going to put me to building fence, digging post holes out there in that old, hard rock [laughs]. H.L. Robertson, the big boss, had come. And he said, "All you boys need to go out there. And Joe, I want you out there too."

I said, "Now wait a minute, Mr. Robertson. I been out here a long time, and I come out here to do nothing but ride your horses. They told me they didn't even want me to work cattle. And I think it would be better if you just figured my time up and let me go on back to Uvalde." Damn! he was a mad sonofagun. He was a bad man, too. Hell, he'd "boom!" kill you. He killed lots of people. That's the way he finally got killed himself. They known he killed a lot of people, and he got killed on that account. They waylaid him. Went into the hotel and shot him in the lobby of the hotel. No open fight either. They went in with a shotgun and "blooey!"

So I went back and was working around home there, and I just had made a deal with a man to break ten of them old, big horses. They had come out from New Mexico. Some guy had bought them and they was kind of poor when he got them, but he'd put them out there on a ranch and let them get fat. Now they was big, pretty horses, six or seven years old and never had nothing on them. He was going to bring them in, and I met him one day after that and he said, "Say, Joe. I been thinking about them horses. Do you think you can ride them?"

So I told him, "I'll tell you what we can do. We can settle that. I don't care anything about breaking the horses if you don't want me to break them, but that riding part we can settle easy. First time you got a little time, you come by my place and get me. I'll throw my saddle in your pickup and we'll go out there and I'll let you pick out whichever one you want, and I'll ride him."

One day when it was misting rain, he come by. I went with him, and when we got there, I knew they'd pick the worst one. He roped out a black horse, a beautiful horse, good-sized. They got in there with a saddle and I climbed on the fence. He said, "Get on down here and help us."

I said, "No. I'm going to ride him. You're going to saddle him." So they finally got him saddled and said to come on down and ride him. I told them I didn't want to ride him in the pen. I said to lead him out yonder into the middle of that opening where they had grubbed all the brush out. Them days instead of bulldozing it, they hired Mexicans to dig it out with a grubbing hoe. Then they piled it up and burned it. We called it a "field," but it never had been plowed. They led him out there and held him while I got on and turned him loose. Well, hell, I was like Shorty by then. Just bring the damn things on. It was all the same to me. I went ahead and rode him out, led him back there and got off.

*Joe Newton*

"Well, that's all right," the man said. "Satisfied me. When do you want them?"

"Anytime you want to bring them in."

"I'll have them there Monday morning. I'll put them in the shipping pen."

Well, about Friday, I'd taken some cattle up for somebody two or three miles out of town and put them in a little pasture, and I come back by the post office and got the mail. In it was a letter from Willis. From Oklahoma. I opened it up and it had two $20 bills in it. He said to take this money and come up to Oklahoma, to Tulsa, that he had a job up there for me. I went ahead and got ready, got my saddle in a tow sack and my spurs in there with it, and caught the train with my suitcase for Tulsa.

I had wrote and told him when I'd be there, so I met him at the depot when I got there. He started to go and I said, "Wait a minute here. I got to go around and get my saddle."

"Your saddle? What have you got your saddle for?"

"Well, you said you had a job for me." To me that meant he had work around there riding something.

"Hell," he said. "I haven't got you that kind of job. You won't need that saddle. I'm going to get you a pistol and we're going to rob some banks. I want you to help me."

God Almighty! I didn't know about that! [laughs]. It had already got warm weather down at Uvalde, so that was in early spring, I guess, of 1920. I had just turned nineteen. Anyway, I got my saddle and put it in the car he was in. A little later on I decided if he could do it, I could too. But that was all new business to me. I hadn't even thought about such a thing. My gosh! I didn't know he was off robbing banks. I knew he was running over the country, and he was supposed to have been gambling. And hell, I know he'd been stealing stuff, but he'd never come down there to Uvalde hardly. It had been a few years before that when he was there last. Then he'd been in the penitentiary. Then he got out and come home and went off thataway somewhere. So that bank robbing was all new to me.

# 14

## ORGANIZING THE NEWTON
## GANG (1919-1921)

"So Doc come to us at Tulsa and
took right in, one of the gang.
Jess joined right after Doc.
I had my bunch then."

**M**e and Joe went on to Omaha, and in a few
days Glasscock, the other guy I was working with, come
up, and so we went out and looked up a job. There was
just three of us then. That's when I took charge. The first
bank we went out on, I said, "Now I'm going in there with
you, and I want you to show me how to shoot it."
Glasscock just stood there and told me and I went ahead
and shot the drum door and shot the bank and everything, got the money, and come on out.

*You kind of got to control yourself when you go to
shooting one of them banks, because if it's an especially
big door, it could be dangerous blowing it, and Willis never
measures the grease. He pours in a lot, and then pours in
some more! [laughs]. And he kind of tipped his bottle that
night. They'd been in there a good little bit, and I was out
on the street and across from the bank, you know. Half a
block or something. There was lights on in the town, so
you could always see. And when these explosions go off,
everything on the inside goes, "bang!" You can hear it
fifteen miles! Then, the banks them days always had
plate glass windows, big ones, maybe six by eight feet on
both sides of the doors. All right, now when this big
explosion goes off, "blam!" inside, why that jars the whole
neighborhood, and just when that sound dies out, all that*

*big glass goes to hitting the sidewalk, the concrete out
there. That makes another noise you can hear for five
miles. It's enough to stampede anybody.*

And that's where Joe, the gentleman, carried all of
the hard money. I had said, "We'll leave the silver."

But Joe said, "Oh, no. I'll carry it out." It was about
a thousand dollars, and we had a half mile to carry it!

*Yeah. Willis didn't want to carry any hard money
himself. It was too heavy. But he told me, "Hell—when I
was your age, I could run that far packing that big of a
load." And he's been telling me that now for forty years:
"When I was your age . . ." Because he was older than I
was, he would say what he could do when he was back
my age. He was about thirty years old then, in Omaha,
and when he got to be sixty, he was still telling me what
he could do when he was forty-five [laughs]. I guess that's
something that never wears out.*

*I know what Willis says, but the truth is nobody give
me orders. My job outside is to protect them in the bank.
I do it the best way I know how, and the way I know how
is to take care of my part. Their job inside is to blow the
thing and get us the money. Mine is to keep anybody from
coming up and shooting any of them through the window.
I never worried about being seen. It's in the dark, in the
dimness, you know, and the only way anybody could say
they seen you is to lie. If you've got a mask, they lie
anyhow. They say it fell down.*

*Anyway, just before this shot went off here come a man
along. He was probably forty or forty-five. Had a
moustache, but back then they wore moustaches as young
men too. Lots of farmers did. But I'm nineteen years old,
and I considered him an old man. So I dodged around and
stopped him just before he got to the bank. He went,
"Whoa" and stopped his team, and I walked over to where
he was at.*

*"Now, mister, I want you to hurry up and get out of the
way. We're going to rob this bank here tonight. They're*

*going to blow it, and some of that stuff might come and hit you." I was trying to scare him up a little.*

*Well, he was kind of dumb like I was right then. "Oh, don't tell me that," he said. "You ain't going to rob any bank." And just about that time "blooey!," it went off [laughs] and after the explosion, the glass went to hitting the street. Boy!, you talk about him getting away from there with them horses. He had them horses in a run, hollering at them to get up and calling one of them by his name. I think of that name sometimes, and then I forget it.*

*So we got the money and went on. That's where I had the big job of carrying that sack of silver, so I put it on my shoulder and goddog! it was so heavy I could hardly carry it. Lots of it in nickels and dimes and quarters and halves. Well, the farther I carried that sack, the lower I'd get. I was wobbling along way back there behind Willis and he was saying, "Come on. Come on. Keep up with us. We've got to get out of here!" The car was a mile or so up the track.*

*We've talked and talked about that robbery, and can't think of the name of the town. It was outside of Omaha, not very far from there. I'm sure people there remember it, that one farmer anyway. I don't guess he'd be there anymore, but I bet he told lots of people about it.*

After that we went back to Omaha and stayed there a few days, and then went over to Glenwood, Iowa, and robbed a bank there one night. The wind was blowing, my God! the wind was blowing. So we went in it. We got $300,000-$400,000 in Liberty Bonds and Victory Bonds and every one of them was registered. Their names were there on the book in Washington, so they wasn't worth the paper they was wrote on to us. You couldn't sell a registered bond nowhere. So we just burned them up. If we'd been there two years before when they wasn't registered, we'd ahad a pile there.

When we went into this town of Glenwood, there was a big bulldog and a Dutchman sleeping down in the basement. We went in there and the wind was blowing so I like to never got up that telephone pole to cut them wires. The wind like to blowed me down. Directly this big dog had got out, so Joe run outside and behind the store he found an old banana crate. He went over to that big dog and just smacked it over him, that banana crate. That scared that dog to death. He hit that basement hollering. And the man sleeping down there with him, he woke up and he wouldn't come out either, so we didn't bother with them. When the dog went in there, we just shut the door.

*It was a real bad night, real windy, and Willis and another fellow went inside and I was on the outside. After awhile, they come out the window and said there was a bulldog in there that kept charging them, and that there was somebody sleeping downstairs in the basement. They wasn't worried about the guy downstairs, but the dog was giving them trouble. Willis sat down on the steps, and the other guy and I went around there and damn if I didn't find a banana crate. So we went back in there and started after the old dog with that crate, and he was just afraid of it. They had a place back there in a closet for him to sleep, and he finally went into that and we shut the door on him. Well, then Willis come in, and we blowed her open.*

*And that's where I dropped a pint of nitroglycerine on my foot. It was real windy, and we didn't have the grease in a flat whiskey bottle like we should have, just a regular old pint bottle. I had coveralls on and had it in my pocket, but when we was leaving, up there apiece was a street light, and we had to go across under that light to get away. One man would go across, then another one would come. So this other guy went across, and then Willis went across, and then here I come. I started to trot out in the middle where it was bright light, and dang if this nitroglycerine bottle didn't jump out of my pocket! And here I was out in the middle of a gravel street as hard as this concrete right here. As it jumped out, I felt it and stuck my foot out, and it hit me right here on my instep and just rolled off. Didn't break or anything. And that was a full pint! I'll tell you,*

*if it had exploded, there wouldn't have been a greasy spot
or nothing left of me right there on that street.*

Well, in the spring this other feller with us and his
old lady headed up to Indianapolis to that race track. Me
and Joe stayed around there and we both had some silver
money. We'd been over in Des Moines and this guy with
us, he'd got some wrappers out of a bank to wrap his
money, and he give us some of them. We rolled our
money, and it had the name of that bank in Des Moines
on it. Joe had just thirty or forty dollars in nickels, or
something like that. I had buried mine before I got back
and my caps and string and grease. But Joe had just left
what little he had in there in our room.

When we went to check out, two laws grabbed us.
The old maid had prowled Joe's handbag up there—there
wasn't a big lot in there but she said we had a handbag
full of money up there. Well, hell, there wasn't *any*
hardly, but it was big money to her. She'd seen all the
money rolled up. So they arrested us and put us in jail
over there with nothing in the world on us.

*Willis had went downstairs of the hotel to eat
breakfast. He said, "Now you wait here for me. I'll run
over to the Studebaker agency there and try to sell the car.
Then I'll be back. Won't be gone over an hour." Well, by
noon he had never come back. I'm an old kid, you know,
so by that time I had got hungry. So I decided that I know
where he was at. I know there's a whole bunch of girls
working in the cafeteria down there, and he's probably
down there eating dinner right now. So I'll just go down
and eat too and see if he's down there.*

*I went down there and looked in the front, and there
he was! And he was going to be back in an hour! Here
he'd come back there and gone in to eat his dinner, and I
don't know when he thought I was going to eat. But that's
exactly where I found him, in that cafeteria. So I go over
where he is and say, "Where the hell have you been?"*

*"Well, I got busy and everything. Let's go back up and*

*get our things and move down to the hotel where we used to stay. I just come by there."*

*"I thought you was going to sell the car."*

*"Oh, I'm going to take a couple of days with that." So we go back up to the hotel to check out, and when we go into the lobby, the law was there, and they corralled us. Off to jail we went. For what, they didn't know. There was a nigger maid and her old man was in jail over there. She was doing everything she could to get him out, and she suspicioned something about me staying around the room so long. So when she come in to make up the room she prowled our handbags. Of course we both had pistols in there. I heard Willis say something about coin wrappers from a bank over at Des Moines, but I don't think that was the trouble. Them big pistols was what set her off.*

They kept us, I don't know, three or four days, then they had some people come over from Des Moines. Somebody had robbed a picture show over there and these wrappers was from the same bank where the theater always deposited money. They come over there and identified us as being the robbers that stuck up the man.

We fought extradition and stayed in the jail a week or two. My lawyers went over to Lincoln, the capital, and finally they said, "Well, take them." They was just building a new city hall in Des Moines. We was the first men that they ever mugged, took a picture and fingerprints of, in the new city hall there in 1920.

So we went over to Des Moines. I had a couple of big diamonds, and Joe had one, and we had some money, I guess one or two thousand on us. You want to know the truth, I believe they just took us for a shakedown! So finally I give one of them this big diamond, about a four carat, and I guess a thousand dollars to drop the case. They really had no case against us, but all we wanted was out. I got shook down more times than one. Of course I still had that charge against me down yonder in Humble, Texas, and I had broken out of the jail in

Ballinger. I had to get out because they could rake up them charges back in Texas, and I didn't want to go. I always paid off to get out as quick as I could. I'd say, "Listen, I got a little money I got no use for. Do you need it? I haven't done anything. I just want to get out of jail. Take it. Tell me who to give it to." And they'd tell me who to give it to, let you know right away that they knew how to get you out. They might not take it themselves, directly, but they had it fixed up. They'd say, "I know somebody who can get you out for so-and-so." Then we paid him, not the police.

*We got a lawyer to fight extradition. They wanted to take us back to Des Moines and try us 'cause a theater over there had been stuck up, and they took a lot of change. A smart detective had seen that big writeup and come over after us. They loaded us up and taken us to Des Moines, and going over there on the train, we were talking with the head man at Des Moines. He was a young guy, and we was talking about this, that, and the other, and making money and all, and he said, "Well, if a man had him a hundred dollars he could take that and buy a new suit of clothes."*

*So that was the opening. Willis, he jumped at that, and he went to propositioning him and did it a dozen times before we got to Des Moines. Every time he did, he raised the ante. Course, they probably knew we didn't rob the picture show over there. They had a good description of the guys that did that, because it was in daytime.*

*We both had big diamond stickpins in our ties in them days. Mine cost me two thousand dollars and Willis' was bigger than mine. I don't know what his cost him. Willis said we'd give him these diamonds. And so and so much money. The deal was he had to turn me loose to go get the money. He did when we got over there, and I went to Kansas City and come back, and he met me down at the depot. I can't remember what we give him in cash, but we give him the diamonds too. I had gone and got a check, and give that to him. He went and called to see if the check was good, and it was. So he told me to wait there and he'd let Willis loose to come down. After awhile he did, and we caught the train for Chicago.*

It was in Des Moines where I got acquainted with my wife. She was working at a big department store. I was over there at her house playing cards with her on the night that the picture show got stuck up. I'd been going with her awhile and she knowed I was over there. She was engaged to marry some wealthy man, but he was fifty years old and she was thirty. She never did care anything about him, but when she had the flu he got a doctor for her and she thought he saved her life because at that time you couldn't get a doctor and you couldn't get a hospital and he had got a doctor and got her in the hospital. And this guy had told her, "Don't you go to Des Moines and testify over there. I don't want nothing to do with him."

And she said, "And I don't want nothing to do with you, mister. You forget it." And then he tried to beg her out of it and she told him to go straight to the devil. She said, "I don't want nothing to do with no people like that. I know the man is innocent and you want to take an innocent man and put him in the penitentiary. And you'd keep your mouth shut and let them do it."

When they finally turned us loose, an old boy come around to see us. I was going by the name of H.S. Scott and Joe was going by the name of Rogers. This old boy said, "Mr. Scott, they made me identify you. I knowed you wasn't the men!" When he said that, these policemen that was standing there jumped him up and said, "You get the hell away from here." See, that's the way they do. Like they done us at Marble Falls, they took us off and come back and made that little boy identify us. That's the way they do.

So when we give them that money and rings, they turned us out of jail and we went about our business. Then we went on, Joe and I, and went to Chicago. The other guy went to Chicago too, and we monkeyed around and robbed one or two little banks, the three of us, and that fall we went back to Tulsa.

At this time Doc was in the Texas penitentiary, and Jess was at home in Uvalde and I decided to get the four of us together. Jess was two years older than me. He worked for Dolph Briscoe and Briscoe's daddy, both him and Tully did. Briscoe was later the governor of Texas. Doc was two years younger. There's just two years difference in every one of us, eleven of us. As a kid, Jess was a big, old larruping, lazy boy. The one you'd call a mama's boy. Big, old, fat, lazy kind, you know. The old man would whip him for not hoeing his cotton good, for cutting out too much, and he'd get right up and walk off and hoe it the same way! Didn't care. [laughs]. He was the best natured one of the whole family, though. He went to school before I did. Went three months and never did get his ABC's. He didn't try. When my daddy went on those trips looking for honey ponds and fritter trees, he'd take Jess with him because he was the biggest one at home. Bud was older, but he was gone.

Doc was still in prison, had been for a good long time. After him and me had got into that cotton deal business with old Tobe Roberts, he run and went to Crystal City and about a year and a half after that, they arrested him and brought him on up to Eastland County, tried him and give him two year. He went down there on the prison farm and stayed ten years, got convicted two or three times for running away, and they'd add on to his time and add on to his time. What they wanted with Doc was to put him to prize fighting. Doc was a bull, see, and he whipped everybody all over that country and in the penitentiary. He whipped any of them.

Finally, the last time he escaped was that fall of 1920, just went and saddled up the dog sergeant's horse, took his Winchester and rode off. He was a trusty, and in a job like he had you could wear citizen clothes. He rode down to Humble first because my daddy and brother had been there, but they had just left. So he come plumb across the country on that horse to Sabinal where he stopped at an old boy's house and told him he wanted to leave his horse and saddle a few days. But he just turned him into the man's pasture, hung up the saddle, and caught him a freight train for Uvalde.

My mother knowed we was up in Oklahoma, but she didn't know where. So Doc went up to Oklahoma but it turned out we was up in Illinois, and we was a little late coming back, so Doc picked cotton up there and hauled cotton and traded horses and stole horses and done everything else until we come back in October. Then when we wrote home, my mother wrote him and told him where we was at, and he come to us in October 1920 at Tulsa. From there he went right on with us, took right in. He was one of the gang.

Jess joined me right after Doc, the next spring. I had my bunch then. We had got rid of this other guy that was working with us, Brent Glasscock, but then I let him come back. He wasn't fit for nothing, just only to drive the car. He knowed all about a car and he was a good driver and I'd take him with me and he'd drive and we'd go through the country and look these places up.

I always went inside on bank jobs. If there was only one bank, I'd go by myself. If there was two, I'd take Joe or Jess, one or the other. Usually I taken Jess because I'd rather have Joe and Doc outside. Both of them was good. One was as good as the other. They'd stay on their post. There was no way of getting them off of it. I knowed when I went in that they'd be out there when I come back. And they weren't going to let nobody come in on me.

We drove nothing but Studebakers. When we robbed the Chicago train, we had some Cadillacs, but we didn't buy them. We stole them because we wanted hot cars to do that. But we used Big Six Studebakers or Special Six Studebakers all the time. That was the best road car in them days, of a cheap car. They was tough. You could just run them into anything. And the Goodyear tires would last ten thousand miles before they'd go to peeling off, and after that we'd drive in and pay six or eight hundred dollars and get a new car. We bought two new cars a year.

We always used four guys because that was the best way. Now I had my own gang there, I knowed what I could do. Jess and me and Glasscock went down to Denison and on down to Glenwood. They had a mail transfer on the Katy and some other little old line that went to Paris, Texas. We had seen some good sacks lifted off there. We watched, and we'd see them come nearly every night. They'd come from Dallas and unload in Denison.

So we figured the sacks would be in a certain mailcar nearly every night. I told Jess, "You go to Glenwood and stay all night in our automobile. We're going to jump in that mail car over here at Bells, when they start out." It was summer time and they left all the doors open. "I'll take Glasscock with me, and we'll jump in that mail car and we'll get all that mail, that money. We'll throw it out and then we'll get out about two miles before we get to Denison. Then we'll walk back up the railroad tracks and hide in the brush. You come the next night and get us."

So the train started out. I jumped in first and there stood a mail clerk right there and he tried to come out with his gun and I throwed my pistol on him and made him go down. When I looked down in there, there was one more clerk who went for his gun and I throwed it on him and he went down. Then I looked down and there was this other one coming out, and I throwed it on him too. And I stood there for two or three minutes putting it on this one and putting it on that one. And that other dirty louse, Glasscock, he was a-hangin' on the door and was afraid to come in!

Finally I hollered, "You son of a so-and-so, get in here!" Then he come on in. Scared to death! And there I was with them three men. When he jumped in, wouldn't you know it, he got tough and hit one of the men. I didn't want to hurt them. I said, "You dirty coward. You hung out there and like to got me killed, and was scared to come in. Now you get in here and you get tough!"

Well, we rode on and stopped the train and throwed

the sacks off, but this time again we missed the big money. We just got a few thousand dollars. Was supposed to get two whole sacks of money, but it had come in the night before, that big money had.

We'd seen the sacks the times we checked out the train. Square, canvas sacks and they were registered. There's a big, brass lock on the registered sack, and they're the only ones that's got a big brass lock on them. In those sacks was greenbacks. Pure old greenback money. That's the way the banks and the Federal Reserve Bank out of Dallas shipped all the money till about ten years ago, in the mail. Just throw it in them sacks. Now they take it to the Federal Reserve Banks in trucks, armored cars. One comes out through Uvalde, Del Rio, and all over that country. Another one goes thisaway, another goes thataway. It's all hauled in armored cars now.

So at Bells, we didn't get much money. Then we went on over to Texarkana where once a week there was a man come from Shreveport on that train with a big express box. He could just carry it when he got off the train. He'd take it into the express office there in Texarkana. We watched that for two months. One night, it didn't come. I said, "Well, wonder why it didn't come that night?" And we had seen it come eight or ten times. We'd watched it two or three months. We knew we couldn't miss it. So we got up, and we got all ready to get it.

We got Joe and he took us to a litle town down below Texarkana. We had a place picked out about eight miles out of Texarkana, and we knowed the train was going to get there about nine or ten o'clock at night. We would get off that train and walk out there and plant in the woods and the next night Joe could come and pick us up.

So it was me and Jess and Doc and, yeah, we had Glasscock with us then, because we needed Joe to come pick us up. So we went to Bloomburg and we jumped on the blinds of that train. When we got to the Sulphur

192

River, I went on over the top and got the engineer and the fireman, me and Jess did. And I told him, "Just when you get that mail car across the Sulphur River, you stop and leave all the rest of the train on the bridge." See, nobody could get off then. So he did, pulled it up just so, to where the mail car was off the bridge, and then he stopped. I jumped back and run up on top. I had a pint of formaldehyde, and one of them little glasses in the top of the coach was up, where they get their air, and I just took the cork off and threw the bottle in the car. The other guys told the mail clerks to come out, that it was poison. And boy!, they throwed them doors open and come tumbling out. I had Doc on the off side. But some smart nigger porter, he tried to get around, tried to get off the bridge. Doc hollered at him, "Don't you come up here, you get back in the train." When he didn't get back, Doc shot right under him. And boy!, he got back on the train then.

I said, "Get out here and uncouple this car!" We throwed the two or three clerks outta there. I says, "Where's that big box that comes in here every night?"

"Well," he says, "Mister, it didn't come tonight. You can look this car over all you want." I hunted the coach out and got two or three registered sacks. We got a pretty good bunch of bonds and stuff, but we had missed that box. They said there was several hundred thousand dollars. Now that was just our bad luck.

We went on up there to the engine and got on. Made the engineer cut loose from the train and leave it on that bridge, and we went to Texarkana, fifteen or twenty miles. We got off and sent him back. We hit the woods and went over to where we had our place ready. We'd showed Joe the day before where we'd hide, and when we got over there on that track, it was dark, my God, it was dark. We was just four or five miles from Texarkana and we walked into somebody. I throwed my pistol on him and said, "Get 'em up!" and he hollered.

I seen he was an old nigger, and I said, "We want you. We been looking for you for a long time." Well, he was so scared he couldn't talk.

Then he said, "My God, mister. I never done no harm to nobody."

"Get around there. Turn your side to where I can see you." I looked him over and I says, "Boys, this is not the man we're looking for. We're mistaken, old man. You're not our man. But I'll tell you one thing, if we ever hear of you telling anybody that you met us here and we're a-lookin' for somebody, we're going to come back after you." That was to scare him up.

So we walked on about ten miles to a good thicket on the creek. We done had our jugs of water and food already there for the next day. Course, they thought we hit Texarkana, thought we had a car up there waiting for us and was gone. But we just laid in the woods out there till after dark the next day, maybe eight or nine o'clock, and then Joe come in. I had a signal to blink his lights when he got close so we'd know it was him. He'd been over to Ashdown and stayed all night and then come back to get us with the car.

We went into Denison that night—we knowed what time the passenger train went out of there—and two of us got on the train for Tulsa while the others took the car and went over and stayed somewhere and come on the next day. We stayed around Tulsa a few days and went to Kansas City. Going up through Nebraska we was looking for some banks to get that winter. This was in the summertime, July. We didn't do any robbing in the summer. Very few times we ever went anywhere on a job in the summer. We'd wait until September and then we'd quit in April. We'd go up there and rob banks till the beginning of cold weather, and about the 1st of November, we'd hit San Antone and rob banks around there. It was cool around them lakes in the North. I'd look things up in the summertime, and then we'd rob them in the winter. We found several that looked pretty good, but the little old banks and things that we robbed all around there didn't amount to anything. We just got enough to stay alive.

*We laid off working while Willis scouted for new jobs. But sometimes we'd spend part of the winter in San Antonio because it was warmer there and sometimes we'd run short of money. Like in the winter of '21-22. We was running short and decided to rob a bank at Hondo, about thirty miles west of San Antonio. Fact is, there were two banks out there and we'd been talking a long time about robbing but never did. So we decided we'd go out there. The night watchman out there we'd known for years. One time he got ahold of me when I was a little kid. I jumped off the steps of a passenger train right under his face. That was the first time I'd ever caught onto a train, and I stepped off and he seen me a minute later. He never seen me get off the train, but he knowed that's the only place I could have come from and he asked me did I ride in on that train.*

*Well, I just said, "No, I come down here to meet my brother." He kept me by him most of the night before I could duck him and run around and get away. He was a big, fat fella. Nice old fella.*

*This night we went out there and located him. He was in the depot. We got around and cut all the wires, and he was still in there, so we decided to let him stay there. It was a pretty cold night and we thought he'd sit tight. But I stayed across the street from the depot, by the bank on the corner there and watched to see he didn't come out.*

*But we was lucky there, because it didn't take too long in the first bank. They'd left the vault door open, unlocked, so we didn't need any nitro to blow it or nothing. They didn't have to do anything but go around and raise up the window and go in there. Then the door to the vault was open, so it didn't take them long in there until they'd cleaned that all out and they come out.*

*The night marshal was still in the depot, so I don't know which one of us suggested it, but somebody said, "Well, we've got lots of time, why don't we go over and try the other one?" Doc and I stayed in the same place and Willis and Jess went down and got into the other one. Anyway, we got that bank too, went and got into our car, and the night marshal, he never did come out of that depot.*

*Later we went and robbed the Boerne bank. Caught the night watchman and cut the wires—that's always the first thing you've got to do. Sometimes if you can't find him, you've got to go on and cut the wires, because it takes so long to do and you've got to have time.*

*But as it turned out, a cold norther blowed in there and we didn't have any trouble. We had caught the night watchman when he come out on the street, and we went around and got close to him—you got to get close to 'em because they've all got guns. He didn't try to use it, though. Only very seldom one does. We tied up his hands and I kept him with me. Set him down over there by a building in the dark somewhere, so someone wouldn't come along and shoot him, thinking he was one of the robbers. I could see him there, but if anybody come along, they wouldn't notice him.*

*They didn't even have to blow the safe there. Even if we made some noise, the wind was a-blowin' and it'd blow something over or bang somebody's door. But I tell you, you'd be surprised. We'd be in some of them towns and it'd be just as still as it could be in the wintertime and in the night, so you could hear a firecracker three miles, and we'd set off an explosion you could hear ten mile, boom! and you'd think it would wake up the dead. We'd put in four or five shots like that and not a soul in town would ever wake up! You'd think it was impossible to do that, but that happened. Yeah.*

*After we was finished at Boerne, we taken the night watchman with us when we left, a little piece of the way, toward San Antone. I guess now you could call it kidnapping or something, because he sure didn't give his consent to go [laughs]. But he was a real nice old fellow. Down towards San Antone, we took him out in the hills there and give him a blanket, told him to build up a fire because it was real cold, and told him to stay there until daylight. Then he could come on out to the road and catch somebody and get a ride. It's a positive thing that he seen us and could have told how many there were, but I never went back to Boerne until just a little bit ago when we went up there to make this film. That's the first time. I don't think he'd have known me. Course the way it happens is that somebody says, "Oh, you're bound to know him. This is the fella," and then he says, "Yeah, I guess that's him."*

We went down to Pearsall to rob a bank one night in 1921. I believe there was two banks there, but in one of them, the safe sat out on the floor. A passenger train come in there about midnight one night and while it was there making noise, I climbed up the telephone pole to cut the wire. The pole was beside the telephone office right across from the bank. I had a hacksaw and boy, I could cut one of them inch-and-a-half wires in two or three minutes. I had one of them .45 thumb busters, single-action pistols in my belt, and when I run down that post and jumped down, it flew out of my belt and hit the sidewalk and shot. Hit it right on the hammer! It's a wonder it didn't shoot me in two.

But with that train there, nobody heard anything at the bank. The safe stood out in the middle of the floor. It was a big old Packer. The front door would only have taken one shot and the next would have taken, oh, two, maybe.

We heard two guys talking at the depot and then they come up to the town, the two men did. We spied on them and they was two Texas Rangers. They had got off there; don't know what for. There was no hotel there and they went down to a rooming house and they couldn't raise nobody there. It was about one o'clock in the morning. So they sat down half a block down across the street on one of them high curbs. They just talked and talked and talked and talked—right in front of the bank. Well, we waited because we thought they'd go back to the depot. If they did, then we'd put a man on them with a shotgun. Rangers don't amount to any more than anybody else. They're not going to run out in the face of a shotgun. But we waited and waited until after three o'clock . By then it was getting too late and they was still sitting there, so

197

we had to walk off and leave the bank. Later in the papers they said something about the wires being cut, but they didn't know what they was cut for. I don't think they ever suspected a bank robbery.

Texas Rangers in general is like anybody else. There's a lot of good Rangers and a lot of bad Rangers. Nowadays they're better people, better educated. See, in them days there would be some old sheriff come from West Texas where he'd killed two or three people and that's the way they got their reputation. They didn't care any more about shooting your eyes out, some of them, than they did taking a drink of water. In them days, there was a lot of tough ones that would rather kill you than arrest you.

*When I first come in with Willis, I had never done anything like that robbing, but by now I was getting so that I could see a good place too. I don't think I was ever scared, but you get excited, kind of "excited" before it starts, when you're going up and looking for the night marshal or cutting the wires before you start doing anything.*

Everything we went on, I done the "casing." All the time. I'd pick the towns and go in the bank and get change and look it over. See if it had a safe we could blow. Then if there was a night watchman, we'd go on a couple of nights and come back and park out of town, watch where he went, who was the first people that come and opened up the bank, and when it was closed at night. After we got all that done, we'd go to driving the roads for a getaway. Glasscock would drive and I'd watch the roads and write them down. Then when we robbed the bank, I set there and read and told him which way to go. I kept all that stuff in a tablet, but when we were all done, we tore those things up and throwed them away. I was in on everything, knowed a hell of a lot more about it than they did. Oh, they could go at night and case them too, but when we went after one, I was the one that always went inside. There was no extra cut for me, either.

Everybody got his own share.

*We usually lobbed all the money together. Didn't even count it. Willis would put it in a handbag or something, and he'd separate the bonds out and take and sell them. Later we'd meet. All of us usually had money, you know, so at our next meeting after that, that's when we'd divide up the money. Sometimes, if it was handy, if he had an apartment or something like that, we'd meet there one at a time or two at a time and divide up the soft money there. He'd keep the bonds until he got back up to Chicago or somewhere where he could sell them.*

When we was working on a bank, we kept a tab of our expenses and then we took that out of the money first. We bought a new car every ten thousand miles. Tires wouldn't last but ten thousand miles, and when the rubber played out, we got rid of it. It wasn't that we wanted a new car all the time, but the getaway is the main thing, see. You got no trouble to get a bank, but you've got to get away after you get it. That means good equipment. Glassock knowed if a car just rattled wrong, a little rattling, he just knowed it and he kept it in tiptop shape. Remember the Santa Claus bank robbery? They were just two ignorant Hoosiers was all they was. Had never robbed a bank, and never done nothing and pulled the silliest trick in the world. And them kind, they just shoot anybody they see. They don't know before they go in what they're gonna do and they don't know where they're going when they come out. Yeah. That's the way they get caught.

*I carried a pistol and a shotgun, both. The shotgun had birdshot in it, but you've got buckshot in your pocket, so if it comes down to anything or you have to use buckshot to protect your own life, why then, you can. But at first, you've got a whole bunch of #7 birdshot in the gun, just enough to scare somebody.*

ORGANIZING THE NEWTON GANG

There wasn't many night men but us. Very few bank
robberies at night in them days at all. Used to be, up till
1912 or so, the old-time robbers walked out of the
country. There was no automobile roads or automobiles
them days. If electric lights burned after twelve o'clock,
an old-time bank robber wouldn't go within a mile of it.
They went to them little towns where there was a bank
and two or three stores and no lights or watchman. And
they usually walked out of the country. When I met up
with these guys and talked about catching a nighthack,
well, they was scared to. I never seen such cowards as
them old-time bank robbers in my life. Scared to death.

And they didn't blow safes until after 1900. I think
the first nitroglycerine was used in about 1905 or '06.
Then you could blow them safes at night. Before they
had that, them robbers would knock the combination off
the safe. You take a Hall or a Diebold, either one, all you
got to do is take a hammer and knock the combination
off and put a pin in there and take a sledge hammer and
hit it one lick. It just opens up! But the Moslers you
couldn't do that with, or the Victor. So the oldtimers
picked banks that had only Diebolds and Halls, I think.
They just went in there and saw the name on the door.
Then they'd get a big old bar and go into the bank and
just take it and hook it on that combination, behind that
knob and strip it right out. Then they had a sledge
hammer and put a punch in there the size of that hole,
hit it, and it fell right off.

Sometime along in there, they put a trigger on them
safes. When you busted that combination, then auto-
matically you locked the door all the way around it. I
tried to knock that trigger in two, but when you busted
that you could hear it go thump! and then the pins goes
in all around. You couldn't get in there then.

A vault—you can't get into the vault without blowing
it. You got to blow the door off. Hell, we hardly ever
monkeyed around with even punching them. Just go in
there and put some nitro around it and blow it out of the
way. What did we care for noise?

For cutting the telephone wires, I'd get a keyhole saw and climb up there. You could take them big old cables an inch and a half through and cut one in two minutes. Both electric lines and phone lines was on the same pole, but you could tell the difference. The hot wires was way up above us. We just cut that big cable that had all them little wires in it. Lots of times there was nearly always some loose wires for long distance and things, and I'd cut this big one first then reach over and whack them with a pair of pliers. I could run up them telephone poles thirty-five foot high. Just "cooned" it. No climbers or anything on, just bear hugged it and went on up.

*Before Doc and Jess joined us, there was another fellow there with us, and his wife had a safety deposit box, so I'd give my money to them and they'd get it turned into soft money, greenbacks, hundred dollar bills, and keep it for me. You have to spend a whole lot of money. Your expenses run up pretty high. In 1922 or so, it cost me twelve or fourteen dollars a day for a hotel, the best hotels, you know. I never knew but one that was up at twenty-five dollars, and that was the Astoria in Chicago. The wife of this old boy with us used to try to get him to go over there. "Let's go and just stay one night," she'd say, so she could tell people she'd stayed there, you know.*

*So there's four hundred a month for your room rent. And it'd cost you three or four dollars a meal for food at the best places. Hell, I was young and hungry, and I wanted to eat! I'd have ham and eggs and toast and what not for breakfast, then for noon, it'd always be something good—steak or fried chicken. And at night it was pretty expensive around the best places even in them days. So meals run me from six hundred to a thousand a month.*

*Course you'd spend money for entertainment too. They had burlesque shows, you know, and it cost about four dollars to get in to see them. They was real good ones. That was the first class thing them days. Lots of pretty girls in a row dancing, besides the other guys joking and this, that and the other.*

*Everywhere you go, you had to have a car or call a taxi. Later on I got to where I liked to ride them streetcars and cling-clang around, but then I didn't know much about a streetcar, so I'd just get me a taxi to go somewheres and get another one to come back.*

*When you went in a barbershop, there was always a good-looking manicurist in there, and in the cafe there was always good-looking girls waiting on you, and good-looking girls in department stores—and when you're young and got some money in your pocket and a hundred dollar suit on, why you can always find somebody that'll go out and have something to eat with you anyway. Yeah.*

*I'd have them ideas once in awhile about quitting this, getting out of it and going home. I know once along about this time, I had decided if I ever got my bankroll up to ten thousand dollars again, I was going to quit, right there. But of course that's like all them good resolutions you make when you're down a little bit. When I got my pockets full again, I forgot all about that. Nobody ever encouraged me to quit. Along in the early part I had the idea two or three times to quit and do so-and-so, when I'd get to thinking of the fun I had heading out on them old ranches there, riding pitching horses. I'd think about how that was a lot more fun than this, but I had to get me some money first. Then as it turned out, I'd get some, but never did quit.*

# 15

## WORKING IN CANADA (1922)

W hile we was staying at a fine hotel in Kansas City, a fellow that we knowed from Chicago came and found us. He'd been in with us once in awhile before. He was one of them old-time bank robbers, one that wouldn't rob but only where it was dark, where there was only a store and a barbershop and a bank. Well, him and his wife had took a trip up through Canada that summer and he'd looked at all the banks, and in Canada they didn't have no round safes. All of them was square and you could shoot any of them. He said if we wanted to go up there, he'd show us. Of course, we had to take him with us.

> "We never worried about the Mounties. Canadian Mounties don't amount to a hill of beans."

So here we go. It was nothing but wheat country back in there and it was August, I guess, of 1922 when we arrived. We drove all over while I looked them banks up, and I never could find anything but only what was called a "mark." That's one you could blow.

*Canadian towns wasn't anything different. There was more of them up there, and practically all of them had safes that you could blow. Down in the United States, they had got to using round ones that you couldn't blow open. For one thing, they was so tight that you can't get any grease in there. And another thing, if you got it in there, you can't blow it open anyway, because they're so thick.*

We went over to Pelican Lake, Manitoba, about the first of September. Nearly all the tourists had left to go back home by then. This old-time robber and me and our wives went down there first. The others, Joe and Doc and Jess—was in Winnipeg waiting to hear from us. The two couples of us rented a cabin, a great big one. I guess there was five or seven beds in it. The owner said just go in there and use what you want. When we let Joe and them know it was okay to come on, they rode a train out there one night and come to Brandon, about a hundred miles west of Winnipeg and we met them there. It was night when we brought them over, and we never let nobody see them there. There wasn't many people around Pelican Lake, and whoever was there thought only me and my wife and this other guy and his wife was at the cabin.

*The reason we stayed there was there was a few banks up there in that country that was close enough to that lake that we could rob them and make our getaway—come back to the lake. This was at a resort, but it was a little past the resort "season" and everybody was gone. Willis said they was going to stay there a little while and fish. So the rest of us come in of a night and went up there and the owner never did know we was there. They thought there was just two men in there and their wives.*

We went out and located a town by the name of Melita that was alright, and we drove a getaway to plan the route. There was roads all over that country, section lines roads, most of them dirt in them days. Then we looked at another town, Moosomin, and drove that one too. And another one that I just can't remember. We got us three places lined up, all about a hundred miles from where we was staying.

When we went into Melita, we cut all the wires and grabbed the nighthack and took him with us up to town. It was a big old two story building. Them days, every bank in Canada had somebody who slept upstairs over it. We knowed they was sleeping here too, but I put the guys in place outside and went in figuring to shoot it. The vault was in the back of the building, and that's where they slept, right straight up them stairs. The living quarters was out in the front part of the second story. I blew that first shot and knocked the door out of there and a man hollered, "Let us out of here! Let us out of here!"

I said, "You go back to bed and stay put and you ain't going to get hurt." This was a Canadian Bank of Commerce, and it took about five shots. You could just get a plate of it at a time and then there's rubber. Then another steel plate, then more rubber. It takes about five shots to peel them.

I put in another shot and run out the door and he heard me. When I run out front, they'd run downstairs. When I'd go back in, they'd run back up. So here we went. I'd put in a shot and run out, they'd come down, it would blow, and they'd run back up. Outside there, somebody showed up and one of our guys hollered to him to go back. When he didn't they cut down close to him and boy! he left then!

*I'm outside, way off over there. You don't get up close to it; some of that glass might get to falling on you. And if anybody comes out there with his gun, he's going to be looking at the bank, and you want to be way back up yonder there where you can see every direction, in the shadow of a building or behind a post. Someplace where you're not right out in the open where they can see you. Then thataway, he's coming up and he's watching the bank because that's where the trouble is at, and he'll walk right up on you and you can catch him. Or, if you want to, you can make him throw his gun down there and go on home.*

*You know before you go there that you're not going to run in there and scoop up the money and go. Hell, sometimes we were there an hour or two. And after you start that shooting, you know that people are awake and know you're there, so then you shoot out all them lights close to you, but sometimes it gets to going so fast and furious that everytime you shoot, you let them know right where you're at. If you run out there to shoot them out and they're shooting at you, bullets are hitting the sidewalk and going "zzz....zzz," you know how they go in the picture show? Well, that's a pretty good imitation. They do the same damn thing out there on the sidewalk [laughs].*

So we went ahead and blowed it and went on out to the highway where we turned the nighthack loose. We had the telephone wires cut so there was no communication out of town. Nowadays you can't cut the phone wires. You can cut them, but it lights up every wire in the office just as fast as you cut them. Them days, with them old crank phones, it didn't show up nowhere.

We pulled out from there and I was telling the driver, "You better look out. You're driving too fast. It's too dark for that without any lights on." He was the guy who had told us about this stuff. Finally we come to where we had to turn and boy!, he just kept going. Right out into the field. We was the luckiest people in the world there wasn't a big ditch there. And I said, "Now, no more. You can't drive with no lights on." So he put them on and we did get back out of there and over to our place at Pelican Lake just before daylight.

There was very few bonds up there that you could get that was any good. Most of them was registered just like they was down here in the United States. We got a few bonds and about ten thousand cash. That was a lot of money to get out of a bank in them days, but the wheat harvest was on up there and that made for more money in the bank. We done had the getaway drove for these others, but there was a lot of commotion in the countryside about the robbery. Newspapers said it was Americans. They knowed that by the way we talked, but they didn't suspect us because they didn't ever see me. We was tucked in at Pelican Lake about a hundred miles from there, and they thought the robbers was coming across the border and running back.

*After we come back from that, the 27th of September it was, we went over there to another one, a second one, at Moosomin, out from Pelican Lake. But before we did that, there was lots of ducks on this lake and we'd go up there and shoot ducks, me and Jess, I think it was. One day I seen something up there, looked like a little feather-legged banty hen, about that size, but prettier than that. I didn't know what it was, so I didn't shoot it. I come back down and was telling about it, and Willis had heard them talking about it, and it was what they call a partridge. So he said, "Show us where it was at and we'll go back up there and kill us some. They say they're awful good eating."*

*So I did, and when we got there, why, he starts in, "Let me shoot first!" So he banged away and killed it and then he went on back. He'd killed him a partridge and he was done. If I wanted to kill me one, I had to find another one. I was circling around back to where we was staying, and one of these things flew up and went down right quick. I come up with my shotgun and shot right where it went down, "bang!" I heard a lot of flopping and went down and there was two of these birds and both of them had their heads shot off. That's a fact. There must have been another one there on the ground, that's why he lit there, and I be dogged if I didn't shoot both their heads off and I didn't even see the one.*

We laid around there and rested up three or four days and then went to Moosomin. All the time we was there, there was no night watchman. I went in and it was a Canadian Bank of Commerce with one of them big steel safes as high as my head. I had never gone up agin one of them, so I give her a good, big shot of grease, about four ounces and blowed the first door off. I cleaned her plumb down to the keester, the little inside door where all the stuff is. The keester inside is about an inch thick. That's the "duster" between the money and the big door. You open the big door and then you got a small, thin door to open and there's the money. I put one shot in there and it peeled off a piece of steel. Blowed it out about an inch thick. The door was solid, but I had some wedges with me. We used to get these old case knives out of the Ten Cent Store and cut them in two and make wedges. They was tough. They wouldn't break. I take a hammer and drive wedges into that crack and spread it a little, then put in another shot. Blam! I'd get another few inches.

*But before you pour in the grease, you get some of the P&G soap, Proctor and Gamble, and I guess it didn't sit up on the shelf so long in them days, and it was kind of soft. You could cut it up and put just a little water with it and squeeze it into a little ball that you could seal this crack up on the outside. Before you poured in the grease. Seal it up on this side all the way around so that you've got the crack sealed good, and then you make you a little "cup" out of the soap up there at the top where you've left a little space for it, and you pour your grease right in there and it runs down through the whole crack about like castor oil.*

I think I put five shots, maybe six all together in that keester to get it out. Somebody had come out and hollered around but with them big nitro shots going off, they all went back and got in a hole. They'd try to ring them phones, you know, but when the phone won't ring, that scares them up and they won't get out of the house. Anybody that's got any sense.

So we got that one. I know just exactly what we got out of it. There was one package of money. A little silver money was in some sacks in there and there was one package of greenbacks, six thousand dollars, every dollar in greenbacks they had in the bank, I guess. There was a few hundred dollars in Canadian money and in silver there, but we wouldn't touch it. We just got that six thousand in greenback. We didn't want to monkey with their money. Oh, we might pick up a handful or so, but most of it we left.

Somebody was asleep in a car in front of the building,

but when we went to shooting, whoosh! he come to, and away he went. He was scared to death.

*He had been asleep in an old car right in front of there, and don't you know, when that went off that he really come out of there! I stopped him a minute and then told him, "Go on. Just keep going."*

And we was getting some trouble from one guy up there with a rifle. You got to be afraid of a rifle, and he wasn't shooting wild.

*I got to thinking I had to do something about that because they'd be coming out of there before long. So I taken around and got up pretty close to him and elevated my shotgun a little bit and shot and that birdshot hit all around him and he left. I never did hear no more out of him.*

Then the engineer over on one of the trains, he got the message some way or another and he just tooted that whistle and tooted it, damn! I imagine for the last thirty minutes we was there.

*It was kind of a railroad town, and somebody had found out about us and went down to the railroad yard and they had a train there and he was pulling the whistle. "Toot, Toot, Toot," just pulling that old whistle as long as he could. The last I heard of that damn train, he was still blowing that whistle, that man down there, but the fellow with the rifle didn't come back no more.*

That bank was a hard one to get. Took us awhile, maybe an hour. Then we pulled out and went back to our place. There's another place the other way too, towards Winnipeg, that we got, but I have absolutely forgot the name of it.

*I think that was at a town called Ceylon.*

Anyway we went down there to that third place and it was a pretty small town, and dark. We had no trouble there. The people knowed we was blowing it, but nobody come out. Some of them would come out, and you holler at them and tell them to get on back and they do. They could have driven to the next town for help if they hadn't been scared to get outside, but by the time they done that, we'd be gone. After we got that third place, we went back to Pelican Lake. I guess we was on the lake there about two weeks getting them three places.

We never worried about the Mounties. Canadian Mounties don't amount to a hill of beans. That's not their business. Mounties can do no more than anybody else, and anyway, they couldn't put guards on the banks because they didn't know what bank was going to be robbed.

But I'll tell you one thing. They quit having people sleep up over them places. They took everybody out, at least in that country they did.

It was about a hundred miles back to Winnipeg, so we goes back and takes the car and ship it to Toronto. Put it in a boxcar and shipped it off. Then we all go on the train. Two of us went on the Canadian National and the other three went on the Canadian Pacific. We took different routes to Toronto where we met.

We put up in them big hotels there and then went out in that country looking for a bank. This was getting late, I think it was October then. First day we was out, we found a good one. Good location and everything, wasn't but twenty-five miles outside of Toronto there. We drove the getaway, working out a route so that we wouldn't run into nobody and could stay off the main roads. There are roads all over that you can take, small roads. When we come to a big road, we had a place to cross it, usually on a section line. On every mile, there's a section line, all over the United States, Canada, and everywhere else. After the country'd settled, they went back and each man that owns the land next to the section line, he's got to give so much land if they want to put a road through there.

*This Texas country's all laid out in sections too, but there's no roads on these sections lots of times. Up there, there's people lives on these small places and they have to have a road.*

Everybody has to have a road. When this Texas country was first opened, you know, those big ranchers tried to take all the land. They'd fence it and then, when a guy'd get in there and get him a piece of school land, a half section or six hundred acres or whatever he could take up, they wouldn't give him a road. So he couldn't get in or out. He was locked in or out.

Well, the state went ahead and passed a law that they had to give him a road. That was done way back there, in the sixties, or eighties. In the North, it's the same way. Every section line, you've got to give a man a way to get in or out, where he owned a piece of land. And there's a little map, they call it a Mendenthal Map, in all them northern states, it showed every section line in that state. And if a road happened to stop, it showed it. We could just take them and miss all the towns.

After you got fifty miles away them days, it was safe. You could take out on any big road then. After it'd got daylight and other people got to travelling, you could get on the big roads and go ahead if you wanted to. Other towns might not have heard about it for four or five days. They'd see it in the newspaper, maybe, but there wasn't too many daily papers then except in the big towns.

Anyway, we went over and got that bank we'd looked up right when we came to Toronto. Then we went after a Bank of Toronto. It was real soft—a one shot bank. I went in and shot the door on the vault. Because there'd never been any bank robberies down in this area, somebody was living upstairs. The first shot, I knocked the door off. And somebody said, "What's the matter, Robert?" Then some woman stuck her head out and said, "Cut that out! Cut that out!" And we laughed about that a hundred times.

Also, that's where the guy with us, the one who had

211

tipped us off about them Canadian banks, run out and left me in the dark holding a bottle of grease with a safe about to explode on me. The way it happened was that I had loaded her up good. It took easy. I drove in that wedge in there and boy!, the nitroglycerin run in there like nobody's business. I usually put two or three or four ounces and it'd run in there. Then I would cut me what we call a cap and string, a dynamite cap and fuse. It burns a foot a minute, you know, and you can cut it in five second, ten second, fifteen second pieces—you know, just how long you want it to take.

*I always cut them long enough to be damn sure I could get away!*

Well, I had several of them short fuses and I had put in about three ounces of grease—that nitroglycerine—that had run away pretty fast. So I got some cotton and stuck it around the cap so the grease wouldn't get all away, then I poured another three ounces in. Inside with me was this oldtimer who had a flashlight to show me how to come out. But when I capped the bottle and lit that fuse and turned to run, he's gone! And I can't see the door, it's so dark! Well, I had about a fifteen-second fuse on it and the safe was just a little higher than my waist. I was as active as a cat them days, so up I went on top of that safe and I put that grease right against me and laid up against the wall with my back turned toward the door. I didn't hardly get up there and get straightened up and blooey! she went. I didn't get much of a jar. It stung my feet a little, but the power of everything went outwards. Nitroglycerine just blows one way, and dynamite blows every direction. If I'd been knocked off the safe, it might have set off the grease I was holding against my chest. It takes a fifty-pound jar to set off nitroglycerine, but it's got to be right against it. But there wasn't no jar on me, hardly, up there.

That was also like the night I stepped off a cliff carrying a pint. I went right off the edge of a creek in the

dark and hit on the sandy ground, so I was okay. If I'd
hit in the rocks I might have exploded the pint. I run
out there from the Toronto bank and I cussed that guy
out! Did I cuss him out.

I didn't know I'd got the door in the first shot. We
run back in and boy!, it'd broke the big door out and the
thin door in. And I had a little bar there, I always carried
a bar, and I just put it in, twisted the little door out, and
there laid our money with one shot, one shot. I guess we
got about ten thousand—it was a pretty good little town.

The car we left about a half mile out of town by itself,
hid in a good dark place. So after we robbed the bank,
we walked back to the car. We knowed what we was
doing. We knowed that there was nobody out there.
People never bothered to come out till an hour after we
left, then they'd sneak out. We had plenty of time to get
to the car.

*Our car was always outside of town. If you got your
car up there close and you get a bunch of people shooting
at you and you get in and start up, all they've got to do is
shoot into the car to kill somebody. So we were afoot.
We'd stay in the dark if there was any shooting going on,
and we've got our car off down there maybe a half a mile
sometimes. So when we get to it, why we're gone. Or if
they should happen to hear it, we're too far away for them
to shoot at it.*

Then we come back to Toronto, and on the edge of
town we knowed where there was streetcars. I'd get off
one place and get on a streetcar and go into town. Then
we'd let another one off down here a ways and the last
man took the car and went on in and put it up. We never
went into town all in a bunch so they'd see four or five
men in the car! That'd look suspicious. You've got to
protect yourself.

Well, that night, two of us caught a train out, and the
next day, two more caught one out, and the last guy takes
the car and goes on to Detroit and drives it on back to

Chicago. We didn't have our license on it. We'd just get a license off of some other car before we went.

On this Canadian trip in the fall of '22, then, was four of us brothers and one other, the oldtimer that we had to take along because he had told us where they was at. See, if a guy told you where there's a mark, it was his mark. If you went to get it, you had to take him in on it. We was always organized from the time that I got Doc and Joe with me. I knowed what to do. I knowed that if anybody come in with us, we'd just put them where we wanted to use them.

*I was young but I remembered everything that happened, each place where we were at and everything. I was young and everything was new to me then. Them towns up there was like what our towns was like here fifty years ago, about the same, little kind of frontier towns like down in South Texas or like the towns out in West Texas back them days. Not like they are now.*

*We stayed around Chicago for a good little piece there, I'm pretty sure, and changed our money. We had to give ten percent to change the Canadian money into American, but at that time, it was worth a little bit more than American money was. We couldn't use it, though, so we had to get it changed into American. After that—that's late in the fall or the winter time of '22—we come on back down to San Antone, or I guess we come on back down to Tulsa and stayed there a little while before coming to San Antone. Everything we're telling you is a fact; it happened thataway. This morning when we were coming in, I said to Willis, "That date don't sound exactly right to me."*

*"Well," he said, "It don't sound just right to me either, but it's somewhere around in there."*

# 16

## UPPING THE ANTE: ROBBERY IN DAYLIGHT (1923)

A"Chances. You've got to take chances."

fter we'd worked around Toronto, then, and gone back to Chicago, it was getting pretty late. That was in the fall of 1922. From there we headed for Kansas City. One drove on down and the others come on the train. Well, down there was a guy that had told us his name was Des Moines Billy, but he was really out of St. Louis. All them old-time bank robbers had some monicker. He was an oldtimer, one I told you that only went into the little dark towns.

Billy had a tip that up at St. Joe, a packing house payroll come in on the passenger train at about eleven o'clock at night and unloaded. Said he had watched it and had seen it. When this train come up to the station, it was on the side where it was all dark and one or two tracks over from the main depot. The other trains come up on the other side, and they was closer to the depot.

He told us that it come on such-and-such nights. It was a small railroad but I don't know the name of it. 'Course I went up to the depot at night and seen it come in myself, seen how it'd come in and what we had to do. So we got ready for it and when it come in there that night and they went to unloading the mail, throwing all them registered sacks off, why we nailed them. Three registered sacks. We thought that was the money, you see. It was supposed to be the money. But the money had come in the night before. He had the right dope on it, but sometimes they switch them things, you know. Maybe

215

they was late getting it out. Anyway, we missed that big payroll. We got a lot of bonds and stuff out of it, Liberty Bonds. There was supposed to be forty thousand dollars in there, in the payroll, but we had got about, oh, several thousand in bonds. That was our third train robbery.

*From where I was, I was supposed to see that no railroad dick run up on them and that no policeman came up. If I seen one come in, I'd have to go meet him before he could realize what was going on, you know. But as it happened, the Good Lord had his arm around our neck for years and years. Nobody showed up, no policemen of any kind, no trouble. So we got the mail sacks, went to our car where we had it close by, and went off there to Kansas City.*

Billy had a market in Kansas City, some banker, some fence, and he could sell them bonds, so from there we went on back to Kansas City. I had a market with bankers from Tulsa to Kansas City to Memphis to Chicago. All the way up, I had a banker I could sell them bonds to. A Liberty Bond was just like a ten-dollar bill. It says, "Pay To Bearer." When they send them out from Washington, it's just like sending money out. They'd send them to these big places and they'd distribute them out, and they ain't even got the numbers, the serial numbers, on them. But if it's registered, you can't sell it. You just have to burn it up.

Anyway, we went on back to Kansas City and let Billy take the bonds and sell them. We split them up, but we never got a big lot out of it. Then we had a bank that we had marked in Gallatin, Missouri, the county seat bank. It was right north, forty or fifty miles north and a little east of Kansas City, in a town of about two thousand population. This was the same town that Jesse James once robbed.

*I don't know whether we even knew or not when we robbed the bank at Gallatin that Jesse James had been there, but it come out in the paper, you know, telling that it had been robbed and that the Jameses had robbed it before that. We sure weren't trying to do some of the same things Jesse and Frank James did. We went in there at night and blowed it open. They rode in on horseback in the daytime and stuck it up. When we get into a daylight robbery, we're getting out of our line. We figured the night was a lot safer. It wasn't so quick and it was a lot more trouble, but it was the safest way.*

So we went up there to Gallatin and drove a getaway from it. Went into the First National Bank, I did, and there set a little square safe back in the back, a little square Steel Pete. Then there was a new bank across the street on the other side. It had one of them round safes. So we went back to Kansas City and later we all went up there again. We still had Des Moines Billy with us, so I put him over behind that new bank. Doc and Joe covered the rest of the outside and I went in and blowed the vault door clear out through the window. There's a big hotel right up the street, and you could see people. It was one or two o'clock but you could still see people up there. The hotel was all lit up and everything. So they commenced to shooting. We had the wires cut, but they got guns and they was just shooting all around that bank everywhere.

Directly I put another shot or two in there. It was one of them little ones that just took about three shots. It was a rotten Steel Pete, an oldtimer, but they've got that rubber in there and the grease will just go back so far, so you had to shoot them a little at a time.

Then here come the old night watchman down there and Doc hollered at him. We was loaded with birdshot, you know. If we had to shoot a guy, we just used birdshot, to make him leave. So Doc hollered at him, "Get back there! Get back there!" And just as I run out the door, Doc cut down on him with some of that birdshot. He turned around and started back the other way. I was right here, so when he turned I run in behind him and grabbed him. Just jabbed my pistol in his side, took his and brought him on back down and give him to Doc.

*There was an awful lot of shooting, an awful lot of shooting. It was coming from the hotel right straight across the square on the other side, shooting over towards the bank. I was on up there a block and a half, so it wasn't anywhere close to me and it was too far for me to shoot a shotgun with #7 shot in it, so that left it all up to Doc. He was down there and he was doing a lot of shooting too, over thataway.*

When I went back in there, we sacked up the money. I had a sack to put the stuff in. We left the hard and only put the soft dough in.

So we got ready to go, and I said, "Come on," and I clucked to Des Moines Billy over there down the alley. "Cluck, Cluck. Cluck, Cluck." And he don't cluck back. We go over there, and there he lays deader than hell. One of them stray bullets had hit him right in the center of the side of the head.

*I didn't know it then, but the night marshal had come out of some building up there and Doc had caught him. Doc kept him up there until they got through, and when they finally did, they come on down where I was at and said, "Let's go." We went down the alley to where our other guy was and we signalled. We had a little signal we'd give, sort of "cluck cluck," and you can hear it a pretty long ways on a still night. When we did that, nobody answered.*

*Des Moines Billy, the guy that had give us the information on them two places, was supposed to be there. It was his own fault he come along. He wanted to come, and we let him come along, but he didn't know anything about this business. There was shooting coming from everywhere, and some stray bullet was bound to have hit him. Yeah. He was shot dead. Shot dead.*

I said, "We can't leave him here." Two of us drug him with us down the alley, and two went back up towards the bank so there ain't nobody could come any further. We finally got him out to where we had left the car, and we dumped him in it and took off out of there. We went on down there to where we had to cross a ferry, down below Kansas City, and when we got in that river bottom country, we took him out and put him in the brush. Then we took the ferry and went on into the city and made a deal with an undertaker that we knowed well. He took a coffin for him and we went with him that night and he put the guy in the coffin and everything and was to bury him and we never asked where. We give him five hundred dollars and paid for the coffin.

*I've thought about that, but it didn't bother me because we figured that was just an accident. It just happened. If he'd been up there where we were, this might have happened, but he was back down there where nobody would bother him. It had to be just a complete "freak" accident.*

Then we come on down to San Antone for the winter, where we stayed at the St. Anthony Hotel most of the time. Sometimes me and my wife would get an apartment. The boys would stay at them big hotels. We didn't go under our name. We went under another name, just any name. We all had to pay our rents you know, and everybody knowed his name anyway. I would use R.E. Baker one time, R.E. Bidwell one time, and R.E. something else the next, on account of my laundry number. I'd let the letters run with it natural, you see.

Well, we monkeyed around there in San Antone, then we went to Comfort to get that bank up there and they had just changed the old safe to a brand new round one. The old safe was sitting there, but we thought they had put the money in the new one, so we walked off and left it. You can't shoot them, see. And come to find out they had never changed the money! We could have blowed that safe.

So we missed that money. The money was in there that night but we didn't think it was because they had the brand new safe sitting there. Some guys come in there four or five years after that and robbed it. I read that when I was in the Leavenworth Penitentiary.

So we hung around San Antone and then we laid out on the New Braunfels job. Where we made a mistake in New Braunfels was not robbing the First National, because we'd have got twice as much money. But I had went down to the New Braunfels State Bank at the center of town, and it was such a lead pipe cinch—you walked in and right on the right was a guy setting in a chair. When you jumped over that little fence, you was in behind there with him.

After we pulled the robbery, I found out we'd have got twice as much out of the First National plumb up on the other side of town, and we could have robbed it and went out at the back door. It was a good getaway, but we'd got set on this other one, the New Braunfels State Bank. It looked so good, and it was right where we could just whip around the corner and take to the hills and we was out of town. I'd been over there at dinner time watching the place, and there was no customers in there hardly at twelve o'clock at all, except once in a while.

*New Braunfels was a pretty good sized town, you know, even then. We thought we'd stick up that bank there. It was about the only thing left around here.*

So we drove us a getaway—wc had us a big Buick— and spotted a place to hide out of town on the side roads away back in them woods there. Our route was to take out over that big hill by Landa Park. Then we would go about four miles out on that big road that cuts across to Johnson City, and duck off on a side road. There was a hill there all covered with thick cedar, thicker than the devil. So I says, "Here's where we'll go. We'll drive our car in these cedars and put the top back—you laid the top back in them days like a buggy—and we'd be careful not to break anything, just pull the limbs back, drive in there, and turn the limbs loose. Then you couldn't see anything from the road.

After checking out our getaway, we went back to San Antone to get ready for the job. We almost had some trouble there, though. There was an old bank robber that I knowed well, and him and his partner had got arrested when they tried to blow the safe over at Bandera. They had made bond and was hanging around San Antone and just as I was ready to get in the car and start out, he hollered, "Hey, Willis." Boy, I jumped in the car and we went thataway. The next time I seen him, he told me he knowed what we had done.

So we went on over to New Braunfels and got there just at twelve o'clock. I said, "Now at ten after twelve, we'll drive right up there. Joe, you stay under the wheel, and Doc you stay in the car too. Don't you get out unless somebody gives us trouble or if somebody comes in to the bank. Then you jump out and follow them on in."

*We drove right up and stopped in front of the bank. All of the cars was parked head in, and I wanted to do the same, but he said, "No, just park crossways here, because we won't be in there but a little bit." Facing toward San Antone. I pulled in behind the other cars, and me and Doc stayed in the car.*

*This was our first daytime robbery. We decided to do that because we had missed out on two or three around there and was getting tired of staying down there. We'd been in this country too long. Willis said, "Let's stick that one up and get some money and go on back. But it's a lot riskier." We knew it was a lot riskier, but we figured we could do it.*

*Doc stayed in the back seat and I sat in the front seat. So naturally Doc didn't do any looking around. He just looked right at the back of me. If they see two of us looking every which direction, they might get suspicious, but I could turn around and talk to him and I could see up thisaway and thataway and every which way.*

*After they was in there a little bit, why here comes some fellow from over towards the courthouse that was behind us. I told Doc, "When he gets closer, you've got to follow him in." Well, Doc took a little bit too much time getting out. It seems to me like he was tying a handkerchief around his neck so when he got in there he could pull it up. I think that's what made him just a little slow about getting out.*

*But anyway, just before he got to the fellow, he went in. So Doc started to run a little and dadgum, he had his pistol in a scabbard in his hip pocket, a pearl handle, silver plated, pretty pistol. And when he struck that trot to go in there his coat come up over that pistol and there was that pearl handle pistol sticking out and shining out like a new moon! You could see it all over town. Anybody that seen that, they'd have known what was happening, see. But that was the only man that showed up. He went in and then started to back out just as Doc got there and course, Doc taken him right on in, you know.*

Jess and I was going in. I told him, "We'll just go in at the door. You be a litle ahead of me. Be getting your money out of your pocket like to get some change for a twenty dollar bill." He walked up to the counter, and as he did, I leaped over this little fence and I was in behind with all of them. I had a big six-shooter on them, there was four or five people there. I talked real rough to them, "Lay down here!" like I was going to kill them any minute. That's the way to do it, and then you don't have to hurt nobody. Boy!, they dropped down and I lined them up heads to tails.

In my pocket I had me a thin sack, something like a flour sack. There stood the safe wide open and there was all that cash and Liberty Bonds stacked in there. I stuffed the cash in the sack endways and then a big row of Liberty Bonds. Then I come out. We hadn't been in there but a minute or two and just then an ex-Texas

Ranger that worked in the bank and had been out to lunch, he come back. As he opened the door, he seen what was happening. He started to turn, and as he did Doc pushed him in the back with a pistol and said, "Get on in there." We brought him around the counter and laid him down with the rest of them.

I gave the sack to Doc and said, "Here, go and get in the car." Then I went up to the cash register, but they didn't have hardly any money in the drawers. I pulled them out and got a handful or two. And there set a tin box. Now, I knowed about some old boys that had stuck up a bank in Houston a year or so before, and when they got ready to leave, there was a tin box and one of them picked it up. It turned out to have sixty thousand dollars in Liberty Bonds in it. So here was this tin box. It was locked, so I reached down and grabbed it. Then we come out and there was people going up and down the street, but they paid no attention to me. I stepped in the car and said, "Go on!"

*When he come out, he was carrying an old, long tin box. He come out the front door, walked to the car, got in the seat just as straight as he could come, and we taken off. That means he was in the passenger side. He had a handkerchief around his neck, but it was pulled down. I guess when he went in there he must have pulled it up or something.*

We didn't wear masks. I had a pair of dark glasses is all I had on. There's no sense in wearing a mask. Anybody can see you're robbing the bank, and I wasn't thinking about being recognized. I just didn't want them to catch me. I never did get recognized. Chances. You've got to take chances. If you go in there with masks, people see a masked man and they know you're robbing the bank. If you haven't got a mask on, just walk along like anybody else and act natural, they won't know what you're doing.

This robbery was in the daytime. That was different for us, but we was going to leave there anyway to go back to Chicago. We started out of town and there was a lot of guys working on the road, but we just went on out of town at about a forty or forty-five mile an hour clip.

*We went either one or two blocks. See, this other street, the one they was working on, had messed us up. We was going to go down the other way and then turn back, but we went thisaway then, one or two blocks, turned to the right, and I don't know whether we went one or two blocks, but then we turned right again and went straight back. We were all watching for our road. So there it was. We turned to the left and right out to the country. Not driving fast, just taking our time. You don't want people to notice you, and even after you get in the country, you don't drive fast, because you might have a wreck. Or you pass somebody and they say, "A car went by here a-flyin'," and they notice it. Especially back them days. Now you'd say it was some crazy kid, but you'd still notice it if it come by like that.*

I read later that they rang the bell, but we was long gone then. We never heard them. The people in the bank stayed there about fifteen minutes. I had told them to stay there or they'd get shot. Later somebody grabbed an old Winchester that they said hadn't been shot in twenty years and run out and shot up in the air and hollered "Robbery! Robbery!" but we was probably in our plant by the time they got stirring around.

So out we goes about four miles, then hit that little road and went about two miles more. I jumped out and opened the gate and we turned off the road and went in. I had a brush all ready and brushed the ground around there so they couldn't see where a car had went in. We run the car into that brush, put the top down, and whacked all them cedars and set in there. Then we got our money and we crossed the road and went on up a little, high hill. It was solid cedars, but we could peep around and see and hear. It was about two or three hundred yards down to the road, and we could see people going by.

*Nobody has any idea what you'd do if there had been a bunch of law run in there. Course, you know something would have happened. But you wouldn't have started to killing them, I'm telling you for sure. We'd have let them get between us and tried to catch them. With some of us on one side and some on the other, with shotguns you know, they'd have been pretty easy caught, I don't care who they were. People is people. And especially somebody like that. They know how dangerous a damned old shotgun is, where some farmer or city storekeeper might not realize it, yeah.*

As we set there, we counted our money and stuff and got that box open. It was full of nothing but the bank's notes. I didn't exactly know what I had. They was just papers. I'm sorry now that I didn't throw it out along the road the next day or two, so they could get them back, but I didn't. We took them out of the box and stuck them into an armadillo hole under one of them cedar trees. Then we put the money and everything else in the box.

We set there, and directly these cars was running by and we could see big hats and they'd meet another car and stop and talk. And directly here come the airplanes! So we run and got under them cedar bushes. They could have been within fifteen feet of us and couldn't have seen us. They flew all over that country, airplanes, all around. They'd come thisaway and run down the road, then cut across the country—I guess for two hours.

*We knew they couldn't be doing but one thing: looking for us. That was the first time an airplane was ever used to look for outlaws or bank robbers or anything down in this country.*

We had something there ready to eat, so we laid there until one or two o'clock that night, when we heard the last of the cars. One of us would sleep and another would listen to them people. Well, just before daylight, it was just peeping daylight, we come out of there and cut across on a little road until we hit the New Braunfels to San Antone main road. When we hit the first streetcar line I got out, then they went a little farther and Doc got out, a little farther and Jess got out, and Joe took the car and planted it. We had stole it.

*We almost never used a stolen car unless we was just going to go do something right on the spur of the moment. Then we'd go out and get one. But we did have stolen license plates that we'd put on there.*

We had already stopped and planted the money and stuff. It was all in the tin box and we didn't want to take it into town with us. In case we got caught, or if anything happened, we wouldn't have it with us. The next night we planned to come back and get it.

I went on home then. My wife had just got out of the hospital. She had her back burned. Clothes caught on fire from a small heater, and burned her back and she liked to have lost her life. If I hadn't been standing right by the side of her, she would have burned up. I was standing right to her side with a milk bottle just fixing to walk out of the house, and her clothes flamed up. I reached up and got her at the neck and ripped everything off her at once. But it had burned her back pretty good, and then she monkeyed around and gangrene set up in it. But she had got better and was in shape to travel. Since we knowed we was going to get this New Braunfels bank, we had moved to a little apartment and rented it for just a week. When the week was up, I could go and get the box, see.

So I went out and got the money and bonds and things and put them in her suitcase. Then she caught the Southern Pacific train out of there to New Orleans. I didn't go with her; I was riding in another car. She got off there and so did I, and when she went to a restaurant to eat, I moved over and sat down and talked to her. That's the way we got together. Then we got us an Illinois Central passenger train out of there to Chicago that night.

We got about twenty thousand in cash and eighty thousand in Liberty Bonds and Victory Bonds. There was about twenty-five thousand in road bonds in there too, but we burned them up, since they wasn't good for anything. That gave us just about a hundred thousand all together. The papers said there was more than that taken, but that's all we got. If they lost more than that, then it was the employees or somebody else at the bank that took it. They do that, you know. When there's been a robbery, they can take cash and bonds and gold out of there themselves and say it was taken in the robbery.

In Chicago I had a place for us to stay, and I went to peddling the bonds. I had told the others to get rid of the car and come up there one at a time. Whoever found the car never knowed it was the one used in the New Braunfels robbery. About a week after the robbery, they all come up to meet me. I had turned all the bonds into cash, and I give everybody his money. My wife had a safe deposit box with my money and she always kept Joe's too.

I don't think we stayed there but about three or four days, and we headed for Denver. Two of us always goes ahead and the other two come after. We was after the bank in Lafayette, about twenty or twenty-five miles north of Denver. It was a coal mining town, and if we had got there two years sooner, we would have got a barrel of money by hitting it at payday. But they had mined the coal all out and had quit, so there wasn't much business around then. There was two banks that had consolidated, and both safes was in the same building.

My wife and I was staying in an apartment in Denver, and I had us a getaway drove and everything. Then the other two came and they stayed at the hotels. We got all

*Boerne Bank, now an antique store*

ready to go one night, and as we was out on the street at Lafayette, we knowed they had a nighthack. We hid in an old barn and watched him flash his light this way and that. He was an old Wop, an Italian. So I said to Jess, "Now, when he gets right here and shines that other way, you just step out and grab him and I'll get the gun on him." When he got close to us, Jess clamped him and you never heard a man holler so! Italian was what he was yelling. He thought some of them other Wops had him and was going to kill him. I kept telling him, "Hush up! We aren't going to hurt you. Hush up!" Well, it was two minutes, I guess, before he calmed down and listened. I told him, "Old man, we aren't going to hurt you. We're going to rob this bank. We just want to hold you until we're done."

"I don't give a damn if you rob the bank," he said, so we went over and I turned him over to somebody, Doc or Joe. Me and the other one, probably Jess, went in at the back, then I blowed the door off the vault and there sat both safes, Steel Petes.

*Double trouble, in other words. You get this one and then if everything is going smooth, you get the other one. But I swear I don't see why we didn't wake everybody up in Denver [laughs]. We was there for a couple of hours, a couple of hours! and nobody come down there. But we could hear them talking all around.*

So I started in on the first one that I had seen and blowed it, and as it turned out, it had all the money and bonds in it, but I didn't know that. So I sacked up what was there, then turned around and went to work on the other one. When I blowed the last door off, there was probably ten thousand in them brand new silver dollars, the first ones that was ever made in the Denver mint in 1921 or 1922. They poured out under my feet until I was knee deep when I swung the door back. I reached down for a handful of them and put them in my pocket. I guess I've got a couple of them today.

We had to leave all that. It was so heavy it would have taken a mule to haul them all, besides the other sacks setting there on the floor.

Joe, who was that across the street when a piece of steel blowed off and tore a corner off the building out there? Was it Doc?

*Yeah, Doc. You had told him to go across the street, but he knew better than that. He went down the street. It didn't hit him, but he hollered, "Hey..."*

He was behind the building. It wouldn't have hit him.

*Well, that's what he always said.*

That was the last shot. When we come out with the sacks, the town was lit up all over, but very few people ever stirred. We walked to our car about a half a mile out on a side road and got on out of there. We circled way around east, around Denver and come in the other way. We had it fixed so that we'd come in to where there was a streetcar and we strung out that way. One could get off, then farther along another could get off, like we did in San Antone.

*We were staying in Denver while we were up there doing that and one day I was in Denver there and going up the street, people just like that, you know, crowded, down in the picture show district, and by gosh! I walked face to face with a little old girl who worked in the hotel in Omaha where we'd stayed before we'd gone to Denver. When we'd got arrested over there in Omaha. She recognized me for sure, and she knew we'd been arrested over there in Omaha too. Couldn't keep from knowing it. Hell, it was in the paper that big! But she didn't run and tell anybody. She was staying up there someplace. I went up there and visited her all of one evening. Never have seen her again until this day, no more.*

# 17

## BLACK GOLD (1923)

**W**hile we was staying around Denver, I picked up a paper that said an oil well gusher had come in, the Dalton Well, twelve miles northwest of Mineral Wells, Texas, making twenty-four hundred barrels of high gravity oil a day, oil that you could burn in a Ford car. I told Joe, "I've always wanted to get in on the ground floor of one of them oil booms. This is it! That well has just come in, and it's a wildcat well, way out there by itself."

> "I've always wanted to get in on the ground floor of one of them oil booms. This is it!"

So we went from Denver, and in five or six days, I was down there. I had gone by Fort Worth where I had a nephew run some kind of delivery service. Had a pretty good education, and I said, "Come and go over with us to Mineral Wells. I'm going to buy some oil leases." And he come with us. Joe, did you come along, or did you go to Kansas City or Tulsa?

*I was over there once or twice, but I didn't stay. The one at Mineral Wells, I went and looked at. It looked like a good lease, but I would have let the man, when he offered me a half interest in the lease to drill a well on it, I'd a-made a deal with him right there and drilled on it. We'd have come out on it thataway.*

So out I go nosing around Mineral Wells, and just half a mile south of this well I got me eighty acres at two hundred an acre. That was cheap! I could have sold my lease for five hundred an acre right then, but it just looked like a lead pipe cinch. It was flat ground from my lease up the creek to the Dalton Well.

*These leases cost so much an acre. I don't know for sure how much these cost, but Willis went down there, him and one of his nephews, and they chased an awful lot of girls. I know it cost me fifteen thousand dollars for the leases we had at Mineral Wells. And that was expense besides what they was supposed to be paying for their own eating. But they probably charged the hotel bill to me, and the girls and all, as far as that's concerned, because that was too much. Anyway, he says, "No, no, no, there wasn't nothing like that," but I know very well what it was.*

After we had been there two or three weeks, nothing was happening so we went to Spokane, Washington, after a bank out there. We had plenty of money left from New Braunfels, and we had got that bank at Lafayette, Colorado, but this was our business. If you had a chance to make ten thousand dollars over here today and a chance to make another ten over there tomorrow, wouldn't you go ahead and make it?

*I had my stake up to ten thousand dollars lots of times, way up there, and Willis blowed it out at Mineral Wells and he blowed it again down at Smackover. I really don't think I stayed with it because it was "fun," though. No. It was a brother deal. That was the whole thing. I'm sure as I'm a-sittin' here if I'd been with somebody else, I'd have quit a long time before that. But this was a brother deal, all of us around together. I'm the youngest and they was older.*

*They didn't try to keep me in, but nobody ever told me I'd better quit and go do this or that because you've got some money now. Nobody never done that. I had good resolutions there two or three times, especially in the first years 'cause I had a lot better time down here. I didn't have as much money, but I always had plenty to spend. I broke horses and I was having a good time all the time. You can look back and see my record where I growed up and all, have you ever seen where I was in jail? In all of my coming up a kid, until I went with Willis, did I ever tell you that I ever stoled anything or my friends did, or that I was ever in trouble?*

*Well, see the difference in the nature of us? That's all Willis had from the time he was ten years old. But I was enjoying myself doing what I was doing. When I was a kid growing up, what I wanted to be was a cowboy, a bronc rider like my brother Jess. And Tull was a good rider too, but everybody talked about Jess all over the country. That's what I wanted to be. Then I'd got up to where I was "it" and Jess'd quit riding. He carried the bankroll and rode around in a car. I rode all them pitching horses and he drove me from one town to another. He could still ride pretty good, but he had got up to where he was about thirty-five years old and he shied off from that. He didn't want to ride anymore, and that throwed it all off on me. That suited him. "Here, old so-and-so brought this horse in awhile ago. Saddle him up and see what he'll do." He didn't saddle him up. He was in that stripped-down red Ford that we had, and he was gone! He was a business agent.*

*I think Jess never really cared about the robbing. Here was our "spark plug," Willis. That's all he ever studied about and thought about in our lifetime.*

*I don't think any of us ever got any "kick" out of it. And I'm sure I was kind of following the leader. I was nineteen years old and I wanted some money. But after I got some, I didn't know what to do with it. Fooled around and let Willis have it, then made some more and let him talk me into that oil deal again. He tried to get Doc to go in with him too, but Doc wouldn't do it. Said, "Hell, no. I'll spend my own money." And he did. To tell you the truth, I only agreed to let him have six thousand. But he had my money. His wife had a safe deposit box and she had my money in there and hell, he took it all!*

Well, that's the way we was, but we decided it was summer time and we wouldn't rob anything. We couldn't find anything to suit us. So we got in the car and turned back across the Snake River south, then down by Idaho Falls, then to Salt Lake. We stayed there for three or four days or a week, then cut back and come across to Cheyenne, and on to Denver.

*We didn't usually rob banks in the summer. It was a kind of "off time" for me. I stayed around Kansas City a couple of years in the summer time chasing the manicurists and waitresses and department store help. Kreske's and Woolworth's and all of them, the help in them days was just solid girls. Then if I'd say something about going home, Willis would say, "Oh, you better not be going there and spending money. You'll get us all in trouble." That was Willis. "Don't go off down there. Better stay here. It won't be long until we'll be doing something." "Here" might be in Kansas City or Tulsa or whatnot. But I stayed around Kansas City more than any of them because it was a bigger town. You never really got acquainted with anybody there.*

*What I was doing then was saying I was fresh off the farm down there in Oklahoma and they'd got oil on my Daddy's farm. I was just off up there running around a little. That was my story. That would explain why I had money, see. We had an oilfield on our old farm down there.*

From Denver my wife and I caught the train for Mineral Wells. When I met my nephew, he said there was another twenty acre lease available right east of the Dalton Well. So I bought that too. Stayed there until July or August while they drilled that offset, and by God, it come in dry! Before that I could have got over twice what I had in them leases, but goddamn, it just looked like a cinch for a million dollars out of that lease! They drilled seventeen dry holes all around that well and never got another gallon of oil.

It was about that time that Smackover had blowed in, them big wells over there, so off I go to Smackover, Arkansas. That over there at Mineral Wells was done

dead, and I'd blowed around thirty thousand dollars or
more when I was there. So I got to Smackover and in the
bottoms there they was bringing them big wells in, gushers, gushers, gushers.

*He went down to Smackover, and he sure "smack-
overed," because he smacked all my money over. God
dawg.*

*Later on, after all this, I was in the oil business myself.
I mean legitimate business in later years, buying and
selling leases. Of course, when Willis took my money and
went to Smackover, I was in the oil business too, very much
in the oil business. Kind of got me sour on the oil business.*

*But that was an honest oil strike down there, one of
the biggest fields in the country at that time. East Texas
and Oklahoma City was the only places bigger than it.
Course, in later years in New Mexico and West Texas there
was hundreds of miles solid with oil fields. So that wasn't
any kind of a "hustle" Willis was in on. Hell, if anything,
it was somebody else swindling him. He must have got
sold some bad leases because it didn't pay out on any of
them.*

I got in there right quick and got me three or four
acres right down in that bottom. I got a man and drilled
me a well, and we was half way down, about twelve
hundred feet, when it began to rain. They was getting oil
at about two thousand feet. But it was the fall of the year,
and it rained and rained and rained, and water stayed
up on my derrick six feet deep. For five or six months we
couldn't drill. Everybody had leases all around us, and
gas is what makes the oil flow. In that length of time,
they'd drilled so many wells around there, the gas pressure was down. I drilled it in finally, and it was an oil
well, but oil had went down to fifty cents a barrel. I could
have pumped two or three hundred barrels a day out of
it, but it cost several thousand to drill it and put in the
tanks and all. Since it wasn't worth but fifty cents, I just
let it set there.

*That driller stalled along for six months and then the river got up and flooded the country, and something else and something else. It would have cost about five thousand dollars to put a pump on it. We could still have come out on it if we'd have went ahead and put a pump on it, but Willis didn't want nothing like that. He wanted a gusher. So he went somewhere else and bought another one.*

*I say it cost us seventy-five hundred apiece at Mineral Wells. He says, no, it didn't cost us that much. But it cost us all we had, practically. Then he went down to Smackover, and he says he spent fifteen thousand of mine, but I say he spent seventeen thousand five hundred. And he spent all of his—more money than that. So whatever it was it cost us, he spent all we had but a few hundred dollars or a thousand. Enough to go somewhere else and "refinance" ourselves [laughs].*

It cost me twelve thousand to drill that well, and I paid another fifteen thousand for the lease. In the meantime, after I had started to drill the well, I had went up to Little Rock and opened up an oil company. J.W. Wilson's Smackover Interests. Wilson was the name I was going by. It was a corporation. Everybody does that, you know, adds "corporation" to it. Joe and I had an office in a building there, with six or eight rooms, and I got in the newspapers and went to advertising. I was selling stock in my well over there. But there had been so many in there ahead of me that I couldn't compete. I stayed with the office from November until the next June, I guess, but I put more money into it than I ever did sell stock.

In May I missed another chance. They was drilling the big Burton Well, and they had it down twenty-two hundred feet and it was dry, where every other well had come in at that depth. So a guy called me up from Pine Bluff and he said, "I'll trade you half interest in the Burton Well, and I'll take stock in your company."

I said, "You come on over and we'll talk." But he didn't. And I didn't go over there. Then it wasn't but about two or three weeks after that they decided to drill a little deeper and after another hundred feet or so, it blowed in twenty thousand barrels. So I missed that.

*When the man offered to drill on it for half interest, that's when he should have let it go. Or even earlier, when he was offered a pretty good profit on it.*

All right I run over there and got me a lease right north of Burton, ten acres, and I paid, oh, around ten thousand for it. Rounded me up a crew and set to drilling. Spent eighteen thousand on that, and it was dry. I'd bought leases all around in that country, me and a guy I had working for me. We'd send papers to this person and that person and we'd get them to sign that they'd give us a lease to drill in some length of time. I don't even know how many leases I had. Another big well had come in right close to the Burton, about four hundred yards from one another, but wouldn't you know, there was never no more oil out of that area than them two wells. People drilled all over there, but the oil was just in spots. So that's the luck I had there.

Joe and me was both in on it. I spent my money and his money. He just turned it over to me. Jess and Doc, hell, they blowed their money. I blowed mine and Joe's trying to make some more, and they blowed theirs not trying to make nothing. They drank and gambled and done everything else. High-played, just throwed it away.

Well, about the first of June, a Jew out of Philadalphia name of J.G. Burns come over to talk to me. He had got a charter for a bank in Little Rock and he says, "You ain't doing nothing with this oil company, why don't we pro- mote this?" He had a big real estate business in Phila- delphia, but he had two brothers that was running it and he'd come down to Arkansas. "I've got some people connected up there in Canada, and through a big oil company there we've promoted a lot of people." Sir

Winston Hughes, I think he said it was, from England.
So him and me got together and began to fix it all up. We
drawed up a regular oil company corporation and worked
in a few big people on it. We got the ex-governor, old man
Hays there in Little Rock, and the ex-senator . . . what
was his name, Joe?

*I guess I've forgot.*

Well, old Hays was the governor and the other one
was an ex-senator. Anyway, we got them into the company and nobody knows who I am, see. I'm J.W. Wilson.
We made Governor Hays president of the company and
the senator vice-president, and I was secretary-treasurer.
I'm the man who was to handle the money [laughs].
Burns and I took the stock then and went to New York
City and he set up a three million share company. We
had priced the stock at one dollar a share. Burns knowed
everybody on the New York Stock Exchange, and we went
up there and registered the company. It wasn't hard to
do in them days, especially with being a big Philadelphia
real estate man who worked with lots and lots of money.
Wilson's Smackover Interests, was the name of the company.

When we was up in the East, he took me around and
introduced me as J.W. Wilson, and everybody knowed I
was okay because J.G. Burns was a big broker and real
estate man. I stayed up there about a week, and he give
me a chauffeur and his special-made Packard car that
had cost him twelve thousand dollars. Every piece on it
was stainless steel. Boy! I was stepping high.

It took him a week or ten days to register that stock,
and before we got back to Little Rock, all them post office
inspectors come in on them promoters for mail fraud, you
see. They arrested people at Smackover and all over that
country for advertising that they had all kinds of stuff
when they had nothing.

Of course I had something, but it didn't matter. I run.
I just left everything with Burns and Governor Hays and

the ex-senator, and me and my wife got our suitcases and things and we took out. See, if they went to investigate me, they're going to find out I'm not J.W. Wilson. I'm Skinny Newton! That blowed up mine and his deal in New York City. My plan was that I would be the man that would handle all that dough, and what I would do is put Joe out buying cheap leases all around over Arkansas. As treasurer of the company, I'm going to pay a big price for them and we could just weed that money out as we go, all of it we want or the biggest part of it. Then we'd disappear. They didn't know who we was. So what got blowed up there was millions and millions in our hands. We just had to walk off and leave it.

If I hadn't been in the Walls before I wouldn't have run, because I had more of my money in the deal than I had the stockholders'. When we got caught for the train robbery, I asked one of the post office inspectors, "Say, did you inspect J.W. Wilson's Smackover Interests in Arkansas?"

"It was all right," he said. "He had spent more of his own money than he took in stock." Then I told them that I'd been Wilson [laughs]. In everything we done down there that had to do with the oil business, we hadn't advertised any lies that amounted to anything. And me and Joe had plenty of our own money in the deal that showed we was interested in it. I guess all my life the things I should have done, I didn't, and the things I shouldn't have done I did. Every time, that was what hit me.

We went to Chicago, me and my wife. And then on up to Toronto, Canada. I had lost over a hundred thousand on the oil deals and had only about four or five thousand left. Enough to operate, to get me where I wanted to go, but I had to set out again to get me some money. We kept it in cash in a lock box. We never deposited anything in a savings account or in checking. We wasn't that kind of people. We had cash, just cash. For our day to day expenses, why, we carried six-seven hundred, or maybe a thousand dollars in our pockets all

the time.  And we wasn't afraid of being robbed either.
No, sir.  That was *our* game.  So when we went on a trip,
the four or five of us, we had probably between three to
five thousand in our pockets.

If you was picked up by the police, the money
wouldn't make no difference.  If their suspicions was up
anyway, they'd arrest us and say, "I got you for vagrancy,"
or something.  So we carried money for when they got us.
It'd give us something to work with.  They wanted that
money.  They didn't want us.  You could always make a
deal with them.  They'd say, "I'll tell you who can get you
out."  Then we'd deal with that man, but of course the
money was going to them policemen, and then they'd
have to give the man they dealt with some of it.  And they
had them a judge that was fixed, so they could take you
in front of him and he'd dismiss the case.  Then he'd get
a little too.  Nine out of ten you could make a deal with.
Nine out of ten.  They'd arrest us and they had nothing
on us.  Just on suspicion or something.   And a lot of
them would take it today too, if they've got the opportunity.  They maybe had a better chance to get away with
it them days than now.  I think it was easier.  Everything
was easier.

# 18

## TORONTO CURRENCY CLEARING HOUSE (July 1923)

> "Every night all the money went into this clearing house . . . . Guys going here and there on the streets with bags . . . . I could hardly believe my eyes . . . so I sent for the boys. . . ."

After losing out on the oil I went to Chicago and then on to Toronto, looking for something to make money out of. Down in the street in Toronto one day, two guys passed me carrying a big heavy bag, one on each side. I looked across and there was two more going down that-away carrying a big heavy bag. It was just after eight o'clock in the morning. So I watched them. One pair went into a bank and so did that other pair. The next morning I went further up the way they had come from, and there was a big, old-time brick building that they went into and went up the stairs. While I stood there, I think there must have been fifteen of them come out at once carrying bags of money, two to the bag. A half dozen of them would be together for three or four blocks, then they'd begin to split up. This was right down in the heart of Toronto in the financial district, and there was banks all over. In them days every bank had its own money, with its own name on it: Toronto Bank, Canadian Bank of Commerce and so on. I know there was eight or ten different banks. And every night all that money went into this clearing house where they separated it. Then in the morning, each bank sent and got its currency back.

That seemed like the silliest thing I ever heard of, but that was how they done it. They've quit that now. I got to trailing them, and I tell you I could hardly believe my eyes. Guys going here and there on the streets with bags that some of them could hardly carry!

So I sent for the boys, and when they got there we watched it and watched it. It looked real easy, but we wanted to give things a chance to settle down so we drove up to Montreal to look at the town. While we was there I bought an automatic shotgun, on purpose to stick up these messengers. When we come back down, I sawed six or eight inches off of it so it would be short and I could handle it easy.

*So I came up to Canada on the train. The other three guys were already there. Willis had gone uptown one morning, and he seen all these people with these handbags coming from some buildings across the street and going this way and that way and scattering and he seen some of them heading for a bank. We watched it and boy!, they come across there with little handbags full, and little briefcases and some of them with big handbags. We didn't know what it was, but we finally decided that whatever it was, there was a lot of it. There was a guard with each two guys, following right along behind them.*

They all had pistols, them little short bulldog pistols that wouldn't shoot nothing. Later when we robbed them, they shot and hit the back of our car two or three times and just made dents in it.

*We figured it had to be money, because if it was checks they wouldn't have had guards. When we figured it must be money, we tried to think of a way to get it.*

Then we got a break. One day when we was on the street, we seen an old boy park his car and just jump out of it. It was a Big Six Studebaker, just what we always used when we was robbing banks. The keys was in it so

I stepped in and drove it off. We had a garage already rented to put it in, four, five, six blocks away.

We had it planned so that we'd pull out right behind the messengers after they'd crossed in front of the car. So here they come. I got in front and Joe drove the car, Jess and Doc was in the back. As they got in front of me I had that shotgun under my coat, and just as I got out of the car I thought I'd better grab my pistol too. It was laying in the front and I had started to leave it. I stuck it in my coat pocket with the barrel up. It was a long barrel.

*We were alongside a curb and they were going to come walking across in front of us, and the one we had decided to get was going to go straight down ahead of us and we was going to pull beside them and step out and grab the money. Well, Willis said, "They're going to come pretty soon. We're going to go around the corner and get them all." When Willis says we'll get "them all," that means ten, maybe twelve couriers. There was a lot of them, anyway, with five or six guards.*

When the bags come across in front of me, I come out with that shotgun and I says, "Give me that bag!"

But they wouldn't give it up. I turned and over there was a telephone pole and I blammed! that post full of shot. I thought that would scare them, but it didn't. One turned to run and I reached over and got ahold of the bag, then one of them jumped on me. I went to shoot the gun at his feet and it wouldn't work! I pulled and pulled at the bolt and and it was hung up somehow. Brand new gun.

I've got this pistol in my pocket, though, and a bank messenger hanging on my back. The other one was standing there watching him. As I pulled the pistol out, the hammer brought the inside lining of my pocket up and I had to let go of the shotgun with my other hand to get the lining of my coat free. I had turned loose of the shotgun and now he had it. When I got my pistol, I

dropped back and turned it on him. "Drop that gun!" I
hollered at him, but he wouldn't. He just come right at
me. He started to come up with my shotgun, and I didn't
know if it would shoot or not. It might have, so I shot
him high up on the right side and he dropped the
shotgun. I could have killed him dead, but I didn't want
to kill nobody.

*Willis jumped out and got right in between them
couriers and the guards! The guards was at his back and
the guys carrying the bag that he wants is in front of him!
I don't know what the hell he done that for, but he did.*

Now I could grab that bag, and as I did I saw that Doc
was tussling with another messenger that had a big bag
and wouldn't give it up either. He was coming out with
his gun and Doc had to shoot him, but he didn't shoot
to kill him. Just shot to hurt him. I went around the car
and the other messengers had run back down the alley
with three or four of them bags. Jess had been a little
slow coming up himself, and when he got there, he had
to run to help Doc. Well, that let them other messengers
go.

*So I'm supposed to not leave the car, sit in the car and
keep that safe. So here come a guard alongside me and
he saw what was happening. He had a shotgun. I could
see that. I don't know where the other guards are by this
time. Everything had gotten real busy. Every guy in our
bunch has got their own guard to take care of. This one
occupied me. That was all I had on my mind.*
*Anyway, Willis got out right in front of the damn guard.
He was a tall, slim boy. I don't know how old he was, but
anyway, as old as I was, I guess, or maybe older. I'm
twenty-two then. Anyway, he stuck his pistol straight up
and went to shooting, "Pow! Pow! Pow!" and I taken a shot
right over at the wall, you know. I thought if I shoot the
brick wall I might attract his attention. But you know, he
didn't pay that a damn bit of mind! He just kept shooting*

*Joe Newton in his Studebaker Special 6 in 1921*

*that until he got his gun empty. Then he stood there a little bit—I don't guess he had any more shells—and then he run. He went down about a quarter or a half a block and stopped and was a-watchin'.*

I threw my bag into the car where Joe was sitting, and just then an old sedan come up that they was carrying money in, and they run right at me. On the passenger side was a guy with a pistol, and he had run the window down apiece and as he went to bring his gun over the window at me, I flipped mine up and shot right through the door. I hit him in the groin and his door flew open and his pistol rolled out at my feet and he scooted out.

*I don't know whether he was pointing at Willis or pointing at me, but Willis had shot him and he rolled out there and his pistol slid off thataway. Later we read that that fellow Willis shot was another bank guard. He had all of his money in the car there, and he said he* should *have been shot for coming back. He was already at his bank with his money and he heard the shooting and he come back and brought all of his money. He said, "I should have been shot for being that crazy."*

By now Doc and Jess had come over with that bag they was after and the other messengers was gone. We only got them two bags.

*Doc got one bag away from a guy, and Willis got one bag. That was all. Just two. Doc got sixty-eight thousand dollars in his, and Willis got twelve thousand. Jess didn't get anything. We should have got $200,000, but you can't get them all. They're going to start running in every direction and you can't get them all.*

We'd hardly noticed it until then, but there was people upstairs that had seen everything and heard everything, and they was throwing chairs, boxes, everything they could find out of the office right down into the middle of us.

"Get in the car and let's go," I told Jess and Doc. They did, and I got in the front.

*As we went by this old boy that had been shooting straight up, well, here the darn sonofagun taken after us afoot. He was going to run us down, stay with us and see where we went. And he stayed close too. We had to turn, there was a lot of traffic and we couldn't go too fast, you know. And he could run along and stay up with us running down the sidewalk. Well, I didn't know what to do, and all at once he was catching up with us a little. He'd have been hollering at us the next thing, and there was a big old plate glass window there, about an inch thick, with some name on it. I waited until he got right at that thing and I shot that glass right in the center and it splattered glass everywhere, some of it back at him and some down at his feet, and he stopped right there. That was the last I seen of him.*

How we ever got away, I don't know. Then we hit a main street going to the right. I said, "Turn right in there," and we got room to cut in. We looked back and they was coming after us in cars trying to shoot, but two or three cars had got between us and them.

We was coming up on the main street and they had a policeman standing there directing traffic. Just as we run up there and I was fixing to jump out and throw my pistol down on him, he stuck out his hand to stop the other cars and told us to come on!

When we looked back, boy!, that traffic was thick, and since the policeman didn't know what had happened back there, he turned the traffic the other way and that stopped them in the cars behind us. I saw that when I looked back.

About two blocks farther on we went right, and at the next main street there was two policemen directing traffic. It wasn't so heavy there, and Joe said, "Stop?"

"No. When you get there, don't go, but pull out on the left of him and I'll holler at him."

We got there and Joe pulls out by the man, and as he does I waved my arm at him, you know? And he let us go on around him! We went down that road, made one turn, got out of sight of them, and then we was going west. After we was out of their sight, we turned and run our car into that garage. They thought we had gone the other way. Then we got out and scattered.

*Doc and me, we went down to the picture show. It was open already so we just sat in there two or three hours and then went back to the hotel. I suppose they had a police dragnet out then, but we was staying at the best hotel there and as far as anybody knew, we was just tourists. We had separate rooms for everybody. They never made any connection with us.*

I had a car parked near there because I'd just come up that morning from Hamilton where they had horse races. My wife was staying there in the hotel, so I got into my car and drove back over there. And you talk about excitement! There was gangs of people everywhere and all you could hear was about that robbery. It nearly made my hair stand on my head. But none of them guards was dead, you see.

I've only been boogered two times in my life. Once was there in Toronto, and the other happened in a melon patch when I was a kid. Those times I was really scared. Felt the same both times. First time we boys was standing in town in Cisco one night and a bunch of boys was talking. There was a grown guy there, Rob Weddington, and another old boy we called Big Ears. They said they was going to a watermelon patch. They got eight or maybe ten of us kids, and one of them was a great big guy, Tom Nashman. Tom was an eighteen or nineteen year old. We didn't know it, but them other older fellows had a trick set up and didn't tell me about it. They planted Rob Weddington out there in the patch before we went, and it was just getting good dark. There was a real tight old wire fence around the field. We crawled through it and I was the head man. If I ever done anything, I was behind nobody. So I was right beside Big Ears. We got us a nice melon and I went thump! thump! thump! and just then bloom! Rob Weddington let go with a shotgun straight up. And, boy!, I leaped and Big Ears hollered, "Get away, boys! I'm killed!" and blooey! the gun went again. By the third time it fired, I was plumb to that fence and I hit it and it throwed me back about six feet. And I hit it again and I could hear that fence screeching, like when cattle run into it! [laughs]. We all of us hit it, tore our clothes off and cut ourselves up with that wire, and finally I got through and there was old Tom Nashman sitting there behind a bush and there was another shot and Tom said, "Oh, my God, they've killed another," and he took off for town to get a doctor. By this time Big Ears come walking over and asked where was Tom. I said he had gone to town for a doctor, and he said, "Oh, somebody catch him and tell him to come back." And then it come out what it was.

But you talk about scared! Oh! The next day I went over there to get me a melon, and when I got in sight of that fence, I took a "buck-acher." I just shook and shook, I was so scared. And I never got another watermelon out of that patch that year. Never could go in there again.

After that I never was scared in my life until up in Toronto on that bank messenger holdup. And it wasn't until two days afterward that I got to thinking about it—I can wake up at night sometimes and that will hit my mind and make me nervous yet. How near we escaped with our lives! It was a miracle, just a miracle. I can get scared about it yet. Get nervous. Will all my life. They'd have stomped us to pieces if they'd got us. Put us to a telephone post right there and hung us, but it was as slick and smooth as you ever seen in your life. Nothing went wrong, after we got in that car and started.

We went back into town right away and seen nobody was dead. I wasn't afraid of being recognized because there was just too many people. They wouldn't ever recognize you. Down at the hotel over at Hamilton there was a big blackboard where messages come in, and it said that robbers had got so-and-so much money, and that there was four of them and one was captured. Well, she was coming to pieces when I walked in.

"Oh, Willis," she said. "I knowed it was you. I was sure it was you."

"What?"

"One of the robbers was captured. Who was it?" And when I said nobody, well, my God! if you ever seen a happy woman, she was a happy woman.

I stayed in Hamilton that day, but the others, they walked all around up in Toronto. Went to movies and everything else. To tell the truth, I don't see how we kept from getting arrested. Anyway, the next day we went back and got the car—it still had the money in it—and we had eighty-four thousand dollars.

249

That robbery was July 24, 1923. We had left the
money bags in the car, so now we went and got it and
went way out in the country, that old sandy country,
about thirty miles. We took a spade and went down into
that sand and raked the leaves back good and dug a hole
and buried most of the money. Covered it up nice and
good.

Then we come back to Toronto and I went and got my
wife the next day and brought her to Toronto just in time
to put her on the train to Chicago. After she was gone, I
discovered that I had left my pistol in her hand bag. Well,
boy!, if you've seen a sick, scared old man, it was me,
because they was going to search her going out. But she
had done discovered it, and she said that she just put it
under some little stuff and put her douche bag on top of
it. When the man went to dig down there, he seen that
and he wouldn't go any further. So he just let it go.

The next day we got us some ducking material that
goes around your body to brace it. Then we took that
money in layers and sewed it all around there. I think
we took about five thousand apiece. Just buckled it on,
you know, and there you was. It was like a vest. We went
and caught a ferry going over to Niagra Falls. That was
another bad thing we done. We all went on the same
ferry, which we shouldn't have done. We should have
scattered out, some of us walked across the bridge over
there.

So we went over to Niagra Falls and caught the train
to Chicago. The first thing I did, I went to the hotel where
I had told my wife to go and there she is, sitting in the
lobby! And you talk about a tickled old man, I was it.
She told me then how she'd seen the gun and how she
fixed it.

We stayed there three or four days, and then in about
a week we went back to Toronto and dug up the money.
We planted it all under the cushions of the car where the
springs is at and drove over to Niagra Falls. I got out
before the car come up for inspection and walked across.
I was just about twenty or thirty feet up on the bridge

and I sauntered along so I could see if anything happened. A man asked the guy driving some questions, then waved he can go right on. We drove out with that money, and in Niagra Falls we put it in one bag and I took it and caught the train to Chicago.

We knowed a fence there that could turn this into American money if you give him ten cents on the dollar. I went and found the guy and he said we had to take it to Detroit. So me and him went to Detroit and he turned it all for me to somebody he knew there. We got shed of all of it.

We monkeyed around awhile and that job had been as easy as snap, so we decided a month or two later that we'd go back up to Toronto and see how everything looked. We should have went just one at a time, but we all went together. That was another mistake. We went up to see what they had done about carrying that money, if they was still carrying it the same way. And when we got there, boy!, there was men on horses, automobiles, machine guns! [laughs]. All around that clearance house up there and down them alleys everywhere they went. I never seen such a thing! Well, boy!, that put the fear of Christ in us. They was all carrying shotguns. Before, you couldn't tell they had a gun. They just had them little old pistols. We would have robbed it a second time if it'd been alright. But it was terrible.

So we went back to Chicago then, and later me and Jess went up to Winnipeg to see what was up there. They've got the same kind of place there, a clearance house. When we got there it was just the same thing. They was riding horses and watching us, watching everybody, and they had machine guns, shotguns, and everything else! And I think it was because of what we'd done in Toronto.

We just stayed around Winnipeg a little bit. We was there right when President Harding died, and Pancho Villa got killed about the same time. Jess was sitting in a barber shop and he was talking to some barber. Of course they knowed from your voice you was from the

States. The barber says, "You've lost two great men this month, just a little while apart, down in the States."

Jess says, "Who?"

He says, "President Harding and Pancho Villa!" I'll be damned! Two great men: President Harding and Pancho Villa! [laughs].

Jess says, "Yeah. I knowed Pancho. He was a fine old guy. Fighting for the poor people."

# 19

## TRAINS, BANKS AND FUNERALS
## (1923-1924)

W"You always know you're liable to
get killed . . . you got to expect
it, just like a policeman."

hen we went back to Chicago after the
Toronto holdup, there was a guy come who said he
knowed where there was two little banks at Tab, Indiana,
right on the Indiana and Illinois line. Both of them was
marks. We could blow them both, one up there on that
end of town and the other one down here in a big store.

*They was getting harder to find, the ones that you*
*could blow open. The new technology was beginning to*
*make it harder for us already.*
*   It was cold weather. Once in awhile we robbed a bank*
*or a train in the daytime and we didn't have to depend on*
*the weather. But we were going to rob these banks at night*
*time, and cold weather was the best time. This other guy*
*with us wasn't a "tipster." He was working with us.*

We went and looked the town over, and he had told
us where there was two more in Spencer, Indiana, so we
had to take him in with us. When we got there to Tab, I
said, "Well, I'll blow this one on this end.  Joe, you all go
up on that end and blow that one." They went on up and
broke into the back and  me and my man, Jess, I guess
it was, broke into this one.  Inside was a big sign that
said the bank was closed.  It had gone busted, mine had.
   Well, I went down there to that other bank and told
them.  I said, "I'll stay outside here with this other guy

here. You fellows go in there and blow it." So they went up stairs to that bank. We had never seen anybody before when we was looking around down there. There was no night watchman. This guy that had give us the mark, I told him, "Stand behind those posts over there now, so if somebody's upstairs they can't see you." I was back down the street here, down on this sidewalk. I could watch any doors if anybody came out of it.

And our guy—it was a pretty light night with some lights on— he just come out and stood around! If there was anybody upstairs they could see him! I was over here on the sidewalk and they was inside. They had put one shot in the thing and knocked one door off. While they was getting ready with the others, somebody raised up the window and seen that guy over there and cut down on him, blazing with a little .22 automatic. The guy turned to run but the man firing at him shot him right in the back. It didn't come out. It went in him.

He had a shotgun and he let it go off, and that knocked all the window glass all over the place about eight feet in front of me, and I hollered, "God damn so-and-so . . . What's the matter?"

He says, "I'm shot!"

I said, "Well, get over here! I told you to stay behind something." And he come to me on the sidewalk and I went around and told the others. He was in awful pain. I says, "Let's don't mess with getting this jug. It'll take us an hour and that man's upstairs and this boy's in bad pain. We got to get him in to a doctor." We knowed a man in Chicago who told us where to take him to a guy that'd get him a doctor. So we took him on to Chicago that day and put him in the hospital, but he never did get well. He died. He died from that shot.

Well, we had these other two banks down here at Spencer that he had told us about, so we go to look them over. But we decided instead that we'd rob a train, the Illinois Central going out of Chicago. I intended to get a map last night so I'd know the name of the town and I didn't do it. It's about seventy-five miles out of Chicago

254

where the line forks, and one goes on to St. Louis and the other goes the other way. We got on at that junction. Went down there and drove the getaway down into Indiana. We knowed an old man from Oklahoma that lived down there close to Terre Haute out on a farm. We could go stay at his house. Make our getaway and drive into his house and we wouldn't have to go to no town.

So we drove the getaway and everything down there and told the farmer what time we was going to do it and when we was going to come to his place. Outside of this town about twenty miles where the junction is, me and Jess caught the train. We had a bridge picked out to stop it on, and after about twenty miles we stopped it on this bridge. The rest of them was down there waiting for us. We took another fellow with us that sometimes we let come along because he was a pretty good driver. Joe and them was parked in the car out in a field about three hundred yards away from where we stopped the train.

We just told the engineer where to stop and leave all the cars except the mailcar on the bridge, so that nobody can get off and come down there. We went back to get in the mail car, but the mail car man wouldn't open her up. I knocked the windows out and still he wouldn't come out. So the engineer said, "Let me in there and I'll bring him out." But after he got in, then he wouldn't come out either! So I just reached down in the axle box where the grease is and got me a big handful of that old packing stuff and set it to fire and throwed it into that door.

Well, boy!, it wasn't a little bit till it went to burning and smoking and it burned and smoked and they began to holler, "I'm coming out. I'm coming out."

I said, "Just stay in there and don't come out this door or I'll shoot your head off!" I made them stay there until it was getting pretty close, and then I said, "All right, come on out, and bring everything out with you."

All they brought out was just two or three small sacks of mail. And this old mail clerk, he was about fifty, a mean old so-and-so. He wouldn't come out. When he finally did, I said something to him, and he pushed me!

255

Well, boy! I rared back and I slapped him. I slapped him just with my open hand. I didn't hit him with a pistol. But we was high up on a dump, and I knocked him head over heels down that dump. He got up though. He was all right.

By now the thing is just a-burnin'. They got out of the train up there and somebody with a shotgun went to shooting. The old shotgun didn't bother me. Somebody up there says, "This is Al Jennings back here," and we said, "To hell with Al Jennings." We knowed who Al Jennings was, a train robber who operated way back in territory days. So, now the train was burning up. We took them small sacks and we went across to the car and this other guy with us had done run, the driver we had with us. Jess seen him run going to the car and took after him. He got away and Jess said he was in the car with it started and I don't know what he was going to do when Jess stopped him. Then the other three of us, we brought them two sacks and got in the car and took out.

*The first train robbery I took part in was some little old thing down at Bells, Texas. There was a railroad crossing there. That was mostly a mail robbery. We got some mail sacks there. Didn't know what was in the sacks or anything. And there wasn't nothing in them of any value.*

*But the first real train robbery was over in Texarkana. We were down there looking around at the depot one day, and the train come in. We saw them take a square steel chest off the baggage car and two men carried it and they had a guard with them and they went over into the depot or someplace with it. So we figured that was money, a payroll or something. We finally decided to get that.*

*Well, there was no roads out of there in them days. And somebody had to let a couple of our guys out where the train stopped, and then take the car and go off somewhere and the next night come back and pick them up at a designated spot. So that fell on me, to take the car and stay all night, and the next evening, a little after dark I'd get to the spot to pick them up.*

So I did that. They had got on the train either at a little town or where them railroads cross. They robbed the train before it got into Texarkana and then got off out there in the country where I picked them up, but the box didn't come! They only got some registered mail and a little money in a registered sack. Not enough to amount to much. Then they got off the train and walked off. First thing they did was rub cayenne pepper all over their shoe soles. You snuff some up your nose and you'll see what it does. That was so if the law figured they was afoot and brought dogs out there, the dogs couldn't trail them.

So that was kind of a fizzle. We had a lot of them fizzles [laughs]. Oh, we got a little out of that. There might have been a small sack going to some bank someplace, but not a lot. We thought we were going to get a lot of money, and I think if the box had been on there we would have.

The third train robbery was at St. Joe, Missouri. They was supposed to take off a lot of registered mail sacks full of money. So we went and looked at it. It was right up on a long platform with a shed over it all along there that you'd get into before you get to the depot. There was lots of trains come through there.

We had it all planned. The train would run up there and stop, and two of us went right in there and got what we wanted and all got in the car and left. You'd think there'd be guards on the train, but I didn't see a soul. Passengers was getting off and on, but nobody bothered us.

When I think about it now, I see we didn't have any sense. Any of us. We didn't have any masks on either. But people like that, they're excited and they can't recognize you later. Anyway, they didn't have any pictures of us. There wasn't no such thing as the FBI. That was before the FBI.

Then, I guess the fourth train robbery was that Illinois Central that we burned [laughs]. Willis don't remember, but we had some little sticks of dynamite to "scare them out" with if the mail clerks didn't come out. Them doors fasten from the outside, so although they had shut the door *we could open it, but they wouldn't come out. So we got the dynamite and cut it off so that it was about like a big firecracker, a big jumbo firecracker, and we throwed them back in there. It wouldn't have hurt them. We didn't want to hurt anybody. So we'd throw it in there and it'd be spewing, and they'd run to the other end of the car [laughs]. Then it'd go off, "boom!" Then we'd throw one in the other end and they'd run this way and it'd go off, "boom!"*

*We could have throwed them in there at both ends at the same time, but we didn't want to take a chance of hurting them. So I think it was Jess come up with the idea. He said, "Let's get some of these old greasy rags out of the axle." So we pulled them out, lit them up and throwed them in there. It taken a little while to catch and for a while they stayed in there, but finally they opened the doors. By the time they come out, though, there was too much fire for us to go in. She just went up like a house a-burnin'!*

*After that, we let the engineer detach from the other cars, and we went ahead and left. So we don't know what they done then, but we could see that fire for a long way.*

We was going to Terre Haute, Indiana. Way on down in there on an old off-road we stopped and built up a fire. It was in the fall of the year. Nobody else come along, so we opened up them sacks. We never got more than, oh, a few hundred dollars and a few thousand dollars in bonds. All the rest of it had burned up. Car, mail, and everything that was there burned up.

There was a lot of niggers operating out of Indianapolis robbing people all around Terre Haute. We didn't know it at the time. So we went on and we met another car and he just pushed us off the road! We thought maybe it was the law. Somebody opened the curtain and said, "Stick 'em up!" They had curtains on the cars in them days and somebody just jerked that curtain off and said, "Come on out there and get 'em up!"

The guy that had throwed down on us, he wasn't watching the front seat so I slipped out of the car on the passenger side and come around and just about the time

I got out this guy that was in the front seat with me, he opened the door and took his pistol and fired at the nigger and busted him. He turned in a kind of summersault, then jumped up and run and got in the car and away they went, up the road about twenty miles right to where we had opened them mailsacks. The gunshot fellow died and the other one throwed him out, right there. So the law found him dead there with them mailsacks and they said the niggers done it. Well, the people on the train knowed better, and the police traced them up, found who this nigger run around with, and we read in the paper that they was hijackers and they got the other nigger and he told them what it was all about. That they had stopped a car to stick it up, and somebody shot this other guy. And that broke up the niggers holding people up.

On two robberies we had men killed. One at Gallatin, Missouri, and the other at Tab, Indiana. But you always know you're liable to get killed, just like that. Out doing that you got to expect it, just like a policeman. If he takes that job, he might get killed. We had that happen to us later, to Doc, but he didn't die. If one of our brothers would have been killed, we would have taken him into Chicago and had him buried in the cemetery. But that wouldn't have stopped us. So we decided we would go back down to Spencer and rob them two banks. We got ready and we went down to this old man's house. We put our cars in the barn. They all had big barns back then.

*So we just went and drove into that man's barn—we had groceries in the car and stuff that we needed—and we stayed in there all day long and the next night, early when it got dark, why we drove on out to Spencer.*

*We had stayed there a little longer than we should have because there was an Elks Convention going on. We wasn't Elks, but everybody was welcome. We was waiting there for our "convention" [laughs].*

*It was a circus, so many people, and they had concession stands and everything to try to make money for the Elks, soda water, hamburgers. They even had a* "jail" there and they'd arrest you and you had to pay ten or fifteen dollars to get out. I didn't get arrested, but Willis and another guy did. I seen it over there and knew what was going on, but they went over there to see what it was and got arrested. They didn't try to search them or anything, and besides, we didn't have any guns. We never carried guns anywhere. Just when we was on "business." So they put Willis and this other guy in the jail and asked them where they was from and they said Chicago. They asked what they did there and they told them what business they was in in Chicago. That come out in the paper in the next day or two: Mr So-and-So and Mr. So-and-So, businessmen from Chicago. Course, the names they give them was bogus.

When we hit Spencer, Jess and me went to the lower bank. There's one on this corner and Joe and Doc went to that other corner where a big old Packer sat on the floor. It was easier to shoot. The other bank had one of them new drum doors in it ten inches thick and not once had one of them ever been shot. Before or since.

But I said, "While we're here, maybe we'll get something if I can knock that big door open." So Joe and Doc went down there and started on that one, and me and Jess went in to that big vault. I took a piece of my case knife and hammered until I made a little opening. Well, I made me a cup and put about an ounce of grease in there and it soaked and soaked. Well, I put me a string in there, a cap and a string, to last about twenty seconds, and I lit her up and just stepped on out the door and around the corner. Blam! she went. That wasn't a very big shot but it had gapped that thing. A great big gap. Well, I put me another cup around it and went to pouring grease and it went to running in. I let about six ounces of grease run in, then I poured in another two ounces, fixed my cap and string, lit it, and out I went. Boy! that went blam! Well, Joe had done shot two or three shots and the glass was falling out of the buildings down there where they was at. When my eight ounces went off that big vault door flew off, hit the floor and went right down into the basement!

Well, there was that vault standing wide open, and the shot had broke out all the windows from where we was at to where Joe was.

So I went in there and the safe had a round safe that you couldn't shoot, but I turned the crank and it wasn't locked! They had that big vault door—it was ten inches thick— and they didn't think that nobody in the world could get that door down. That's the first one and the last one of that kind that was ever blowed. I went there and opened that thing. I got about eight thousand in cash out of that safe and just shut her back up. They was still shooting down at the other bank. We went to walk down there and we caught the old man that was the night hack there. He was over at the courthouse. And he says, "What are you boys going to do?"

I said, "We're going to rob these banks."

He said, "Oh, you can't rob the one up here on this end." We tied him on a stool and set him out in front of the courthouse light where we could see him. I said, "When this stool turns over with you, you can say we robbed the one up here." And boy!, you talk about biff! blam! blooey! when that shot went off! We could still see him over there. The telephone man run down there and we grabbed him. Joe had the other safe open and was sacking up the dough.

*I got through a little ahead of Willis, or practically about the same time. I'll bet he put half a pint in that big door and it liked to blow my building down! I heard it down there where I was at and I was down there busy. Willis said that the wooden floor in the building was rotted out, and when the big door blew off it had knocked a hole down through the floor.*

*I had to fire a lot of shots to get my door off. Some of them doors is real tight. You've got to be sure that your grease don't leak at the bottom and run out on the legs of your safe. Because if you shoot those front legs off, why the safe'll fall over on its face and then you might just as well walk off and leave it. You can't ever lift it back up. When you light the cap, you get on out of the vault. You certainly do. You don't want to be anywhere around it. You go back around on the side there. I never had no narrow escapes. You know what to do and the door's right there. Hell, I never had no trouble.*

Then we all went down the back alley. You could hear people, guns a-shootin' in every direction, but we was going down a dark alley you know, where nobody could see us. We went all down that alley to where we had our car parked, and that old man was still sitting over there on that chair.

We drove to this old man's house to lay up and stayed there two or three days. He had had some hogs over at his place and he lost three or four to some sickness. He was just a poor farmer. So when we was robbing the banks, I said, "Boys, let's carry the hard dough away from here, all of us carry it and give it to that old man."

So we carried, between us, a thousand dollars in hard. We got in the barn that night and left everything there. Went in and slept until ten or eleven o'clock the next day. Then we got up and brought the two sacks of hard in and give them to that old man. And boy! that was the happiest man you've ever seen in your life. He was seventy-some years old, and I thought he was an old man then, and I'm ten years older than that now! [laughs]. He come out and he grinned and said, "Well, I lost my hogs, but boys, I'm a happy man. I'm saved. I'm all right now." We stayed there until the next day and then come back to Chicago.

*In that town, we got both banks. And we got. . . now see, that's another thing, it's been so long ago, but I guess we got thirty-five or forty thousand anyway, out of the two. See, there wasn't so much money in banks then, like today. God dawg, we'd have been millionaires.*

*You're always nervous, a little nervous before it starts.*

*But after it starts you don't even think about that. You're*
*too busy doing something. You know what you have to do,*
*and if you don't already know what you have to do, you*
*can see it as it comes up, you know.*

*I didn't have sense enough back then to think that I'd*
*be killed [laughs]. If I'd had any sense back there when I*
*had a lot of money, I'd have "resigned," and turned the*
*business over to my older brother. But I was young and*
*they was my brothers. I guess I was just staying in it*
*because they was there. Doing all that stuff and carrying*
*that nitroglycerine around—I should have been scared, but*
*I wasn't. When I look back on it, I see how dangerous it*
*was. Why, now you couldn't get me to carry a bottle of*
*nitroglycerine from here to downtown. Lord, no.*

This was in November—October or around the first
of November 1923. About November, I guess, when we
got Spencer. So we went on back to Chicago and hung
around there, and then pulled out to Texas to winter. We
come on down here in 1923 just before hunting season.
We sold that car and bought a new car, a Big Six
Studebaker, down here.

In January, we went up to San Marcos, the fourth
day of January 1924 and blowed that bank there. The
legislature just convened that day. They didn't have a
high explosion law in Texas. It was just the same as
burglary and theft, twelve years. Then they went right
ahead and passed a law that made it twenty years for
using high explosion. That's what give us the twenty year
sentence for high explosion in Texas. Robbing the safe
in San Marcos. Legislature thought the law wasn't hard
enough and they just wanted to scare people. It didn't
do any good. They don't know what they're doing. That
don't keep a man from robbing a bank. If it was *fifty*
years, he don't expect to get caught. That's the main
thing. Them old long sentences they'll give it to some old
boy that hasn't done nothing! Like they get some old boy
convicted for the third time for some petty larceny thing
and they give the man life! Ain't that a pitiful thing. They

never stopped nobody in their life.

They don't reform people they send to the penitentiary and jails. They go down there and learn more. I hadn't done nothing in my life the first time they sent me to prison, had never violated a criminal law. They sent me down there for nothing for five years. I got out and tried to do right, and they wouldn't let me. All I learned down there was . . . this guy told me this and that guy told me that, and the bank robber I turned out of there, later I met up with him and that's when I started robbing banks, when I met up with him. You've got all them guys in there and they all tell you what he's in for and what he done. Well, you put young kids in there and they just eat that up. They just eat that up.

Before we blowed the bank at San Marcos we went up there and picked us out a place. We couldn't drive the getaway at night in a car because there wasn't enough roads. So we went up there and picked us out a place about two or three miles out of town on the highway. We took a party over there and showed him where we was going to hide. We put us some chuck out there, and the next night they was to come at a certain time and pick us up.

*This was the same thing we did like when we used to go into them cornfields. We'd just walk off from a robbery and have somebody pick us up the next night. If it was that time of year in Illinois, the corn is high and there's corn for miles. You get in there and everybody lays down and goes to sleep except one. He had a beat to walk. Had to continue to walk all the time. To keep from going to sleep.*

*And it was cold. A lot of people were out in the cold. We've been out in the cold most of our lives, as far as that's concerned. Then we had a spot where the car would come and pick us up at a certain time the next night. But any time we were in the corn, they never did suspect us and there was never a search for us in the cornfield. Now, I'm sure that when the man went to gathering his corn—you know they pulled it off by hand and throwed it in a wagon in them days—he might have seen all the tracks there and the trails beat out if it didn't do a lot of raining between the time we was in there and harvest time. And he might have thought that that was where them bank robbers were. But I don't know that for sure. I know I'd have thought something like that, if it was right out from the little town where the bank had been robbed. They couldn't hardly have kept from tying it together.*

So we went up there to San Marcos to rob the bank and a cold norther was just a-blowin'! We couldn't find no night watchman even though we looked all around. And San Marcos was a pretty big town. So I went down and cut the telephone wires right down the street.

The courthouse was right across from the bank, and that was all one big yard planted in shrubbery. You could get over there in that shrubbery and see down the street every way, could see if anybody was a-comin'. So I set my two guards out there to watch. They was in the shrubbery. Me and the other guy went in and it was a pretty heavy drum door. It wasn't one of them old cracker box doors, so I put about six ounces of grease in it and blowed the door plumb through the window and over to the other side of the street on the sidewalk. I thought there was just a square safe inside the vault, but there was a round safe in there too. Well, I started in on the square safe. It took me about three shots. It was a small Steel Pete. Just took me about three shots to get it. Well, I got between twenty and thirty thousand in money and Liberty Bonds out of it. I sacked that up. I guess there was ten thousand or more of silver, just sacks and sacks of it up and down the vault wall. We never bothered it. The round safe, that was the reserve. They said they had about thirty-five thousand cash in it, but we couldn't get it.

As I went on out, there was two news kids with sacks for their newspapers. I said to them, "What you boys doing out this time of the morning?"

"We're getting our papers over there."

"There's no use in selling those nickel papers. If you go in there and look, you'll find thousands in money all over the floor. Just go in and and help yourself." And they still stood there. I went on over to the shrubbery where the other two guys was and we left with the sacks.

We went on down the street this way to let them kids see us going, and when we got to where it was dark we turned back the other way and went down and hiked out the railroad track two or three miles to a road crossing then turned and hit the highway. Then we went down the highway to where we had our plant. We laid there that night and our pickup come out the next night and winked the light at nine o'clock. We jumped in and went on in to San Antone.

Ten years ago I come through Abilene and stopped to get my car serviced at the Cadillac place, greased, and tuned and oil changed. When I went to get it and gave the man my credit card, he looked at it and said, "J.W. Newton. You the Newton from Uvalde?"

I said, "Yeah."

He said, "You know who I am?"

"No, I don't."

"Wasn't you in charge of robbing that San Marcos bank?" I said yeah.

"You know the two newsboys that was out there waiting to get their papers? Well, I'm one of them." That was forty or fifty years later. He was working there at the Cadillac place in Abilene. Isn't that funny to run into somebody like that? He said, "I'm one of them newspaper boys." Then he asked me, "Was that really a frameup with the banker? They thought it was."

"You can tell everybody that banker didn't know no more about it than you boys did before you come down there. There was no frameup or nothing about it."

# 20

## AMERICA'S BIGGEST TRAIN ROBBERY, RONDOUT, ILLINOIS (June 12, 1924)

> "Maybe we shouldn't have tried one like that, but I'd always wanted to do a million dollar job."

❖ ❖ ❖

Editor's Note: The Newtons' successful career as robbers came dramatically to a climax on the night of June 12, 1924. The four of them, together with one other, acting on inside information provided by a postal employee and corrupt politician, held up the Chicago, Milwaukee & St. Paul mail train at Rondout, Illinois, about twenty-five miles northwest of Chicago.

The contents of more than sixty bags of registered mail, approximately $3 million, was seized, making this, in the words of the Chicago *Tribune*, June 15, 1924, "the greatest of all mail robberies."

Joe was opposed to the robbery from the first time it was discussed, arguing that the amount of money involved would put enormous pressure on the police to keep after them relentlessly until they were caught. Willis never cared much for moral patterns in history. Every story he tells hints at his feeling that he would always prove the exception. He maintained the operation would be a "lead pipe cinch," because they would hit the train in a lonely, rural setting and at night. The clerks, he said, could be taken care of without anybody getting hurt.

For an armed robbery of this scope, they needed more hands. Brent Glasscock, whom Willis refers to as John, was chosen because he had worked with them before and was familiar with their procedures.

This temptation laid before them was the archetypal "job to end all jobs," and a payoff sufficient to make any material desire realizable and any subsequent robberies unnecessary. If all went as planned—and Willis stubbornly insisted there was no way to fail—they would be fixed for life. The amount of money envisioned would buy all the Newtons ranches somewhere out of sight, in Texas, Arizona, or even Mexico, where they could settle and go straight.

It must also have promised to be, at least for Willis, the kind of crowning achievement he had sought restlessly all his acquisitive life. Making a million dollars could be the realization of the American Dream as he conceived it.

The tactics for the robbery were worked out with utmost care: when and where to stop the train, whether to use gas or force the clerks out without a fight, how to make it possible to search through a gas-filled mailcar, how to get the several dozen heavy mailbags loaded into their automobiles, how to drive the getaway route, where to "lay low" thereafter.

Everything did in fact go precisely as planned until the engineer overshot the spot where he was ordered to stop the train. Willis believed the man was terrified by the guns trained on him. In the confusion that followed, Glasscock, for reasons that remain incomprehensible even to the Newtons, shot Doc four or five times.

Both police reports and Willis' and Joe's own narratives concur that it was Doc's near-fatal shooting "that blowed up the deal."

As a result of getting medical treatment for him, Willis and Joe were arrested in the apartment where Doc struggled for life. The high-placed, Chicago political strongman who had helped organize the job from the inside was also nabbed. The police improved their under-

# Chicago Daily Tribune

## $1,000,000 Train Robbery Near City

### 25 Armed Men Stage Holdup on C. M. St. P.

### TRAIN BANDITS' LOOT MAY REACH $3,000,000

Arrests in Milwaukee and Chicago Total 26, but Robbers Are Apparently Still Free.

### MAY HAVE USED AIRPLANE

## WALL STREET FUNDS IN GAS BANDIT LOOT

Chicago Officials Admit Train Robbery Plunder Is More Than $3,000,000.

### CONDUCTOR'S WIFE DEAD

News of Husband's Peril Causes Fatal Shock—Police Hunt for Cached Treasure.

## SEEK DEAD BANDIT AS CLEW

## PECIAL SESSION COURT PROBES BANK ROBBERY

Apparently Being Drawn Around Perpetrators of Most Daring Robbery in History of State.

ANTONIO IS THE BASK OPERATIONS

THINK MAIL ROBBER SLAIN AND CAST ASIDE

Big Man Hunt Covers Wide Range.

RECOVER PART OF MAIL LOOT

SIX ARRESTED; ONE IS DYING; WOMAN TALKS

standing of the robbery daily; as they did so their dragnet widened, pulling in one after another of the individuals actually involved as well as many persons who in fact had no part in the operation.

Few of Willis' convictions were stronger throughout his life than that which told him the system is infinitely corruptible. "There's always a fixer," was a major item in his creed. He thought he could bribe the arresting officers into letting them go, "the way I'd done many times before." To that end he asked his wife, Louise (later styled the "bandit queen" by Chicago newsmen), who was waiting for him in Wisconsin, to bring $20,000 from their safety deposit box. Willis' basic belief remained unshaken, and even fifty years later, he claimed the police would have gone for the deal "if it hadn't been for that dirty old chief named Schoemaker." Their account continues:

❖　❖　❖

A train was easier to rob than a bank because at night you had them trains out there in the dark and in the country. There was nobody to bother you. All you had to do was break the windows, tell them to come out, and usually they did. Banks meant a lot of work. They was hard work—and dangerous. Trains, you could just plan your getaway before the job, watch the train, do it, and scatter. It was a lot safer.

With trains, we always tried to get a big one, but we kept missing them. Then we did get that big one when we robbed the Chicago, Milwaukee & St. Paul railroad at Rondout, Illinois, just twenty miles or so out of Chicago, on June 12, 1924. That's a day I'll never forget. We got $3 million in cash and bonds, and it was the biggest train robbery ever in the United States, before or since.

But Doc got shot in that robbery, and almost died. Maybe we shouldn't have tried one like that, but I'd always wanted to do a million dollar job. And if it had come off, we was all planning to quit our business and go to Mexico, where we could buy ourselves some ranch land and live like kings. Besides, it looked like a sure thing.

I'll tell you why. I knowed a guy in Chicago named Jimmy Murray. Jimmy Murray was a big beer runner. He run beer from Peoria to Chicago. This was during Prohibition. Murray had learned about a post office inspector in the Chicago area and this post office inspector said he'd like to make some money. Jimmy sent the wife of a coward tipster to find me, and she come and told me if I wanted to meet the inspector and talk to him, he'd tell me the layout. She said that inspector could tip us off to anything in the world.

So I come in for the meeting, and he told me about it. He says, "I can tip you off to the money that goes everywhere out of Chicago. There are mail trucks that use the depot down there about eight o'clock. They go down there to load that mail train and they all carry loads and loads of money."

We went down there one night and watched them trucks, how they went. There was six or seven of them, one right behind the other. We followed them and every one of them went down there and loaded the mail on that train. We watched them a few nights, but we knew if we stuck up these trucks here on the street, we was liable to have to shoot somebody.

*We had gone up there to Chicago to rob a truck, a mail truck, that taken the money from the Post Office down to the depot. That was our first idea. We went up there and stayed around and got everything planned out and went down there and watched the truck pull in there—just two blocks from a police station! Right there in the heart of Chicago with people walking the streets.*

*So we got all ready and I said, "Don't you think this is a little strong down here? There's a police station right up there."*

*"Oh, we'll be gone before they can do anything," Willis says.*

*Well, we wouldn't have. Everyone of us would have been killed right there. Or else we'd have killed half the policemen in Chicago, if we'd tried it, the original plan. We was going to run the car in front of the mail truck and stop it, and then we was to take our bolt cutters and cut off two locks on the back of it. Then run the car up there behind it and load the mail out of the car. Now, what do you think them other people was going to be doing when we was doing all that [laughs].*

*But you know the Good Lord has had his arm around our neck many a time, and he had it around it for sure right there. Because when we actually went after it, here comes that truck, we're over here, I'm over there, somebody else is over there, somebody else is over there, and the car is supposed to run in front of it and stop it. Well, in the first place he'd have probably rammed us and run right over us with that old big truck. Then we'd have been afoot! [laughs]. Some of us was to go to the back end, I was to get the guard because I was on this side, and somebody else was to get the driver.*

*Well, we're all ready. We're in the crowd. Some of us got shotguns under our coats, some ain't got nothing but pistols, some's got the bolt cutters. I guess there was five of us, same as on the train robbery. Well, anyway, here come the old truck and instead of turning right here where we was going to stop it, he went straight for another block and then turned! We was all set! We was there, waiting for him! Yessir, now that's a stroke of luck right there. That's the best luck we ever had.*

*I didn't think it was too good an idea at the time, but we thought there was a lot of money on there, and Willis wanted to be sure to get a lot of money.*

So I said something about that the next time I seen our tipster. "Listen, they put them mailbags on that train there. If we wait until it's loaded on the train, we can get every one of them and be out in the country to do it. So how about getting the train?"

"Oh," he says, "I don't know. You can't do that. You

can't do that."

He wouldn't think about doing anything big. He was a coward. So I hushed up. Never said anything more to him about it. I went on back and said to my guys, "Let's find out anything we can about that train. This other fellow, I'm not going to mention it to him anymore."

*There was talk even then about them putting marines to riding the trains because there was so many robberies. After we got the Rondout train, then they put the marines on. That's what I think, because there wasn't any marines on the train at Rondout. As it turned out, they shot up a lot of hoboes and things and they finally had to take them off. Yeah, they got on there and every poor old hobo that caught a train up there, hell! they'd shoot him. All they had to do was tell him to get off or come down here, but whoever put them marines on there give them orders to shoot anybody that caught a train, and they did.*

*The idea for the Rondout robbery first come from another old bank robber. He was a guy that we all knew and he said that he could get a tip on a good train.*

I said the devil with that mail truck, and I went to work on this train. I says, "We can get this train and stop it out in the country where there ain't nobody but them. I can take three fifteen-year-old boys and rob it out there in the country. We won't have to shoot nobody."

So we went to studying that train: where it went out: where it went to Milwaukee; the best place to stop it; where and how they loaded it at night; how they went out; if any law was watching the train. Everything. We worked on that, I guess two months. While we was working on it, when we first started, this coward come to me one day and says, "There's a payroll going out to Cicero, Indiana, every week with about forty thousand dollars on it. It gets out there real early in the morning and the post office is a quarter of a mile down there in barely settled country. Just one guy's got that truck."

That sounded awful good, so we went down there and

looked and saw that truck. It loaded up mail and went way down there in that country to the post office. The post office inspector had told the coward about it, and he'd told me. He said, "There's three sacks of money goes down there once each week. I think there's forty thousand." So on the morning we had picked, I told the coward, I said, "Well, you ask the inspector to go and look through the windows." And he told us there was three canvas sacks of money in there in that bin set to go down there in the morning. They put them in the mail sack. Then they put that registered sack in a parcel post sack and draw it up so you can't see it's registered. But we know it's on there.

So we drove on down there in a Cadillac, and when the truck came, why I was standing over there and somebody was over there, and the other guy just drove the Cadillac right in front of the postal truck and we all had guns on the truck driver before he could turn around.

*I went to the back of the truck. We had bolt cutters to cut the lock off the back of it. I snipped it off and somebody jumped up in there and throwed out sacks.*

He had about ten sacks. We unloaded every sack, so we'd be sure to get the right one. We piled them all in that car and jumped in and pulled out. They thought we was going back to Chicago, but we went about fifty miles south of there way down in the sandy rough country where nobody lived, on little offroads. We had a place to go to, an old shack way back in there where we could lay out during the day, and sure enough there was three sacks with thirty-five thousand in them. We burned the sacks and buried all of them locks. Right there at the end of the house. We split up that money so we each got about five thousand and the coward and the inspector split five. There was five of us and them other two, that made six shares all together.

*For our getaway, we went off down into Indiana in place of going right back to Chicago. Of course, they thought we'd double back into Chicago, but we went the other way. There was an old strip of that sandy country down there with one house here and another one there. We pulled in behind one of them vacant houses and stayed until night, and then we come into Chicago.*

*Well, wouldn't you know that still wasn't enough money for Willis. He wasn't satisfied with that. So somebody said, "Well, how about the train?" Well, when we started thinking about it, almost everybody except me was for getting the train, because we was going to stop it out in the country. I thought it was too much money. We'd bring down too many police on us, but we started going down there to watch the train. The same ones couldn't go all the time so we took turns.*

We was living on the south side in the Strand Hotel and the Blackstone Hotel. That's when we went to riding in our cars and watching the Rondout train. We watched for about two months, I guess. And there's a town away down there and this fellow with us had a uncle who owned a paint shop in an old factory down there. It covered three or four acres of ground and you could just drive into it, any door anywhere you wanted to. He made a deal with his uncle to close up his paint shop that day, and we was going to come in there with the mail that we got off this train. That would give us a place to stay all day and then we'd go on the next night.

Well, we studied and studied that train, watched it and watched it, watched them mail trucks bring it down there. I'd get close enough that I could see them brass locks, fifteen or twenty or thirty sacks of that registered mail. By the twelfth day of June we had everything ready—we had already went and stole two Cadillacs and put them in garages. We just went down the street and hooked a chain onto two Cadillac cars and towed them off and took them on to some garages where we pushed them in. We either got a key or we wired them up. It don't make any difference. Them days you could start a car up by wiring it. You just get down there and tie two wires together. Didn't have to have a key. So we put them in the garages and kept them until we got ready for them. We had them planted a month or so.

*We had two Cadillac cars. One was a seven passenger, had them little extra seats, and the other was a regular five-passenger. We had stole them down in the apartment part of town, in Chicago, and we had garages rented to put them away in. They had lots of garages for rent them days. People would live in apartments and rooms—everybody had a sign up to rent a room—so you could go rent a room in some private residence and then, if they didn't have a garage, they could tell you where you could rent one in the alley over yonder where you could put your car of a night. It got so cold there of a night, you know.*

*Everything worked perfect when we stole the cars. We drove around until we found somebody that had left the keys in them. They was all late model cars, I don't just remember which year exactly. They'd have been '23 or '24, I don't remember which. I had to start them to see if the battery was alright and see that they run alright, that the lights and the taillights worked, because we had to go plumb across town in them, you know, before we got out of town. Then we had to fill them up, chuck full of gas, on the other side of town.*

We got ready to go on the twelfth. All of us met down there at a certain little place in Chicago. Joe, Doc and John [Glasscock] was to go on ahead out there to where we'd stop it. They knowed just what time this train come, and when they seen the train coming they was just to pull up on the crossing by the track and stop. We could load the mailbags out of the train into the cars there.

They went early that evening because it's about thirty miles out there toward Milwaukee to Rondout. The road crossing was about two miles the other side of Rondout right on the lake to Milwaukee.

We couldn't catch the train until dark when it left. Me and Jess was going to get on behind the engine in the blinds. That's right behind the engine in the first car. We got on at the station in Chicago. We run and jumped on this car and we had caps on and coveralls, and when we jumped on, there was five or seven tramps on there just going to ride that fast train to Milwaukee or someplace and they thought we was lawmen. I said, "Get the hell off of here!" and I went to kicking and they was a-jumpin' and I was a-bootin'. Boy!, they just fell and rolled out of there in every direction.

The plan was, when we got to Rondout, me and Jess was going to climb over the tender and get the engineer and the fireman. Out at the crossing where the others was waiting, they put Doc on the ground on the other side, on the far side of the train, so nobody could come out of the door, see? We had them covered on his side. And the front car to the engine carried all the registered mail. We seen which car they unloaded all that registered mail in, and in the registered mail is where the money is at. It was seven or eight cars long, a solid mail train. Second fastest mail train in the United States. There's one that runs from New York to Boston that runs just a little bit faster.

This old train runs so fast that in no time we got to Rondout and the engineer whistled for the town. Well, that was our signal to go over. Jess grabbed the fireman and I went for the engineer. When they looked around, I had my gun on him. Boy!, he throwed his hands straight up and went to hollering. I said, "I'm not going to hurt you. I want you to stop this train at that two mile crossing up here."

But he was just scared to death and kept his hands up there and the train kept running. Finally I stuck my gun back down in my pocket here and grabbed him and I said, "Get them hands on that throttle and stop this train." Jess had throwed his gun down on the fireman and he said, "Mister, don't point that gun right at me. I'm scared to death."

Jess says, "Bu-bu-by God, you ain't scared any worse than I am!" Old Jess was just that comical. And he *was* scared too. By the time I got the engineer's hands down, he couldn't stop it on that crossing and he run by. I wanted him to stop that mail car right on the crossing, because our cars was setting right there, but instead he run by the whole train length.

Well, Doc followed the train on up, I guess, when it passed him. I said to the engineer, "Back this train back there and spot this mailcar right on that crossing." He moved her on back there. We got off, and I told them, "Now cut that car there. Cut the train right there behind that engine." That was so nobody could slip up there and get in the engine and run off, you see.

*We waited and waited and finally we heard the train coming and we knew where we was going and all. Doc, he left and went over on the other side. All he was supposed to do was if somebody opened a door on the other side and tried to jump out, the mail clerks or somebody, why he would tell them to go back and shut the door. Then I heard them shut the throttle off on the train, like they was going to stop it, so I knew that was when Willis and Jess had come over on the engineer. So I told Glasscock, "You know you're supposed to come and go with me, and we're going to the back end of the train." We thought there was some guards on it. Sometimes there was four or five guards that rode it.*

*And he said, "Yeah, yeah, yeah," just like that. So we got back down there, and the damn thing didn't stop like it should. It run by. So we taken out running after it, behind it. I was in the middle of the track and he was on this side. But when the old train stopped and we caught up to it, this guy Glasscock just kept a-goin'. He went up that side just sailing. I went to hollering at him, but, hell, I couldn't take after him! I had to stop at the back, and there was a brakeman and a conductor that come to the back. Conductor was an older man. Brakie come down and jumped off and he said, "I better get off so I can flag a train."*

*I said, "Well, you better just flag it right back up that railroad, and if you see one up yonder, why you flag it." I knew what he'd do. He'd head for Rondout, but it was about three miles away, so he taken off with the red lantern up there, up the track behind us.*

*Then I told that old man, the conductor, to come down because we was going to rob the train. He said, "Well, it's cold out there. I'm not going to come out. I'm going to get my coat." I said he wasn't going to freeze, but he said, no, no, he had to get his coat, so I said, "Where's your coat?" and he said it was right there in a big box with a lid on it, see. So I said, "Don't you lift that lid up. If you do, I'm going to shoot you." I didn't know but what the old sonofagun might have a gun in there, you know. And would you know, he paid me no mind [laughs]. He went ahead and raised up that box lid up and reached in and got an old, heavy coat and he put that on and come on down [laughs].*

We got down there by the mailcar and I didn't see nothing of John [Glasscock.] I said, "Where's John?"

Joe said, "Hell, he run off up ahead somewhere. I don't know where he went."

I said, "Punch them windows out up there," and Joe smashed them out with a shotgun. He had a bottle of formaldehyde and I said, "Give me that." Then I told them guys, "If you ain't coming out in half a second, I'm going to throw a bottle of poison gas in there and you'd wish you'd come out." Well, boy!, they jerked that door open and there was seventeen or eighteen of them in there. I said, "Just drop them pistols as you come out here." They was mail clerks, but they nearly all carried pistols.

*I had a bottle of formaldehyde in my pocket and I gave it to Willis in the hole in the glass. He says he didn't throw it, but I still believe he did. Anyway, they started coming out. There was seventeen of them. If they had any guns, they left them in there when they come out. So here they are. I had them all. One of the newspapers said we lined them up, but, hell, you couldn't do that! I was running amongst them all the time. You couldn't tell me from them [laughs].*

*I got them over there as far as from me to you and I watched them. Of course we was talking back and forth, yeah, and so this one big, husky, wide-shouldered guy—I'm sure he was an Irish from the way he was built and because there was more Irishmen in Chicago than anything else—he just leaned over to make a run for me. So I told him, "Don't you try to come over here."*

So they all come out. They piled the pistols and I told them, I said, "Put that bunch of pistols over there in the back of that car." They did it, and I says, "Who's the chief clerk on here?"

A guy says, "I am."

I jumped up in the car and I says, "Come on up in here," and he did. I said, "Now I'm just after the registered mail and I want every damned sack of it." I knowed where it was at. "If you don't give me every sack of it, you're going to get in trouble, serious trouble, because I'm going to find the rest." He went to digging around and he says, "Here's the Milwaukee and here's the St. Paul and Minneapolis. We ain't got no mail for nowhere else."

We piled out sixty some odd sacks, and as we piled it out, I told them, the other boys, I says, "Have them guys load it up in the back of them cars." We had the two Cadillacs ready, and as they was loading it, this clerk says, "Is that your man got shot out there?"

"There ain't nobody got shot out there."

He says, "Yes there was. I opened the door and I seen somebody shoot a man." Well, I knowed just Doc's supposed to be out there. I run over to the door—he had closed it back up—and I pulled it open and leaned out and hollered, "Doc!"

Then I heard, "Ah-y-'m sho-o. . ." like that. His tongue was shot and he was lying out there on the ground somewhere. "Ah-m shot . . . Ah-m shot." So I went back there to where the others was and I said, "Go out there and get Doc. He's shot on the other side." As Jess went to crawl under the train, John [Glasscock] shot at Jess too, but it missed him. He must have knowed by now that he had shot somebody.

I hollered, "John! Come back. Get over here." I still didn't know for sure that John had shot him. I thought that somebody else might have shot him. So I said to come on back and Jess went on over and got Doc. I said, "John, did you shoot Doc?"

He said, "No, no, no. I shot a Hoosier. I shot a Hoosier." We called a "Hoosier" some farmer or some ignorant guy or some working stiff. "I shot a Hoosier. I shot a Hoosier."

I said, "The hell you did. You shot Doc," and that was the last I said about it.

*I never remember hearing a shot. Glasscock, that was supposed to be with me, he had headed for the front of the train, but it was too far. I'm sure he crawled under it and got over on Doc's side. Yeah. I've crawled under a million of them. Didn't you crawl under a train when you was a kid? It was stopped, see. Standing still there, and he had to go up there and crawl under to get to where Doc was. Excited, I guess.*

*Maybe in the dark he didn't recognize Doc. He must have knowed that for one of us to get shot was the best way in the world for him and all the rest of us to get caught.*

*Then what's even harder to understand is he seems to have left Doc there! Maybe he was mistaken and shot him once and then he thought that we'd have to take him to the hospital and he'd get caught or something, so he decided he'd just keep shooting and sure enough kill him and figure we'd bury him somewhere and nobody'd ever know.*

We got Doc back there and loaded him in the car and we loaded all that mail. I said to the clerks, "All of you stay right here on the ground until we get away from here," and they did. It was light around there and we could see them as we drove off. The getaway had been planned for a long time. Joe and Jess rode in the back car, they had Doc there, and the other two of us was in the front car, this guy John [Glasscock] driving and me. We had most of the bags of mail. It must have been ten or eleven o'clock. After we'd drove a little bit, we throwed all them pistols out, over the ground. Of course they found them the next day.

Every thirty or forty miles—it was over one hundred miles to our hideout—we'd stop and see how Doc was. He was still a-goin'. I said something about getting him some aspirin, but he said, "No, that might weaken my heart. I don't want any aspirin tablets."

So we went on. And a damn sack of that mail fell out of a car, it was stacked so high. It's a good thing it didn't fall out right close to where we was going. They found that sack of mail the next day too, but we went on to this old paint factory and drove in there and this fellow, Jimmy Murray, come out of Chicago and met us there. He come in there just after we pulled in. We told him what had happened to Doc and he said, "I can get a doctor."

*So we left. I didn't drive no more. I got in the back with Doc. He was conscious and bleeding like a stuck hog and we was worried he was going to die. Then we went on to our hideout, about sixty or seventy miles, and stayed there until, oh, probably nine o'clock. It had been an old gin, but this wasn't the time of year for a cotton gin and it wasn't operating then. It was the better part of a whole block itself, on the edge of, oh, I forgot what town. A little town there. We slid the doors back and drove inside and shut the doors. We got into the money a little. Didn't know exactly what to do. Cut the mail sacks open and we had a lot of money, but there wasn't much rejoicing because there was Doc and we figured we'd lost him.*

*After we'd got settled down and everything, we said, "Well, Doc's got to get a doctor or he's going to die." Well, me and one of the other boys, we said we'd take him into Chicago and see about getting a doctor. So we did. We drove to a garage we had put cars in and run in there with him. Then we contacted another fellow we knew there, a*

*beer runner. He located a doctor and we taken Doc over
to the house of one of his hired men, and carried him up
there. About dark the doctor come and treated him, gave
him lots of shots and cleaned his wounds out and
everything. He knew there was no such thing as taking
him to a hospital. He had to be treated right there, and he
said he'd come back tomorrow. I don't remember how
much we paid him. He probably knew something was
fishy because Doc wasn't in a hospital, but I don't think
he knew he was shot in the train robbery or we probably
couldn't have got him to come out there.*

They stayed in that garage while Murray inquired
around from some of them hoodlums about another
doctor, and they had all read about this man being shot
at that train robbery. Finally he got the doctor, but the
law went to grabbing these hoodlums around there.
Some of them said, "By God, you don't need to grab us."
They was mad, you see, because they figured it was
outside people. And they didn't have guts enough or
sense enough to do anything like that themselves, so one
of them snitched. He says, "They got a doctor out to
so-and-so's apartment this evening to see somebody
that's hurt."

*Then in the night sometime, or early morning,
somebody rapped on our door and it was all the law.
Somebody'd told them. We'd carried Doc sitting in a chair
up the back stairs and somebody'd seen us carry a man
up there. They was picking everybody up off the streets,
see, and some snitch, he said, well, why are you picking
me up? Why don't you go to . . . a certain place where I
seen a wounded man? Well, hell, that was all they wanted.
When they got there they could see all the blood so whoosh!
here they come and got me.*

The police just went on out about night time and went
in the house. It was after dark and Jimmy Murray was
there and Doc, and this boy who had the apartment, and

Joe. Joe had told Murray to tell me when I called the next day, if he didn't answer the phone himself, for me not to come out there. But Murray got arrested and he couldn't tell me. I knowed what apartment they was at, and after we come in that night and I got something to eat, I just pulled on out there. I called Murray's house, and his wife didn't even know he had got arrested. Well, I was anxious to see about Doc and I went on out there about nine or ten o'clock and started to knock on the door and they throwed it open and there was more policemen that I had ever seen. They grabbed me and we had it around and around and around. I saw they could kill me. I had no gun and there was too damn many of them. I seen it was no use.

After that we sat down there and they had done taken the others all to jail and was just waiting to see if anybody else came in. In five minutes there was sixteen newsboys that had done gotten their papers running up and down them streets telling about where they'd caught the robbers! In five minutes! Now that's my bad luck! Just five minutes, there was ten newspaper boys run around all that house hollering, "Read about it! Read about it!" Now, that's my bad luck.

Well, I set there figuring, and finally I started to make a deal with these policemen to give them twenty thousand dollars to turn me loose. They was all for it. But old Schoemaker, the chief of police—he was a dirty old rat—he wasn't in town and didn't know they had me. I had called my wife in the morning in Wisconsin as I come on over there, and I told her to come on down to Chicago. I knowed what train she was coming in on that evening. My deal with these policemen—there was three of them— was to hand them twenty thousand dollars so they'd turn me loose. I said, "I can get the money, but it'll be tonight before you get it." So they never took me in. They kept me there all day. They wanted that money. And about five o'clock, just before we got ready to go to the depot to meet her, that gawdamn dirty old Schoemaker, that old rat, he come in. So they had to tell him the deal. He said all right. He sided right in with them. In his heart, though, he wasn't. He wanted the arrest to go through, so he made out like he sided in with them.

So we went on down to the depot at six o'clock. I said, "Now, I know a woman—I didn't tell them she was my wife—that's coming in that I can borrow twenty thousand off." So I met her and two of these old laws was with me when she got off the train.

I told her, "I've got some friends that's in trouble and these are their lawyers. I want to know if I can get twenty thousand off of you."

She said, "Yes, I can get it, but I have to go out to the bank."

Then they said, "Alright, we'll take you." She didn't know they was laws. She thought I was telling her the truth, because she hadn't known that we was going to rob that train.

Old Schoemaker and the other guy, they was pretty sly. They didn't come in with us, but they stayed outside and watched us. When we got in the cab and went out there to get that money, they followed us. It was dark when we got there, but them safe deposit boxes stayed open until ten o'clock at night. She went in and came back with twenty $1,000 bills, and when we got in the car, that dirty Schoemaker drives up. One of the laws says, "Hell, let's throw him out right here."

"If any of you throw him out, I'm going to take you in his place," he said. "We're not turning him loose. We're going to take him to jail, and if you run him off, I'm taking you in instead." Well, that killed it. He had just made them think that he was going to turn me loose until he got a look at the money. I think he wanted to see if I had money, or maybe to see if I'd turn up with some money from the train. But they couldn't do anything with that money, because it wasn't mine. I had borrowed it off my wife, and she didn't know that I was giving it as a bribe.

So they took my wife one way and me the other. Finally I wound up at the Chief of Police's office and she was there too. She said, "What have you got him for?"

"Robbing a train."

"My God," she says. "I know he didn't do that." We got to talk a little bit there and then they took me on out to some little county jail at Wheaton or somewheres, about twenty miles away, put me in there and didn't take me back to the city jail anymore.

They didn't file any charges against my wife.

*After they arrested us, they put Doc in the county hospital out there, and they put me in a precinct jail right where I was at. Old Captain Schoemaker, he was a captain of the city police, he was going to whip the information out of me and I was going to get twenty-five years in the penitentiary! The old sonofagun, if he'd tried soft-soaping me . . . see, if he'd said, "I think I can get you out of this," or "I'll help you if you'll just tell me so and so and so . . ." he might have got it to work. But, oh, lord, did he hit me? For seven days and nights . . . .*

*After I come into Chicago, they kept the money down there at the hideout, I guess, and then later they brought it on in, Willis and two or three other guys. Well, I really don't know what they did. I was in jail [laughs]. A bunch of it—see, Jess taken several thousand dollars. And Glasscock taken his and Willis' and mine to Tulsa to some of his kinfolks and hid it in a wall. They didn't even know it was there [laughs].*

*After seven days, the Chicago city police took me down and turned me over to the federal Post Office Inspector. Back then there wasn't no such thing as the FBI and the CIA and all that baloney. At the time they did that, I hadn't made any sort of "deal." Hell, how was I going to agree to give anything back when I hadn't admitted to doing anything? That man wanted me to admit it and get twenty-five years? You think I want to do that? Admit it and get twenty-five years? I didn't know then that we had to give the money back. In fact, I never even thought about the money. They kept telling me that Doc was going to die, but I was suspicious of that. They wouldn't let me see a paper or nobody else. Had me back there by myself.*

*But it turned out they finally arrested everybody. I never did see Willis, but he sent me word that they was going to "trade out." That Post Office Inspector told me that. They'd brought Willis and the other guy in and let them talk, and they decided the money was no good. Hell, we'd have been in the penitentiary the rest of our life.*

*I'll give old Schoemaker credit for one thing. Even though he acted like he was going to kill me hisself, and he hit me and broke my nose on the inside, and then he tried to punch my eyes out, I guess he thought I had sense enough to dodge, because he didn't slow up any [laughs]. If that wasn't bad enough, he had a big, husky, Irishman there about twenty-eight or thirty years old, oh, he was a big one. And every time Schoemaker would knock hell out of me, why, he'd want to put his hand in, and Schoemaker'd say no. Tapscott, I won't ever forget his name either. T-a-p-s-c-o-t-t. If Schoemaker'd let him loose, why he'd have killed me! He was a big son-of-a-bitch as stout as a mule, you know, and he meant business. He'd come at me all riled up, you know. And if he had got to me, they wouldn't have done nothing to him, either.*

The next day after I tried to bribe them policemen, they brought in the chief clerk off the train, and hell, before he even got to me he come a-laughin' and said, "There's the man, right there." And they had identified Joe. Doc they knew, of course, because he'd been shot over there. There was no way to keep from identifying him. So I get to figuring. I know if I don't get loose somehow, we're dead fish. Jess, he don't know anything to do but run. He's scared. The other guy, Glasscock, I know he ain't going to do anything but try to beat us. When we had come in from the train the night before, me and him and Jess had gone to a friend's place where there was a barn. We took about ten bales of hay out of a stack in there and hid the mail and money in a hole about the size of two bales, then covered it back nice.

Then I had got arrested and Jess was gone, because Glasscock give him thirty-five or forty thousand in bills.

I know it was that much, because he lost thirty-five thousand right outside of San Antone when he got drunk and buried it and never could find the place again. The police had no idea who had been with us, see. So I figured and figured of a way to talk to Feahy, the Post Office Inspector. He was the main man, and I wanted to talk to him to try to work out a way for me to get away.

Nobody in our gang knew who Feahy was but me and Glasscock. Doc and Jess and Joe, they didn't know Feahy. They never had no contact with him. The city police had arrested me and after they kept me three or four days, they turned me over to the post office authorities and Feahy was the head inspector there. He knowed about the robbery all along, of course, but he was afraid they'd get suspicious if he talked to me. Hell, he ought to have knowed I'd never snitch. I could have snitched on him anytime. I knowed him and had talked to him before. I wasn't trying to snitch on him.

I started stringing them a line, and I said, "Yeah, the guys that was with us was Harry Wilcox and Sam Grant." Harry Wilcox was that first burglar that had the stolen stuff hidden under a house down there in Texas, and I hadn't seen him in twenty years. "Sam Grant," I told the police, "he's escaped from the Walls where he had a life for murder. I'm supposed to meet him in a saloon in St. Louis in a night or two at ten o'clock. If you take me down there and let me go in and meet him, why you can get them both."

All I wanted was a chance to talk to Feahy alone, but that dirty rat wouldn't ever get off by himself with me. I'd wink at him and do everything else, but he thought I was telling the truth. What I framed up was for him to take me over there and me and him to go in there. Make the rest of them stay out. Then he'd let me run out at the back door on him. But he never would give me a chance to talk to him without them others being there.

They all took me over to St. Louis to catch these other two guys, but that was just a lie I was telling, and Feahy got the word out to the press. That night when the evening edition come out, big words right there said they was bringing one of the train robbers down to catch a fellow by the name of Greenberg and Sam Grant and Wilcox. Greenberg was a thief out of New York City that I'd done business with. My story was good. Maybe too good, but with headlines like that in the paper, there was no use in taking me over there then, so they took me back to Chicago the next day and put me in that little jail out at Wheaton. It was a good, tight jail, but it sat on the ground. Feahy knows I'm over there, and about that time Jimmy Murray has got out on bond. About two weeks later, they come over to transfer me out of Wheaton and up to Rockford at night time. Feahy and three more inspectors. All he had to do was get hold of Jimmy and he could have got a couple of guys and when they went in that jail to get me at night, they could have stuck them up and turned me loose! But he wouldn't do it. He wouldn't try to help us.

So I knowed if anything was to happen to help us, I was going to have to do it, otherwise we was dead fish. But goddamn, if they didn't take me out to Rockford, Illinois, and put me in the county jail there in the death cell, up on the third floor by myself. Never give me a newspaper, never let me get a letter, never let me see nobody for five long months.

Meantime, they went down to Texas where Jess was and traced him around. He was drunk, over in Mexico, spending his money. But all that money was old money. None of it was marked and they couldn't tell it from any other money. Jess had come back into San Antone and went up in some hills and hid the money under a rock. Dug a hole and then put a rock over it. When he goes back the next day, he don't know where he was at, whether it was eight miles, six miles, what hill, or anything else. In daytime everything's completely different, and he never could find that money.

With the few thousand he had left, Jess went out to Uvalde, then over into Mexico where he was staying drunk day and night, day and night. He's a whiskey drinker. They went over there, a couple of them inspectors, and drank with him and every time he'd spend a bill, they'd pick it up. But like I said, it was old money and they couldn't tell nothing. Finally they told him, "Listen, there's a bronc over in Del Rio that nobody can ride. We think you can ride him, Jess, and we're betting five hundred dollars on you. Will you go over tomorrow and ride him."

"Hell, yes," he says, so the next day, Jess come over to ride this horse and they walked up to him saying, "Well, we're Post Office Inspectors and we want you." They took him to San Antone to jail and he got him some lawyers. He fought it and fought it and fought it, but finally they brung him back to Chicago.

Jess, he was so comical that everybody that got acquainted with him liked him. He didn't know anything about who we was dealing with on the train robbery, and pretty soon they come to be sure of that. They had an idea it was an inside job.

Feahy was going with some Dago woman out there and had gotten pretty thick with her. Her old man had been arrested a year before for a mail robbery, and Feahy was the one who was pressing the charges against him. She was a good looking heifer, and after she throwed in with Feahy, she found out quite a bit about him. He began drinking, I think, and he had talked too much. Anyway, she found out enough that the inspectors put somebody on his trail to see where he went, where he got his money and everything. This other fellow that was with us, Glasscock, the one that drove the car and that had shot Doc, he gave Feahy and Jimmy Murray their part of the money, $500,000 in money and bonds. That's what they had coming, one-sixth of what we got.

When all of us landed in jail, Glasscock had all the money. He planted a lot of it in jars right there in that garage where we took the car. Dug a hole and left it right there. Then he took the $500,000 I told you about and gave it to Feahy and he had at least another $500,000 in brand new Liberty Bonds that he didn't know what to do with. The series was numbered one, two, three, just like that, right up. He went out to Tulsa to his brother-in-law's place where he tore a board out of the ceiling and put them all in there, then fixed it back like it had been. He knowed it would be a long time before we'd be able to do anything with them new bonds. Then he left that country and went over into Michigan.

Meantime they got to working on Jess. They were pretty sure he didn't know everything, but they went to dealing with him. "If you'll tell us everything you know about this, Jess, we'll get you off with a year's sentence," they said. They figured they might get something about Feahy out of him.

"I'll tell you what I'll do," he said. "I'll tell all of you right here the whole story, everything I know about it."

Another inspector working on me had hinted that that was what they was doing, and I didn't care. I said, "That's alright. If he wants to do that, just tell everything he knows and nothing else, let him go ahead." I knowed he didn't know nothing but that we had robbed the train. He didn't know who we was connected with. So when they asked about this man Feahy, Jess could say "I never heard of no such man in my life," and he hadn't. My brothers never asked me any questions. Doc, the only thing he'd ever say was, "Boys, do you know the money's there?" and Jess told them, "Hell, the old man— they used to call me 'the old man'—he never told us anything about it. All he said was 'Get ready to go,' and we knowed he was working on some kind of deal."

Joe didn't know anything about it either, not about Feahy. He was just a kid. It was just me and Glasscock, and even Glasscock had never seen Feahy in his life. He knowed who he was alright, but until I pointed Feahy out to him in the courtroom when they brought him back six or eight months later from Michigan, Glasscock had never laid eyes on him.

The man handling the case was called Aldridge, and he was from Texas. He got acquainted with Jess and Doc and Joe and he liked them all, but I was up there in that death cell by myself for five months and never seen nobody. They thought I knowed where all the stuff was at and they didn't want to let anybody talk to me because I'd tell them where it was at and they'd go and carry it off. I did know where it was planted, or most of it anyway, where we had first planted it.

What it come to was they didn't know anything on Feahy except what this woman had told them. She give them a lot of evidence, and they followed him and got a pretty good line on him. About three months after the robbery, they arrested him. I don't know what all he had said to the woman, but he'd talked too much. She never testified against him, though, but they had seen him and Jimmy Murray meet when they followed him and that's what first got him in jail.

So there I sit for five months. Joe and Jess was up in the Wheaton jail, and Doc was in the main county jail in Chicago. They had trailed up who we run with and they knowed that Glasscock was with us. Finally they put out a picture on him and had it up in every post office in the United States. He was over in Battle Creek, Michigan, staying out at some house. He'd have been better off if he'd stuck around a big hotel where he wouldn't have been noticed, but he was one of these guys that got acquainted with everybody, and he got thick with a twelve or thirteen year old kid out there. When the kid was at the post office one day getting his mail, there was Glasscock's picture up in front of him and he run and told the law. They grabbed him and brought him and his old lady back to Chicago.

Glasscock had got away with, I guess, fifty or sixty thousand, but when the post office inspectors questioned him, he told them he give Jimmy Murray more than he really gave him. He took the $500,000 to Murray to go to him and Feahy and he sat tight on it. He didn't want to give it back, so when he said he didn't have the money, the inspectors couldn't really tell where the money had gone and they had to take Glasscock's word for it.

Old man Aldridge told me, "If we can recover that

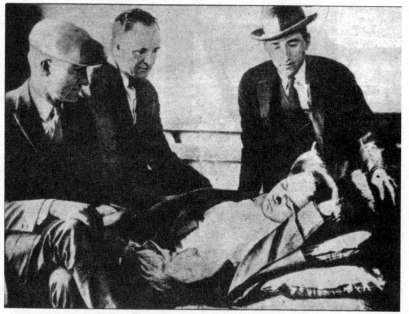

*At their trial, the wounded Doc Newton is brought into court*
*with his brothers, left to right, Willis, Jess and Joe.*

money, I can get you boys off with a lighter sentence and
you can get out. But if we don't you'll get twenty-five
years." The robbery called for twenty-five years flat. The
insurance company wanted that money back real bad.
But there was another old inspector told Glasscock that
if he'd testify against Feahy and Murray, he'd get him off
with five years. So Glasscock blabbed his guts. He told
them where all the money was hid in jars out there and
they went and dug that up. Then he told them there was
another $500,000 in new bonds down in Tulsa at his
brother-in-law's place. He took them down there and
they tore the wall out and recovered that. So they had
nearly all the money and bonds back.

Glasscock had never seen Feahy in his life, remem-
ber, but he knowed about everything I had done with
Feahy. When we went into the courtroom, he asked me,
"Where's Feahy?"

"There he is. That little jug-headed fella," I told him,

and he looked at him good so he would know him, then he got on the stand as though he had done all the framing up with Feahy. I couldn't say he was a damn liar. I had to keep my mouth shut. With that case against them, they convicted Feahy and Murray and give them twenty-five years apiece. The police took them right on to Atlanta.

The inspector told Aldridge that he'd promised to get Glasscock off with five years, but Aldridge said, "We can't do that. We can get Willis and Doc and him off with some kind of lighter sentence, but it won't be five years. We can give them twelve years apiece. I'll recommend Joe for three years—he's just a kid, twenty-one or twenty-two years old—and Jess told us everything he knowed and we told him we'd get him a year, so that's what we'll do."

So they was going to take us up for sentencing, but in the meantime, Joe and I had got a lawyer who come up and says, "You better not take these fellows up in front of that judge or he'll give every one of them twenty-five years. You go to Washington to the Attorney General and tell him what sentence you want to give. He'll make a recommendation that you can give to the judge."

That's what they did, and that's the sentences we got. We never went up before a jury. Just pled guilty up in front of the judge and that's what he give us.

From there we went to the penitentiary at Leavenworth, Kansas. Jess only served nine months on his year and a day sentence. Joe served a year on his three years and then got a parole. Glasscock and I stayed four years and two months before we was paroled. Doc stayed there six years and something because there was a "hold" on him in Texas for escaping from down there. Poor old Doc.

Now, Murray had planted all them bonds and the money that was his part and Feahy's. They went down and made a deal with Murray to give all his bonds and stuff back and they'd commute his sentence. He did, and they let him out. He'd been in Atlanta about five years.

But Feahy, the Post Office Inspector, he stayed fourteen years before he got out. They had it in for him. Said if it hadn't been for him, there'd never been no robbery and they wanted to make an example out of him so nobody else would do that. When he got out, I heard that he lived in Chicago until he died a few years ago.

I was doing one-third time, so I got out the end of February, after four years and two months in Leavenworth. For two and a half years I was the head cutter in the tailor shop that made the discharge suits for them that was getting out. I had all them patterns and I marked and cut any suit that they wanted. I'd never done anything like that before, but in a week or two I was as good at it as anybody ever got.

I took to hurting on the inside when I was there. I had adhesions on account of the flu when I was a kid. They had growed back together, but I walked stooped over and couldn't hardly straighten up. I was working at the steel shop where I'd been transferred. They made all kinds of stuff out of iron. I sat there and gave them their tools and checked them in and out. After about six months there, I went to the hospital where they operated on me.

They went in and cut these adhesions apart. They had growed up together all in a lump. They put me back in the bed but wouldn't give me no morphine or nothing, and I got to hurting so bad, I just rolled and pulled every way. I was pretty near dead, and the head convict doctor in there, Bill Evans, got me a shot of morphine. I had tore them adhesions loose again, and they growed back and I was all humped up. In a month or two, the doctor sent my clothes in and told me to check out. I said, "You take them back and give them to the doctor. Tell him if he wants to check me out, to go ahead, but I know when I'm able to go and when I'm not and I can't check out yet."

The warden down there was old T.B. White, who had been a Texas Ranger. He'd come over and see me and talk to me about Texas and everybody knowed that, so they just let me lay there. I stayed right there in that hospital for three or four months until they built another big room and put cots in it for people that wasn't able to work, old people, like. They transferred me there, and I stayed there a year. Never come out, because we was fed right there too and lived there.

Bill Evans, I've got to tell about Bill Evans. He give me the shot when I was in such bad shape. He and two more boys had got twenty years in the Indiana Penitentiary for robbing the bank down at Spencer, Indiana, the bank that we had robbed! The law told this boy in trouble how it was done and said if he knew anything on Bill, to tell them and they'd turn him loose. So he said, "Yes, Bill Evans robbed it and I was with him." And he didn't know any more about it than you do. We'd done it. Now that shows you when somebody turns state's evidence on you, you think it's the truth. The other two guys was still in the Indiana Penitentiary and Bill had got out on bond, but he was later arrested for counterfeiting and got ten years in Leavenworth.

I found out who he was and we got to know each other. Like I said, Bill was the head doctor or prison nurse in a ward where they kept patients that was pretty bad off. They got nearly everything in the world they wanted or needed. So he got the doctor to transfer me over there and I laid in the bed there and just ate and slept. Prison didn't really bother me. All I wanted was out, but I like to starved to death the first year. Oh, the food they give you is rotten! Jesus, the stuff they give you is old hash, and it stunk and everything. I went from 185 down to 155 that first year. Just pure starvation. Then they had an investigation out there and got to feeding them a little better, and I got over into the hospital and Bill fed me everything I wanted.

I laid there six months until I got my parole. My wife come in a taxi and hauled me out. She had been staying with her mother up in New London, Wisconsin, where she was raised. I went up to the Mayo Clinic and they examined me and said I was in better shape than any doctor up there, but I still had them adhesions that didn't show. It still bothers me a little. It gets sore sometimes, but it never did affect me any other way.

# 21

## LIFE AFTER LEAVENWORTH
## (1929—1976)

"Tulsa had the worst reputation in the world, I tell you, when I went there. . . . I made a good lot of money during the Depression"

After my wife picked me up there at Leavenworth and I went to Mayo Clinic, I come back and bought me a piece of property out there in Tulsa and went into business. About six or eight months before the train robbery, I had bought an apartment lot in Chicago and give ten thousand dollars for it. Them smoke trains turned around out there, and about the time I went in the penitentiary they made trains electric and property just doubled and tripled and went sky high. I had been in the penitentiary about eighteen months when my wife sold the property for thirty thousand. I took some of that money and bought a corner place in Tulsa, put a filling station on it and went to selling gasoline. Tulsa had been my headquarters the whole time before we got in the penitentiary, Tulsa was. Also I had a big nightclub there. In prison, I had made up my mind that was what I was going to do. I've kept that property ever since, had it forty-three years.

Tulsa had the worst reputation in the world, I tell you, when I first went there back in 1919 after I had broke jail over at Ballinger and left Texas. Tulsa was the crowdedest place you ever seen in your life, day, and night. That oil business—it was oil, oil, oil. That's when it was the greatest boom.

It was the oil boom brought all the people there. If

they didn't make money in oil, they'd rob a bank. It brought the drifting crowd of people, you know, the gamblers, drifters, honky-tonkers, and such like that. The gals and the whiskey. The country went dry just when I got there in 1919, and I paid twenty-five dollars for a mini-quart of whiskey.

In Oklahoma you could do anything you was big enough to do. Any law'd take money. Anybody. It was just grafting and thieving and oil wells and joints and gambling halls and everything else. It was twice as wide open as Texas ever was. Why, during World War II, up there, you should have seen it. Honky tonks, beer joints. See, Roosevelt had a ceiling price on everything, and it didn't cost you nothing to live. And people was making all kinds of money and had to spend it. You never seen such as it was up there back then.

In '32 or '33, I forget just which, whiskey was made legal in the United States. Oklahoma, like some other states, voted to stay "dry," that is, legally, but that didn't affect the heavy drinking there. People still bought and drank a lot of bootleg whiskey.

I was in the gas business in Tulsa for three or four years. Then I built a big nightclub and went out of the gasoline business. See, gas was cheap, you know, and I was underselling the big companies. I had four stations and I'd sell from three to five thousand gallons a day at every station, for eight to twelve cents a gallon. And the big companies, they didn't want to go that low. But I was managing, I was managing. I was manufacturing most of my gasoline. It cost me four cents a gallon. I was taking and putting different stuff in and manufacturing my own gas. Good gas too. It was better than a lot of them that was selling then.

And so Texas Company and all them, they was after me and just raising hell. See, they'd put their gas up at fourteen cents and when the customer'd come in, they'd cut it two cents. Well, when I found that out, I just dropped it down below them.

So I'd been there about three years in business—and

I was doing some kind of business—and this one old boy knowed that I was out of the penitentiary. I was selling so much that this old boy working for the Texas Company got to talking with them about me and he said, "Why, don't you know who Willis Newton is? He's a big train robber, ex-convict. He robbed a train in Chicago, and he's out on parole."

I was out on parole, but then I had got pardoned. But them big companies went to the Oklahoma Tax Commission and said, "You know what Willis Newton is going to do? He's going to get in debt to you in taxes and all, and then he's going to close up and leave the state and you're going to hold the sack!"

And they stopped me! They stopped me from buying gas wholesale, that Tax Commission did. And it wasn't even within the law! They couldn't do that! I could have sued the hell out of them if they would have sued me, but you couldn't sue the state then unless they sued you first.

Well, I just owed six thousand. I'd been paying twenty-five or thirty thousand every month. Never was delinquent in my taxes at all. But I owed six thousand when they stopped me. So I went to my lawyer and he says, "We'll let them sue you to collect that, and then you can sue them." But they wouldn't do it, because I'd have sued them for half a million dollars for putting me out of business! So I was forced out of the gasoline business.

That winter and the next spring, I had a drive-in on the corner. Even though it was still prohibition, I put beer in there and went to selling whiskey for six months right over the bar, pints and everything else. And I had all the whiskey business. There was a guy made whiskey, had a big distillery over in St. Louis, Missouri. He made whiskey just like bonded whiskey, all put up just like you see. Everybody thought it was regular bonded whiskey. They didn't know it was bootleg, but it was just as good as the other. And boy!, I was going to town. I tell you I was.

The law knowed I was doing it and they never bothered me. But all them bootleggers around there was getting mad. One day the federals come out and grabbed me, and the man told me, he says, "Willis, those bootleggers is calling me to come on out here. I didn't want to come, but I was a-catchin' so much heat from bootleggers, I just had to come out."

Well, that stopped me in that. They arrested me for selling whiskey and took me down and put me under bond. An old justice of the peace looked at me and he said, "You're Willis Newton of that famous train robbery. I'm going to set your bond at thirty thousand dollars"—it was just a two-thousand bond was all it should have been. And they throwed me in jail. I stayed there for three days.

The third day, this dirty old judge got impeached for taking a five dollar bribe off of some niggers! Three days later! They throwed him out of office for taking a bribe off of niggers, a five-dollar bribe. Next day they cut my bond down to two thousand and I got out. Then Prohibition was repealed before my case come up, and they throwed all them cases out. That next year, in 1934, I built that big nightclub on my property. That was called the Buckhorn Palace.

When we were little we all learned to play cards. Every one of us knowed how to play cards, seven-up, pitch, poker, stuff like that, ever since we was big enough to pick up a deck of cards. After I got in the penitentiary, I played cards. I was the champion cooncan player. Never had nobody beat me playing cooncan in my life. My grandmother Ivy was a fortune teller with cards. She learned it as a girl. She could take a coffee cup and swirl it around the sides and tell you more things—me and another old boy stole a cow up in Cisco one time, and I said, "Grandma, tell me my fortune." That was a week or two after, and she swirled that coffee cup around and said, "Skinny what was you and that boy doing with that cow?"

"We ain't got no cow."

"I see you both right there, one leading the cow and the other driving it."

"Oh," I said. "It's so-and-so's old milk cow over at Cisco. I went with him to get it and take it home. He led it and I drove it" [laughs]. Every one in the family who ever used a branding iron, they put "I V" on it. That was my grandmother's brand. Tull's got the branding iron right now. She used to have horses and cattle all over the country.

Anyway, I built the nightclub on my property and run a gambling house. In the back of the nightclub was a room where we shot craps. All craps. No poker. Craps is a fast game. It's the most popular game there is, shooting craps. Lot of people that come in there was rich, but that was during the Depression when nobody didn't have too much money. But, God!, we had some games. I made a good lot of money during the Depression.

I was out of the city limits, and I was the only nightclub and they wouldn't let the taxi cabs go to them places. They had to unload way off. I had that drive-in down on the corner, about three hundred feet away and a guy says to me, "Willis, what'll you charge me to put a cab stand on that corner?"

"I won't charge you a damn thing. Just put as many as you want to." And he went down and made a deal to put a cab stand there and put it all through, and they didn't even know where it was at! [laughs]. It was right at my nightclub. And you'd see, like fifty cabs at one time parked there. If they didn't scream and holler! But he had his permit and everything and they couldn't do nothing about it. I was the only place in or out of town that had a place for cabs to take them to.

People carried the whiskey in. I had my own, but I let people bring whiskey in, and I'd have a little bowl, a little ice bowl. It would hold about one-eighth of a pound of ice for thirty-five cents. That was enough to go around for about five set-ups. I never allowed the waitresses to pour the water out. They'd bring the bowl back with the water in it, and we'd put more ice in it. I'd get a two hundred pound block of ice and have it shaved up and put in a box. Cost me two dollars, and it brought me a hundred dollars every Saturday night. Just that ice. If they didn't have whiskey, they bought it from me. I sold it for eight dollars a pint and twelve dollars a fifth.

To be in the place, they paid forty-five cents a head and played their own music. Forty-five cents a head. And every Saturday night I'd have a thousand to fifteen hundred people in there. I had a juke box in both ends. They'd just pile those boxes full—they put so many nickels in there, I'd take fifty or a hundred dollars every night out of those juke boxes.

I took all the earnings. I was the house, I was the man that owned the place. I had men working for me, throwing the dice, pitching the dice, everything. If I had cheated there that six months I was operating the gambling house the first time, I could have made myself twenty thousand dollars. But I wouldn't cheat. I made them use square dice. They're "square" dice when they're not cheaters. Others is crooked dice. Customers didn't care because they could bet either way—whether the dice won or whether the dice lost. They couldn't kick because they could bet either way.

When we was buying whiskey, we got it in Joplin, Missouri, out of them whiskey houses. That was after Prohibition but Oklahoma was still a "dry" state—you know a state that voted against liquor even after Prohibition had been removed in other parts of the country. To get the whiskey to Tulsa, you had to cut across the country. That's how I got caught with a load and got a year in the Federal Correctional Institution down at Texarkana—when I was hauling my own whiskey. I sold it there in my club.

When I first went to hauling whiskey, I was paying twenty-six dollars a case. Well, in four to six weeks, I was paying sixty a case! Them saloons over there, they raised the price. It was the black market. They got rich.

You could hold fifteen to twenty-five cases, depending on how big your car was. That's what I put Doc on, and he got to making too much profit and getting drunk. That's when I got my year down there, when my nightclub was going full bloom. Of course, when I went to McAlester prison, there was nobody to tame Jess and Doc, and they went wild drinking that whiskey and fighting and everything else and got my club closed up until I got out. Jess was supposed to sell whiskey around there, and Doc wasn't supposed to do anything but haul whiskey for this other guy. But he'd come out to my place every night and get drunk and raise hell. Jess shot some soldier in the leg out there. Then he let a pistol go off over at another place, with some little old gal he was monkeying around with. I had a big place, and I was getting so much business, everybody else was jealous. And they closed me up. If I had been there, it would never have been closed up. But it was my wife, and she wouldn't fight it. Doc and Jess was raising so much disturbance around there, she said just let them close it up until I come back. When I did, I opened it again.

I got soldiers from all over the country. That's the reason I had so much hell. In town, they had to close at twelve o'clock week nights and two o'clock weekends. I stayed open till daylight. I was in the country. I got my land off an Indian, and they never did put it in the city limits, on account of they got no taxes off them Indians.

Them soldiers—they come in droves. And girls, they was there in stacks, in stacks, them gals was. Yeah. Little old gals, sixteen, seventeen—if they was under sixteen, I wouldn't let them come in. And they come in bunches, twenty in a bunch. They come from town. See, Tulsa's a big town, and there's lots of gals there. They wasn't in the army, and all the boys that lived there was in the army. They come to meet them soldiers.

Transporting whiskey into a "dry" state was a penitentiary offense. The night I got caught, somebody had tipped them in Joplin and they were down the road waiting for me. You had to be suspected, or get snitched on—just like what happens about all this marijuana.

I had pulled into a little restaurant to get something to eat, and they was waiting. They was parked out there and seen me. I went in and sat down, and here come a big guy in at the door. He seen that I was suspicious, but he got in there before I could get out the back door. Well, I went out, and stepped in the car and "Rommmmm!" throwed it in reverse. Boy!, they scattered in every direction. Then "Rommmm!" down the road I went just a-flyin'. But they shot at me and one bullet hit my tire and I liked to turn over. Well, I jumped out, and there was this corn patch. Miles of it! Little, low corn. I hit that corn and them after me. I had to duck down, but they could see me and they run me down and caught me, four or five of them.

It was the federals that got me for hauling that whiskey, but they didn't care about me selling whiskey here in town. They just hunted for people bringing it in. They never raided people round town with all that whiskey business. The state done that, and the county. Federal, all they done was patrol them borders to keep you from bringing it in. That's all they done.

But then a bank was robbed in Oklahoma, and when they couldn't find out who did it, they blamed me and Joe. Somebody had caught that old ex-sheriff up there and taken him and tied him up and robbed the bank. They robbed it with a torch, cut into the safe with a blowtorch, and I never had *seen* a torch in them days, didn't think a bank could be robbed with a torch, but somebody did it. They didn't have no evidence it was us but we had been sent to the federal penitentiary at Leavenworth for robbing a train, so they said it had to be us. It was our reputation that did it.

"Maybe you didn't rob this bank, but you robbed other ones that you got away with," one old law said. That's the way it is, once you been arrested for something. When I was young and went to jail in Eastland County, old man Boyd, that Texas bank inspector, would jump me up for bank robbery everywhere I went after that, and I couldn't rob a kitchen safe at that time. My reputation was made and that's the way they thought about me. What was there for me to do? So I got me a big pistol and I said I was going to make me some money.

And I did make money, but I spent lots of it. When I wound up, I didn't have anything. When they put me and Joe in the penitentiary in Oklahoma, it was for doing nothing in the world. Our reputation was all that put us in.

*It was kind of a political deal. The guy that was sheriff up there had been in office for years and he got beat. Somebody run against him who said, "Elect me and they won't come in there and rob the bank and capture me and do this, that and the other. Elect me and I'll protect your town. I won't do like your sheriff now that you've got." So that campaign beat the guy that was sheriff there when the bank was robbed. The new sheriff was a good fellow. A young fellow. I got well acquainted with him after that. It was under that old sheriff that we got picked up.*

We didn't do that robbery any more than you did. And everybody in Oklahoma knowed it. Fifteen businessmen that had lived in Tulsa forty or fifty years, all their lives, when I went up there and they called my case to trial, all of them businessmen come up there. The attorney general appointed Sam Latimore to prosecute me. Him and the old ex-sheriff that was accusing me— the one that had got tied up that night of the robbery and it had hurt his feelings—they kept that courthouse open until two o'clock for two nights getting witnesses. They would go out and say, "I know he done it, but I can't convict him with all these businessmen testifying for him, but I know he done it and I want you to swear so-and-so." And so he fixed the jury.

That old ex-sheriff even told a friend of mine after that that he had fixed the jury. These men who pulled the robbery was masked, but he got some kids that had come down there and an old woman that worked there at night to swear that the mask fell down.

*You know, our pictures was the first pictures that was showed to anybody when a bank was robbed anywhere!*

305

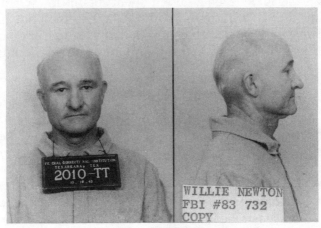

*FBI photo of Willis Newton*

*They taken our pictures over and showed them to everybody and nobody would know us. Then they come back later on after they had framed up some of them old kids and a woman to say, "Yeah, that was him. Yeah, he had on a mask, but just as he walked under a light, an electric light, his mask fell down and I seen him. It was Joe Newton!" [laughs]. My lawyers said, did his mask ever fall down after that? And they said, no, no. It was just that one time that he run under the light [laughs]. Hot damn.*

So he got all these kids to swear that, and then they give me twenty years. Joe hadn't been arrested then, because it was early in the case. He was in Mexico where he had a gold mine he was working down there.

So I appealed my case, but everything was fixed up to frame me. I took it to the Court of Criminal Appeals, and every time we came up with an error, they called it a "harmless error." It come out in the newspaper that they had admitted there was seventeen "harmless errors" in my case, but then they affirmed the conviction and said I ought to be in the penitentiary

About this time, Joe was coming back out of Mexico

*FBI photo of Joe Newton alias John H. Rogers*

into Arizona and some old boy snitched on him, somebody that was working for him that had got mad at him,
and they went out there and arrested him.

They brought him back and tried him, and there was
six to turn him loose and six to convict him. They held
out thataway for three or four days. Finally six of them
come over and said they would agree to convict him for
five years. So then the others agreed, but they said, "We'll
leave his sentencing to the judge." That's where they
killed Joe, because I'd already done got twenty years.
When they left it to the judge, he give Joe twenty years
too. The judge said the reason he give him twenty years
was that I had got twenty—to be "fair," I guess.

I had a little money when they put me in the penitentiary there at McAlester, and I could have got out right
away if I'd have give them ten thousand dollars. They all
knowed I was innocent, the old governor and all of them,
but they wanted ten thousand to give me a pardon and
I wouldn't do it. So there I sat for seven years and six
months—for *nothing*. When Governor Phillips got in, he
told me, "Willis, I'm going to give you a parole. I know
you're innocent." So the governor cut my time to fifteen
years, and since I had already served half of that, I was

done.  But Joe was still in prison.

I served seven and a half years in McAlester Penitentiary and Joe served ten years.  He served all of his.  You get "good time" so he served it out in ten.  He served nearly all of it out as a trusty, about eight and a half years.  I served five and a half years of mine out as trusty.  He went to Vinita and worked in that big hospital there for four or five years of his.  He was a kind of foreman over other help there.

*As it turned out, I actually sure as heck did have to spend ten years in the McAlester penitentiary, yes, sir.*

But we had no more to do with the robbery than you did.  And half the people that had anything to do with our case knowed we didn't do it.  Evidence showed we *couldn't* have done it.  But they just framed a jury to convict us and then framed the Court of Criminal Appeals to confirm us.  Old Sam Latimore did, and he was a big deacon in the Baptist Church.  Like them two fellows on the Court of Criminal Appeals.  Them deacons stood together.  They said we was "bad men," and that if we didn't rob that bank that we had robbed a lot of others.  They didn't have nerve enough to rob one themselves, I guess.

*It crossed my mind at the time we were first convicted for the Rondout robbery that when I got out I didn't want to do any more bank robbing.  And I didn't do no more.  I come home and went to work for thirty-five dollars a month.  That's a month.  Then I got to breaking horses, but after a good long while fur season come on and furs went real high.  Here I was working for thirty-five a month and I seen them paying ridiculous prices for them hides.  My gosh, I thought, I know as much about hides as they do. More than most of them.  I didn't have but five dollars, but I went to buying hides, and when I quit—I just bought for forty days—when I quit I had fifteen hundred in cash in the bank and I'd borrowed my brother Tull's old pickup* and spent $250 on it, and in the meantime when I made a little money, I went to the store and bought $250 worth of clothes. I didn't have any decent clothes.

I also bought a meat market in Uvalde with my fifteen hundred and was in the meat business, making good money. And that's where I made a big mistake. I left and went back up to Oklahoma. If I'd a-stayed there in Uvalde—I had my meat market and had a business going, see, and I didn't want to do anything else. I wanted to stay right there. I'd got married in that chunk of time too.

I had met my wife in Uvalde. Her father was a section foreman and they lived right there by the depot. She was living with him then because she was young. Well, we was all young in them days, it's been that long ago. A cafe had opened up right there on this side of the depot where them old buildings have been tore out, and she was working in that cafe after school. I lived right across the street, a hundred yards from where she did. It wasn't no trouble meeting her, because I was in and out of there all the time. Everybody knowed everybody, you know.

Anyways, this head inspector in New Braunfels told Jess to tell me to go away somewhere before my federal parole was up because they were going to put me back in jail down here in New Braunfels for that bank robbery back in 1923. That inspector said to tell me to go away somewhere, because they would arrest me and send me to prison again sure as hell.

The district attorney in New Braunfels was running a big bluff. He thought that we had committed the robbery in New Braunfels and he was going to run a bluff and try to make it stick. He had come out to Uvalde and got me, and he had me sitting up there in the courthouse, and then I got a writ of habeas corpus and he had to turn me loose until my federal time was up. I still belonged to the federal.

So then when that federal time was up, this old inspector and Jess told me to leave, and that's where I made my mistake. I left and went back up to Oklahoma.

*I should have known they couldn't try me and convict me. On the New Braunfels robbery, I sat out in the car and not a soul in the world seen me. Besides that, one time, I stopped in New Braunfels and went up to the clerk's office and said I'd like to read the record on the Newton boys' bank robbery indictment. I read it and there wasn't anything in there about me being identified. Hell.*

*When I run up to Oklahoma, I farmed for a year. When Willis got out he come over to Tulsa, and the first thing he did, he bought two gasoline stations. When I come over there, he sold me one of them. Didn't need two, he finally decided. So that was my job then, and I stayed there and run that station and that's where I was at when I got arrested for the Oklahoma bank robbery. The one that I got sent to McAlester for.*

I made a lot of money up there in Tulsa, but eventually as I got old I decided to come back to Uvalde. I had always liked Uvalde. That's where my Ma and Pa lived in their last days, that's where Joe and Jess and Doc were living, and that's where I wanted to spend my last days. I liked the weather there. I liked the Nueces River where I could go fishing when I wanted to, and I liked bees. Uvalde's the honey capital of Texas, you know. There's a lot of chaparral around there with flowers and I would say that the *huajilla* honey you can collect around Uvalde is the best in the world. I don't rob banks any more, but I sure can rob those bee hives. Both me and Joe likes to mess around with bees.

My daddy, he died in Uvalde two years before my mother did. They both was seventy-nine when they died. He died on the porch of my mother's place. They wasn't divorced or nothing. He just went up there to North Texas for some years and she stayed here. He had come back to Uvalde, though, in 1935, and was at her house. He laid down on the porch one day to take a nap, and when she went to wake him for dinner, he was dead. Then she died two years later with pneumonia.

# 22

## LAST THOUGHTS

"I wanted something . . . and I knew I would never get it following a mule's ass and dragging cotton sacks down them middles."

After I got out of Leavenworth I never thought of organizing the gang again. We wasn't really a gang. It was just us brothers. A "gang" is what hangs around town shooting people. We wasn't a gang like that. We just acted like businessmen. We didn't want to kill or hurt anybody. All we wanted was the money, just like any businessman does.

Before the train robbery, we always knowed if we ever got a big piece of money, we was going to buy us a ranch—Mexico, Texas, Arizona, anywhere—and settle down. Nobody would ever have bothered us. We was above suspicion. There was no way in the world to suspicion us, if they hadn't caught us on account of Doc getting shot. No way in the world they'd ever suspicion us, old farm boys, cowpunchers from down here in South Texas.

When Jess got out of Leavenworth—he only stayed there eighteen months—he went to Texas and worked around on ranches down there around Uvalde until he died in 1960. He was seventy-three when he died of cancer of the lung. He'd gone up to the Veterans' Hospital at Temple on and off for about two years, in and out, in and out. They couldn't tell him what was the matter with him, so he'd come back home. I tried to get him to go to a good doctor in San Antone. I said, "Jess, if you'll go to San Antone and go through one of them clinics, I'll pay the bill. Let them find out what's the matter with you."

311

"No," he said. "I can go up here and stay in this hospital and I'll gross $250 a month besides staying there."

Well, finally, the last time he went back, they told him, "One of your lungs is eat up with cancer and the other is half gone. You just got ninety days to live." And that was after he'd been in and out of there for two years. Every doctor I ever talked to outside of there said if they had found it when he first went in there, when he was strong, they could have cut that lung loose right now and helped him.

While he was in prison, Doc didn't do much of anything. For one thing, he was all shot up. One shot had torn through his tongue, one went through his chest, and he had been hit in both arms, so for a year or two, he just laid in the hospital. Then he got a job in the hospital where he worked around for two or three years as a yard man, I think it was. All he done was stay out of sight. The warden told him, "All you got to do is keep out of the way back in there behind this building, and that's your job." So he laid low until he got out [laughs].

When he got out of Leavenworth, two years after the rest of us, Doc went down to his farm in Oklahoma. He stayed ten or twelve years before he sold the place. He didn't farm, he just had a farm. Stayed out there, raised some cows and hogs and finally traded it for an apartment house over in Oklahoma City. Him and his wife moved there. Then he traded that apartment house or sold it and bought a home out there and his wife went to work at that packing plant at some kind of job and Doc, he bought hogs and cattle and things and sold them and brought them into that stockyard for two or three years.

After that, he come up to Tulsa and I put him on that whiskey job where he could make two hundred dollars a day running it from Joplin, Missouri. But Doc couldn't stand prosperity. He got to drinking that whiskey and it wasn't but two or three months until the law knowed he was hauling whiskey and they was watching him and he had to quit. They never arrested him. They was following him and he knowed he was under suspicion. He just quit and went back to Oklahoma City and stayed there.

He was about fifty when he met his wife over in Wilson where he was on that farm this side of Oklahoma City. She was twenty or more years younger than he was and a fine woman too. A German. He got to drinking and running here and there, so she quit him and sued him and got a divorce.

Then he left Oklahoma City and come down here to Texas. Down here he didn't do nothing. Well, he made a little money and he'd go back up to Oklahoma and trade bulls and cows and he sold a few. Then he was arrested for trying to rob a bank in Rowena, in Runnells County, in 1968. That ain't been long ago. He was living right here in Uvalde. He'd been working as an iron worker down in Corpus Christi with my nephew for about five years and he paid that big income into social security, but then when he quit when he was sixty-five, all he got was two hundred dollars and something off that. He was living up there in North Uvalde in my mother's old house.

Maybe I ought not to tell this. It's the first time I've ever told it. Doc and this other old boy got together and got to drinking. The other guy was forty-five years old and never been arrested in his life. He was a cow buyer and had credit at the bank for a hundred thousand. They didn't go to Rowena to rob no bank at all. They just had a brace and a bit and a jimmy bar. There was a big gun store joining this bank, and Doc had been up there with a fellow selling onions in this town and he saw some guns in this store that he liked. He went in the bank to get change, and he thought there was a door from the bank into the gun store. So he and this other old boy went up there to get all them guns. They had an old pickup or something parked right across from the bank, hooked up to a trailer. They was going to get all them guns and put them in this old pickup and go back to Uvalde.

The people from the bank said there was never nothing touched in there. Nothing. They went in there trying to find that other door where it went into the gun store.

A man who lived across the street seen them breaking
into the bank. They had a telephone burglar alarm, the
first one that ever was used there, that ever caught
somebody. Somebody had been breaking into them
stores, and they didn't know who it was, so the man
hooked up this telephone alarm to the bank. When you
open the door, it rings your telephone. The man slept in
a whiskey store across the street. Doc had looked in the
bank and didn't see no burglar alarm, but that telephone
woke that man up and he seen them.

They couldn't have been trying to rob the bank! How
could you rob a bank with an eighteen-inch jimmy bar
and a brace and bit? Neither one of them knowed
anything about cutting a safe. So the man woke up and
went to the phone and called the sheriff over in Ballinger.
Him and two deputies jumped in a car and they was there
in seven or eight minutes. Doc and his partner was still
working in there, looking for a door, and there wasn't no
door. About the time they got ready to come out, the
sheriff run right up in front of the door. They like to shot
that door down. Shot that bank all to pieces inside with
machine guns. Course Doc and that guy was down
behind them brick walls, and they couldn't hit them. Oh,
they tore that man's bank up! They said that old German
come down there and he was the maddest man in the
world. Said, "You damn fools! You done all this for
nothing."

And as they come out, that old sheriff knocked Doc
in the head with his pistol, knocked him cold. He never
did get over that. He was bleeding and that German that
run the bank, he was a nice old man, he saw Doc was
about to freeze to death. He made them get something
and cover him up. And he ate that sheriff out. Said, "You
done this for nothing."

When they walked out, they wasn't fighting or nothing, and they had left their guns inside on the counter
and walked out with their hands up. That's some of them
dirty old laws. They just wanted to hit somebody on the
head. The doctor over at Ballinger, oh, he was mad. He

said, "That's the dirtiest, brutal trick I ever heard tell of a man doing." He said Doc had a concussion on his brain. Doc was about seventy-seven years old then, you know.

After that he was—I don't know, it seemed he was never the same. He just seemed like he was kind of dazed at times, and his head hurt him a lot after that.

This is the first time I've ever told what they was doing. Doc and the other guy was under federal bond and under state bond. Well, the state court come up first, and Doc's partner pled guilty and got five year. They transferred Doc's case out to Fort Stockton, and he went out there. He was never tried. Just pled guilty in front of a judge. Well, after he was convicted, the federal government couldn't try him. You can't convict a man twice for the same thing. That killed the government's case, and they dismissed it.

The judge tried to give him probation, but this old prosecutor down there from Fort Stockton wouldn't let him do it. Then the judge wanted to give Doc two years probation because he was sorry for him. He tried every way in the world to turn him loose, but he couldn't get that old county attorney to do it. Everybody in Fort Stockton was for him.

So Doc went down there to prison and done eight months in the hospital. Never was out of the hospital. Then he come back to Uvalde and stayed there until he died in 1974. He got cancer and died when he was eighty-three years old. He had went to a nursing home in 1972. He really wouldn't have had to go, but his head kept bothering him and he began to get where he wouldn't take his own medicine. He'd forget. Then he laid down there two years and a half. It got to where he couldn't walk after he went there, just like my legs is getting. When he died there was only two left of the Newton boys gang, just me and Joe.

Joe, he went down below Uvalde and worked for old man West on a ranch there until he worked his parole out. Took him about two years. He also has a butcher shop and a drive-in in Uvalde. Then he farmed up in Oklahoma awhile too. He was on Doc's farm until Doc got out. Joe and my Daddy grew cotton and corn.

Sometimes people ask me if I'm sorry that I ever robbed banks and trains. I think Joe might be sorry. He would've made a good Baptist. But no, I'm not sorry. I'm sorry that sometimes, for one reason or another, we left a lot of money in those banks and that the Rondout train robbery blowed up on us.

If I hadn't gotten into the penitentiary that first time when I was accused of stealing the cotton that Doc really stole, I'd have been a farmer probably. I was raised on a farm and I didn't know nothing but a farm. When I got out of the Texas pen the first time, I farmed for a year or two, went up there and picked cotton for that man over at Bronte. That's all I knowed.

But I couldn't make no money working on a farm. I picked that old cotton for fifty cents a day, ten dollars a month after I got up to nineteen or twenty years old. Those farmers I knowed when I was a kid worked hard all their lives and you know what happened to them when they got old? Their kids or somebody else would put them in a little shack behind their house and that's where they usually lived until they died.

I didn't want to die that way. I wanted something, something more than that, and I knew I would never get it following a mule's ass and dragging those cotton sacks down them middles. I might never have robbed any banks, though, if I hadn't gotten in with those bank robbers in the state pen.

When I heard that banks were covered by insurance, that settled it for me. Those insurance companies used to sell policies to those poor farmers out in West Texas and promise them everything. But then, if something happened, just try to collect. Insurance companies is the biggest liars and thieves in the world. They didn't care if they hurt us poor farmers, so why should I care if I hurt them?

Me and the other boys was planning to go straight

some day, but we knew that the insurance companies and some of the banks never would, because they'd buy bonds from us at a discount and they knew they was stolen.

We never robbed individual people and we never wanted to hurt them if we could help it. That's why we usually robbed banks in small towns and at night time when there was nobody around. You couldn't go to them big city banks and rob them because there was policemen all around and burglar alarms even in those days. You had to go to the little ones. Whenever there are lots of people around, you run too much of a chance of killing or hurting somebody. Every time we went to a job, my first word was, "Boys, don't shoot nobody without you have to. You've got the first shot, and if you have to shoot him, shoot where you won't kill him." Once you kill somebody, like Bonnie and Clyde did, you're in trouble.

Robbing banks is hard work. There's no fun in it. I never done it for the excitement. I done it only for the money. Oh, you'd get excited on a quick getaway or something. But I was never more frightened robbing a bank than picking down a row or plowing a field with mules. I just made a business of it.

Seems like there was always more bank robberies in Kansas, Nebraska and Missouri than anywhere else. There was getting to be lots more banks in this part of the country, and it was more wide open than back East. Wasn't so thickly populated, so it was pretty easy to get them. And the country was settled by people that had done something somewhere else, lots of them had, and then run from there to here. So their kids come to find out what the old man had done back there, and maybe it didn't seem so bad for them to rob something or even kill somebody theirselves. There was so many people in this part of the country in those days that was just out for themselves. If you robbed a bank and went around a corner and run into a law, if you just gave him a hundred dollars he'd let you go and go after another guy.

Banks didn't have much money in them. There was

317

a lot of little ones that I never mentioned here, where I got a thousand or fifteen hundred dollars, me and a couple more guys the first year out. We'd just get it and get out of sight. This was out in them little towns, out in them oil fields and country towns. There wasn't a lot of money, but it was a lot for them days.

It was just snatch and grab, snatch and grab. It's still snatch and grab today, only it's gotten bigger. Now it's the "skinners," the smart guys, and they've taken to other fields because there ain't nothing in bank robbing now—not like we used to do it—and it's too dangerous. Burglar alarms and vaults in concrete all over the United States.

There's lots of good and bad in everything nowadays. But I would say there's more bad than good. And that's true from Washington on down to the justices of the peace and constables. It kind of starts in Washington. That's the top. It influences people when they see the President and all of them in Washington being corrupt. Sure it does, sure it does. When I told you about them wet ropers, the big crooks trying to run the little ones out, that's just like it is today. All them high kudoos passing all them strenuous laws against petty larceny crime, and if they went down to their own doorstep, they wouldn't know where real crime was at.

In Omaha once in 1920, I went into a garage there to get my car all slicked up because we was going out to hit a bank. Well, it always cost just fifty cents to get a car washed and waxed, and this colored guy that did the job charged me one dollar. I says, "Say, what about this?"

"Well, I tell you, mister, that's a pretty high price. But this graft, it starts in the White House and it comes on down. I gets you, and you gets somebody else."

"Alright. I'm fixing to get me somebody tonight," and we did too [laughs]. Went on out and robbed one that night.

They say people in this country were more sympathetic to each other back in the twenties and thirties. I don't think it was that people was more sympathetic with each other then. To find that sympathetic stuff, you got to go way on back to 1900 up to 1915. After the First World War, the whole country changed around. Before that, if a farmer got sick, the neighbors come over and plowed his ground if it was spring, or picked the cotton if it was in the fall. They'd even take up donations sometimes and go and buy him some chuck.

Everything changed during the First World War because there was a lot of people that had never been out of the country. They had never been anywhere and they was so ignorant, they'd just been whipped down. But when they got out, them old country boys, and saw what the world was, they got a taste of a good life and that changed everything.

I been around a long time and I've watched how things are. You've got to have policemen, but this stuff about "stopping crime," that's just the bunco. That's the old hokum. I guess it don't hurt them to go ahead and say that. They're big men and they need to say something, but it don't make any difference.

'Course, we got to have right, we got to have law, we've got to have the Bible, we've got to have churches. People would be eating each other if they hadn't got civilized. That's what civilized the country, the Bible and the law. But there's no difference now. Anything you go into now, half of it's unfair. The laws—we got good laws, but we got so many bad ones. Preachers—we got some good preachers, but we got lots of bad ones that don't really believe the Bible. They do it for the money.

There'll always be crime, there'll always be lawyers, there'll always be bankers, there'll always be doctors, there'll always be preachers, there'll always be hypocrites, there'll always be some good people and some bad ones. The Post Office Inspector who tried my case where they put me in prison for the train robbery, he says, "Willis, the only thing bad about this train robbery is that you got caught. They do worse than rob a train in Washington every day."

But this world, the way it is, won't change. It ain't

319

a-goin' to. It's driving itself on pretty bad. I don't know what it's going to come to, but I won't live to see it. The Bible says that man will finally destroy hisself. That's in the Bible, and a lot of other things that are in the Bible have come true.

*Willis (top) and Joe (bottom)*

# EPILOGUE

Willis and Joe celebrated the American Bicentennial in 1976 with the release of the documentary film, "The Newton Boys: Portrait of An Outlaw Gang," which, for the first time, gave their own versions of their careers. As Joe said, "Lots of things have been written about us since the Rondout robbery, but most of it was either wrong or hearsay. We're the only ones who knew everything that happened, because we were the only ones that took part in everything. This is the first time we've ever spoken for ourselves."

Having made that statement for the record on film and audio tape, Willis and Joe, in the years that followed, went back to relative retirement. Both spent a lot of time "messing with" their bee hives, their favorite hobby. Periodically, they would come to San Antonio to visit with us, sometimes bringing us jars of honey; and when they had birthdays, we went to Uvalde to celebrate with them.

Willis died on August 22, 1979, at the age of ninety. Joe, the last of the gang, died ten years later, on February 3, 1989, having celebrated his eighty-eighth birthday the month before.

Willis had suffered from a variety of ailments, most of them, like his difficulty in walking, deriving simply from old age. "I never thought I would live this long," he often said, shaking his head. In his youth, in the last decade of the nineteenth century, few had lived that long, particularly bank or train robbers. But he was scrappy right up to the end. We visited him often in the Methodist Hospital in San Antonio, and he "cussed out" the doctors there with the same vehemence he had used to "cuss out" the laws. Once he asked us to bring him some mineral oil, saying that the doctors didn't know what was wrong with him, and when we handed him the bottle, he turned it upside down and drank it all, one swallow after another. Though he was obviously in pain, he never complained. The man in the bed next to him, who was recovering from a heart attack, said, "I like that old man. He's got a lot of courage."

Willis was buried from a church—the Uvalde Methodist Church—but the minister didn't dwell on the deceased's unconventional life. He limited himself to reading from the Psalms to the small group of mourners. Willis was buried in the Newton family plot in the Uvalde cemetery next to his wife, who had died in 1959, and near other members of the family: his brothers Jess, Doc and Tull, and his father and mother, Jim and Janetta Pecos Newton. Willis and his wife Louise had no children, but she had a son from a previous marriage who came from California for the funeral. He also had an adopted daughter, to whom he left most of his estate, with a request that she give her two children "a good education."

In his last years, Joe suffered from heart trouble, and also from nearly constant pain in his back, probably the result of the beating his spine took when he was riding broncs as a young man. But up into his seventies he rode his horse, Old Paint, in local parades. Then when his doctor told him he had to give up riding horses, Joe switched to sitting on a bale of hay in the back of a pickup truck. His popularity in Uvalde was attested to by the way the crowds lining the streets for the parades yelled to him as he passed.

Joe always maintained that his career as a train and bank robber had been a mistake, but he obviously enjoyed the local and national notoriety it brought him. Until two years before his death, he took part annually in the Texas Folklife Festival in San Antonio, demonstrating how to backpack mules and signing autographs for wide-eyed kids while at the same time warning them not to follow him in his career. One of our deep regrets is that we were unable to participate in the last rites for Joe because of an ice storm that hit the San Antonio area in early February and made all roads west to Uvalde impassible the day of the service.

Today we ourselves wonder what kind of epilogue can be written about Willis and Joe and their brothers, Jess and Doc, now that all of them are gone.

We can almost guarantee that, had Willis been born in the latter part of the twentieth century and gone to school like other kids, he would have been labeled "gifted and talented" and probably would have won scholarships to Harvard or Yale. This might have been true of Joe as well. Born in a time and place that was still part of the frontier, they yet embodied modernity in a way that anticipated many later developments of the twentieth century. In this curious combination of past, present and future, they became a kind of outlaw such as this country had not seen before.

Most old time outlaws were renegades who cut themselves off from society because they had killed somebody in quarrels, or out of revenge, or because they were violence-prone sociopaths. What set the Newtons apart from this type of outlaw and what made them "urban modernists" was that their primary objective and motication was money—exactly what everybody else in modern society, from businessmen to doctors and lawyers, wanted. To get that money without killing anybody or being killed themselves, the Newtons were smart enough to know they had to be "professionals" in every sense of the word. Thus they operated in the most modern and efficient manner possible, obeying every rule of safety called for by their mercantile objective.

With hindsight, we now recognize the extent of their involvement in what we today call "systems analysis." They were continuously immersed in the study of banking operations, of law enforcement systems, of security systems, of communication systems, of criminal justice systems, and of systems of demolition. They knew their "times" and took advantage of every asset the new technologies afforded: nitroglycerine to blow safes, the best-built and fastest cars to make their getaways, the latest road maps on which they could trace the getaway routes, and efficient weapons which each of them made sure they knew how to operate with maximum effect.

Conversely, they analyzed carefully and used to advantage the relative absence of technology that characterized small town banks and the small towns themselves. Although most banks in big cities had already gone to round safes which "screwed" into the walls of the concrete vaults and were thus virtually unblowable, small towns in the 1920s for the most part used square "lug" safes into whose cracks nitro could be poured, detonated with a dynamite cap, and the door literally peeled off. In addition to bank safes' being blowable, small towns at that time could be isolated from one another fairly easily, especially in Texas where in the opening decades of the twentieth century, two-thirds of the population remained scattered in rural areas.

Still, granting the Newtons their intelligence and ingenuity, what can we say of their illegal activity? Does it justify a career built on armed robbery when Willis says that he "wanted something" out of life and he knew he wasn't going to get it "following a mule's ass down those middles"? His words begin to give shape to a free enterprise ethic which is fundamentally American, one built around the notions of initiative and fierce, even aggressive independence. In itself, that ethic arouses our respect, yet we must give it grudgingly, because the "something" Willis felt driven to pursue was articulated almost exclusively in material terms. He wanted money. Always more money.

Was Willis merely being clever when he said that what he and his brothers did was "just one thief robbing from another," indicating that the banks and insurance companies were bigger crooks than they were, and the moral difference between them was merely that he and his brothers planned one day to stop robbing, while the banks and insurance companies never would? Our sympathies for the "little guys," for the farmers and underdogs, might tend to align us with Willis on this matter.

Yet a moment's thought leads to the contrary realization that his is a sly semantic argument that depends for its persuasiveness on an audience's not recognizing that whenever banks are robbed—even insured banks—the little people are always ultimately the losers.

Times were certainly tough in the rural milieu in which the Newtons grew up. As W. J. Cash writes in his classic work, *The Mind of the South*, it was almost impossible for most Southern farmers to make a living on the small cotton farms typically dotting the landscape in the early part of the century. The price of cotton went up and down—but mostly down. The land in West Texas, which historian Joe Frantz says could be purchased by the section for agriculture for two dollars an acre and for grazing for one dollar an acre in 1895, had become progressively eroded and worn out from continuous planting of cotton. If rainfall didn't materialize in a given year, there would be no crop at all. Where the Newton family lived, droughts were recurrent, and the no-crop scenario tended to be the rule rather than the exception. Add to the uncertainties of weather and marketplace the supposedly slack character of Jim Newton, the boys' father, "a good man but nobody could ever say what he was good for," and the elements of an equation likely to produce little or nothing in the way of material gain and still less by the way of hope are clearly in place. It is indeed a bitterly discouraging fact that the Newton family actually *owned* land only once or twice, and even in those cases it slipped quickly away. For most of their lives they remained deeply, irretrievably mired in the debt that attends upon tenant farming.

Yet Joe, notably, never accepted Willis' rationalizations for the lives they led. "We were all raised the same way," he said. "Why was Willis the only one who wanted to rob banks and trains? Until I went to join Willis in Tulsa, I had never broken a law in my life." The same was true for the great majority of other men and women who grew up in West Texas under the conditions that battered the Newtons. True, other Southwesterners became notorious outlaws, individuals such as Bonnie and Clyde, Pretty Boy Floyd and the Santa Claus bank robbers who robbed the First National Bank in Cisco, Texas, dressed up like Santa and his helpers. But the great majority remained hard-working, church-going, socially respectable people. Certainly there was among them less crime per capita than there is in the urban areas of America today.

Without doubt, Willis was different temperamentally from Joe and his other brothers. He had tremendous energy that demanded expression, and a will which was not to be denied. As a small boy, he was in his own way the most enterprising member of the family, eager for an education, walking for miles to a post office to pick up newspapers that he could sell back in his home town of Rising Star at a penny or two profit per paper. During the few weeks that he went to school when he was eleven, Willis attacked his studies with the same zest he was later to display in casing banks, and he covered the classwork of several grades in a short time before he was forced to quit because of his family's poverty. His mother was proud of Willis' get-up-and-go, but she also recognized that he was not the same as her other children. According to Joe, she worried more about Willis than she did about all the others.

Willis himself often bragged about his initiative—an initiative which, compared to the others, quickly found its way into anti-social enterprises. "I was the leader, the starter. I stayed busy doing something all the time. Old man K.P. Aldridge told my wife, he said, 'Well, one thing about old Willis, if he wasn't robbing a bank or train, he was looking for one to rob.'" While Joe, Jess and Doc usually took a vacation in the summer months—watching professional baseball games in Chicago or Kansas City—Willis literally never stopped scouting for "marks."

When Willis, bristling with professional pride, set himself and his brothers apart from audacious amateur outlaws such as Bonnie and Clyde ("They never robbed a bank in their life, they just robbed filling stations and stores and run from place to place"), he made what we consider to be a crucial distinction: the Newtons weren't killer types or sadists who took pleasure in brutalizing others.

Undoubtedly the Newtons did maintain certain of the dominant attitudes of the frontier outlaws. Like their runamuck forebears eternalized (as even the Newtons themselves) in books such as *The Album of Gunfighters* and Frank H. Bushick's *Glamorous Days,* they believed intensely in personal freedom and their inalienable right to do whatever they had the courage to do. During the period in which they plied their trade, even though the area of Texas, Oklahoma and the rest of the country west of the Mississippi was rapidly being settled, Willis and his brothers still regarded the scene as a kind of open range in which the money in banks and on trains, like the wild cattle and horses of the old days, was there for the taking by whomever had the skill and pluck to attempt it. Willis often said that many others would have liked to do what their gang did, but they "just didn't have the guts, and they wouldn't have known how to do it. They couldn't rob a kitchen safe."

The enthusiasm with which modern audiences responded to Willis and Joe whenever the old men appeared to tell their story also bespeaks something of modern values and attitudes. The desire for money in today's world is something everybody understands and almost everybody identifies with. Professionalism, efficiency, enterprise, safety—these too are values highly prized in our time. Finally, frankness, as well as a recognition of the corruption that exists today in high places and low, in institutions and within individuals, is becoming not only more and more acceptable but more and more desirable—if only to protect the interests of those who have to place their money and trust in such institutions and individuals. No matter what audiences have watched the Newtons' documentary film, at the point where Willis claims insurance companies are "the biggest thieves in the country," and that what he and his brothers did was merely "one thief a-stealin' from an-other," invariably the viewers' response has been to clap and cheer.

Thus the story of the Newton boys represents not only a microcosmic example of the history of rural, frontier America, but also hints at the emergence of a pragmatic, professional, modern, urban America whose values are still in flux and remain to be articulated in a more positive, constructive way than they are at the present time.

Willis' and Joe's legacy to all who follow them is this complex, subtle, and compelling family narrative. In the process of telling it, they were obviously trying to order and validate what would otherwise be the chaos of their lives and those of their ancestors, as we all try to do in one way or another. We ourselves compiled this record not to create new myths about American outlaws or to perpetuate old ones, but to preserve, with as much authenticity as possible, the raw materials out of which myth may form, becoming a part not only of a people's literature but also of the largest patterns of history itself.

# Geographical Index

Abilene, Tex., 11, 38, 39, 83, 87, 135-40, 266
Albany, Tex., 30
Aransas Pass, Tex., 68
Ardmore, Okla., 95, 150
Ark., 2, 9, 11, 17-18, 19, 23-24, 57, 84, 104
Arma, Kans., 154-55, 156
Ashdown, Ark., 194
Asherton, Tex., 65
Austin County, Tex., 112
Austin, Tex., xvii, 63, 107, 129

Baird, Tex., 22, 37, 83
Ballinger, Tex., 68, 139, 143, 164, 187, 299, 314
Bandera, Tex., 58, 221
Batesville, Tex., 71, 72, 73, 74-75, 109
Battle Creek, Mich., 292
Bells, Tex., 133, 191-92, 256
Belton, Tex., 6
Big Bend, Tex., 132
Big Foot, Tex., xv
Big Springs, Tex., 38
Big Wells, Tex., 66
Bloomburg, Tex., 192
Boerne, Tex., xiv, 196-97
Boswell, Okla., 149, 151
Brackettville, Tex., xv
Brady, Tex., 48
Brandon, Can., 204
Bronte, Tex., 106, 316
Brown County, Tex., 7, 9

Brownwood, Tex., 7, 66, 79
Buffalo Gap, Tex., 136-37
Burnet, Tex., 107, 109
Calhoun County, Ark., 17
Callahan County, Tex., 1, 9, 19, 37, 53, 54, 83, 91
Camp Wood, Tex., 55
Carrizo Springs, Tex., 62, 65
Ceylon, Can., 209-10
Cheyenne, Wyo., 234
Chicago, Ill., 1, 158, 188, 190, 199, 201, 214, 215, 216, 227, 239, 250, 251, 254, 263, 267-96, 297
Chickasha, Okla., 8
Cicero, Ind., 273-74
Cisco, Tex., 30, 34-35, 36, 37, 39, 42, 43, 44, 49, 50, 51, 69, 83, 97, 248, 300-1, 326
Cleburne, Tex., 84
Cline, Tex., 99, 101, 135
Cloudcroft, N. Mex., 31
Coleman, Tex., 30, 49, 110-11
Comal County, Tex., xiv
Comanche, Tex., 47
Comfort, Tex., 219
Commerce, Okla., xi
Corpus Christi, Tex., 313
Cottonwood, Tex., 1, 9-10, 11, 13-14, 15, 19-20, 23, 24, 28, 30, 33, 34, 35, 44, 49, 52, 91
Crandall, Tex., 164-65

Cross Plains, Tex., 79, 83
Crystal City, Tex., 60, 61, 62, 63, 65, 66, 68, 69, 71, 72, 79, 103, 104, 105, 109, 114, 169, 189

Dallas, Tex., 1, 9, 164, 165, 166, 191, 192
Del Rio, Tex., 192, 290
Denison, Tex., 133, 134, 147-48, 191, 194
Denver, Colo., 227, 229, 230, 231, 234
Des Moines, Iowa, 185-88
Detroit, Mich., 160, 213, 251
Dodge City, Kans., 8
Dryden, Tex., 171-72
Durant, Okla., 104, 148

Eagle Pass, Tex., 72
Eastland County, Tex., 68, 83, 189, 304
Eastland, Tex., 39, 43, 44, 83, 84, 85, 86, 88, 89, 118, 126, 128, 133
El Paso, Tex., 72
Eldorado, Tex., 143
Eskota, Tex., 138

Fayetteville, Tex., 114, 118
Flatonia, Tex., 114
Fordyce, Ark., 7, 17-18
Fort Lancaster, Tex., 4
Fort Stockton, Tex., 315
Fort Worth, Tex., 9, 19, 31, 69, 84, 95, 98, 111, 231

Gallatin, Mo., 216-17, 259
Glenwood, Iowa, 183-84

Glenwood, Tex., 191
Goliad, Tex., 2
Gunsight, Tex., 44, 45

Hamilton, Can., 248-49
Hamlin, Tex., 68
Henryetta, Okla., 153, 160
Hondo, Tex., xii, 195
Houston, Tex., xvii, 107, 110, 112, 115, 122, 132, 223
Hugo, Okla., 149, 150
Humble, Tex., 110, 121, 132, 135, 186, 189
Huntsville, Tex., 89, 111, 170

Idaho Falls, Idaho, 234
Indianapolis, Ind., 185, 259

Johnson City, Tex., 220
Joplin, Mo., 302, 312
Junction City, Tex., 7
Junction, Tex., 55, 56, 144, 145

Kansas City, 215, 216, 217, 219, 231, 234
Kerrville, Tex., 145
Kingsbury, Tex., 116

Lafayette, Colo., 227-30, 232
La Pryor, Tex., 60, 73
Lampasas, Tex., 6, 7, 108
Leavenworth, Kans., 294-96, 311, 312
Lincoln, Nebr., 186
Little Rock, Ark., 156, 236, 237, 238
Lometa, Tex., 47

Luling, Tex., 114, 115

Marble Falls, Tex., 106-7, 110, 188
Matador, Tex., 95, 98
McAlester, Okla., 150, 303, 307-8, 310
Melita, Can., 204-6
Memphis, Tenn., 155, 156, 157, 158, 160, 216
Menard, Tex., 56
Michigan, 161, 291
Milwaukee, Wis., 273, 276-77
Mineral Wells, Tex., 133, 231, 232, 234, 236
Mingus, Tex. See Thurber
Montreal, Can., 242
Moosomin, Can., 204, 207-9
Motley County, Tex., 95

New Braunfels, Tex., xii, xiv, xv, 147, 148, 220-27, 232, 309, 310, 312
New London, Wis., 296
New Orleans, La., 226-27
New Ulm, Tex., 112
Nolan County, Tex., 13

Oakville, Tex., 2
Odessa, Tex., 172
Okla., 1-2, 8, 104, 111, 117, 133, 147, 148, 159, 161, 180, 190, 298, 302, 304, 305, 309-10, 312, 316
Oklahoma City, Okla., 312, 313
Omaha, Nebr., 167, 181-83, 230, 318
Ozona, Tex., 144

Palestine, Tex., 94

Paris, Tex., 191
Pearsall, Tex., 197
Pelican Lake, Manitoba, Can., 203-4, 206, 207, 210
Peoria, Ill., 271
Putnam, Tex., 23, 50, 51

Quitaque, Tex., 96

Ranger, Tex., 43, 135, 140
Rising Star, Tex., 44, 79, 80, 82, 87, 88, 326
Rochester, Tex., 53
Rockford, Ill., 289
Rocksprings, Tex., 55, 57, 58
Rondout, Ill., vii, xix, 267-96, 308, 316, 321
Round Rock, Tex., 5
Rowena, Tex., 313-14
Runnells Co., Tex., 313
Rusk, Tex., 90, 94

Sabinal, Tex., 99, 117, 189
Salado, Tex., 6
Salt Lake City, Utah, 234
San Angelo, Tex., 68, 106, 107, 110, 143, 145
San Antonio, Tex., 4, 6, 65-66, 69, 98, 101, 116, 130, 140, 143, 145, 147, 150-51, 156, 160, 170, 174, 194, 195, 196, 214, 219, 221, 266, 288, 289, 290, 311, 321, 322
San Marcos, Tex., xiv, xvii, 264-66
San Saba, Tex., 47, 48
Scurry County, Tex., 11, 12, 34
Seven Hundred Springs, Tex., 56

Sherman, Tex., xvii
Shreveport, La., 192
Smackover, Ark., 148, 232, 234-39
Snyder, Tex., 11, 106
Spencer, Ind., 253, 255, 260-64, 296
Spofford, Tex., 102-3, 145
Spokane, Wash., 232
Spur, Tex., 97
St. Joseph, Mo., 215, 257-58
St. Louis, Mo., 215, 288, 299
Stephenville, Tex., 39, 43-44
Strawn, Tex., 42, 43
Sugar Land, Tex., 93
Sweetwater, Tex., 11, 12, 13, 53, 68, 106, 138

Tab, Ind., 253-54, 259
Taylor, Tex., 69
Temple, Tex., 311
Tenn., 2
Terre Haute, Ind., 161, 163, 255, 258-59
Texarkana, Tex., 192, 193, 194, 256-57, 302
Thurber [Junction], Tex., 41, 42
Tin Can, Tex., 35, 51, 52, 66, 68
Toronto, Canada, xii, 210, 211-13, 215, 239, 241-52
Tulsa, Okla., 145, 153, 155, 157, 160, 161, 163-64, 166, 180, 189, 190, 194, 214, 216, 231, 234, 286, 293, 297-308, 310, 312

Uvalde County, Tex., 109
Uvalde, Tex., vii, viii, xiii, xiv, xv, xvii, 1, 49, 54, 55, 57, 58, 59, 61, 63, 65, 69, 74, 77, 99, 101, 110, 116, 117, 145, 147, 151, 160, 169, 172, 177, 180, 189, 190, 192, 266, 289, 309, 310, 313, 315-16, 321, 322

Valiant, Okla., 149

Waelder, Tex., 145
Weatherford, Tex., 97
Wheaton, Ill., 287, 290, 293
Wichita Falls, Tex., 38, 68
Winnipeg, Can., 204, 209, 210, 251
Winters, Tex., 136, 148, 151, 164